SPMgroup Ltd.
Strategic Project Management

3266 Yonge Street, Suite 2022,
Toronto, ON, Canada,
M4N 3P6
Tel: 416-485-1584
Fax: 416-481-4903
Web: www.turq.com/spmgroup
E-mail: moreinfo@spmgroup.on.ca

The New
Project Management

J. Davidson Frame

The New
Project Management

Tools for an Age of Rapid Change,

Corporate Reengineering,

and Other Business Realities

Jossey-Bass Publishers · San Francisco

Jossey-Bass books and products are available through most bookstores. To contact Jossey-Bass directly, call (888) 378-2537, fax to (800) 605-2665, or visit our website at www.josseybass.com.

Substantial discounts on bulk quantities of Jossey-Bass books are available to corporations, professional associations, and other organizations. For details and discount information, contact the special sales department at Jossey-Bass.

 Manufactured in the United States of America on Lyons Falls Turin Book. This paper is acid-free and 100 percent totally chlorine-free.

Library of Congress Cataloging-in-Publication Data

Frame, J. Davidson.
    The new project management : tools for an age of rapid change, corporate reengineering, and other business realities/J. Davidson Frame. —1st ed.
      p.   cm.—(The Jossey-Bass management series)
    Includes bibliographical references and index.
    ISBN 1-55542-662-X
    1. Industrial project management.   I. Title.   II. Series.
HD69.P75F73   1994
658.4'04—dc20   94-8104

FIRST EDITION
HB Printing 10 9

The Jossey-Bass
Management Series

To Veronica and George

Contents

ix

Preface

The New Project Management was written for men and women working in a broad range of fields, who find themselves struggling to manage projects in a chaotic world. Whether undertaking conventional projects in construction or the defense industry or pursuing information-age projects in such areas as information systems, finance, research and development, marketing, pharmaceuticals, or insurance, many of these men and women have discovered that conventional wisdom about project management is only marginally relevant to them in these turbulent times. They know that there is more to project management than mastering scheduling techniques (such as PERT), budgeting techniques (such as S-curves), or resource allocation techniques (such as resource histograms).

I wrote this book to explore concepts and techniques that are not generally covered in conventional project management texts. When I began, the book carried the working title "Beyond PERT." I created that title in a frivolous moment. It has long bothered me that project management is so closely associated with a set of standard tools developed decades ago—for example, PERT/CPM networks were developed in 1957 to 1958, and Gantt charts were first used prior to World War I. It has reached the point that when someone asks, "Do you know project management?" what they mean is "Do you know how to calculate the critical path on a PERT chart?" When I reflect on my own project management experiences, I sense that what is taught in conventional project management texts played a fairly small role in determining whether my projects succeeded or failed.

The New Project Management focuses on the key concerns project professionals face today. These men and women operate in an environment dominated by chaos and uncertainty. Their jobs are undergoing tremendous transformation as their employers undertake radical efforts at corporate reengineering. They can no longer function as mere *implementers* of projects but must assume the role of *initiators*. To help project managers function effectively in the new environment, this book examines such key issues as assuring customer satisfaction, managing complexity, coping with empowerment, managing contractors, managing managers, and dealing with risk. Readers interested in acquiring more traditional project management insights can get these from a large number of basic project management books, including my own *Managing Projects in Organizations* (1987). Readers who already possess a copy of that book should view *The New Project Management* as a companion piece that fleshes out some of the ideas hinted at in the first work.

The contents of this book are strongly influenced by recent experiences I have had. Since *Managing Projects in Organizations* was published, three experiences have dramatically affected my outlook on project management. One is the immense increase in the volume of training and consulting I have conducted in recent years. Since 1987, I have trained some 4,500 managers throughout the world on project management topics. Some of this training has occurred in large corporations, such as AT&T, 3M, and NCR; some in highly dynamic midsized companies, such as Freddie Mac, Fannie Mae, Fidia Pharmaceuticals, and CUNA Mutual; and some in government agencies, such as the Defense Information Systems Agency, the Agency for International Development, the Smithsonian's Museum of American History, the Beijing Institute of Chemical Engineering Management, and the China State Shipbuilding Corporation.

The point is, I have had an opportunity to meet large numbers of people working on projects in a wide range of environments. Some of them are in growing industries, others in declining industries. Some build highways, others write software, still others process mortgages. To many of these people, downsizing, organizational flattening, outsourcing, and empowerment are not abstract concepts but facts of life. From these people I learned about organizational experiments with total quality management, self-managed teams, economic value added (EVA), and reengineering, long before they were discussed in the press and grew into fads. Most of the ideas I deal with in this book were stimulated by my interaction with these diligent, earnest project workers.

A second experience that has colored my outlook on project management has been my work as director of certification at the Project Management Institute (PMI) since 1990. PMI is the world's leading society of project workers. In 1984, it launched a certification program in an attempt to professionalize project management. The program is growing exponentially, and thousands of project professionals are now certified. Upon assuming the position of director, I suddenly found myself deep in discussions about the core competencies of project professionals. To what standard should they be certified? I came to appreciate the work of scores of PMI members who over a number of years have devised and revised the Project Management Body of Knowledge, a document that attempts to define the core competencies of effective project professionals. PMI members have identified eight areas of project management competency. The first four are obvious: project management professionals should be competent in the areas of scope management, time management, cost management, and human resource management. No surprises here.

The second four areas of competency—risk management, quality management, contract/procurement management, and communication management—are more surprising. They reveal that project management has moved beyond its traditional concern with the famous triple constraints of time, budget, and specifications and that the skills and insights required of effective project personnel are far broader today than in the past. Personnel must know how to assess risk, produce quality goods and services, operate in a contracting environment, and communicate competently with their managers, customers, vendors, and staff. Any project management text that purports to be relevant to the needs of project workers should give serious treatment to these new additions to project management wisdom.

The third recent experience that has colored my outlook on project management has been my extensive exposure to project management practices throughout the world. Although I have worked intensively with China since the mid 1980s and am quite familiar with Japanese efforts, until recently my exposure to project management practices elsewhere was fairly limited. However, during my 1992 to 1993 sabbatical I had a chance to work in Singapore, Hong Kong, Sydney, Buenos Aires, Toronto, Paris, Frankfurt, Madrid, and Birmingham. I also worked closely with project managers from Colombia, Mexico, Holland, Denmark, New Zealand, Malaysia, Ghana, Nigeria, Bangladesh, India, and Egypt. I have seen firsthand that project managers worldwide experience identical challenges. My travels have confirmed my belief that the majority of the problems faced by project staff are universal and totally predictable.

Audience

A number of different audiences will find this book useful. Certainly individual managers who want to acquire knowledge of current key practices not generally treated in the project management texts will find the book edifying. They can quickly get up to speed on important topics—such as configuration management, integrated cost/schedule control, contracting principles, project metrics, and risk management—that are normally discussed only in hard-to-comprehend, inaccessible, arcane literature.

Project management trainers interested in teaching advanced topics will also find the book useful. The material contained in it can serve as the core of a course that goes beyond teaching the basics of budgeting and scheduling. The book will also work well in university-level project management courses. It can be used to supplement standard texts or as a stand-alone text in second-level courses.

Overview of the Contents

The book's introductory chapter describes the business environment in which project workers currently function. It shows how the traditional approach to managing projects does not work effectively in the new environment, which is characterized by complexity, chaos, and uncertainty. It describes what new project managers should be like if they want to survive and thrive in such a messy environment.

The book is then organized into two parts. Part One deals with new project management realities. It contains four chapters. Chapter Two points out that an important characteristic of today's business world is *complexity*. People face a bewildering array of options even when making the simplest decisions. The systems they work with lie beyond the ken of even the smartest individuals. Even when people achieve mastery of some aspects of their work, rapid change makes their hard-earned knowledge obsolete. The chapter presents several ways to cope with complexity of projects.

Chapter Three deals with the constancy of change. Technology is changing, people are changing, budgets are changing, resource scarcities suddenly appear, new regulations invalidate old practices overnight, and so on. Project personnel must become, in the words of Rosabeth Moss Kanter, *change masters* (Kanter, 1983). They should develop an appreciation of the inevitability of change. They must learn when to resist it (for example, through configuration management) and when to go with the flow (for example, through rapid prototyping).

Chapter Four deals with one of the hottest of the hot buttons in today's project management: the management of risk. It describes the role that risk plays in projects and outlines a risk management process that can be employed. It also highlights some risk management techniques, such as Monte Carlo simulation, that are being used with increasing frequency and success.

Chapter Five examines the enormously important role that customers now play in project management. It addresses the important issue of learning how to identify exactly who the customers are.

It offers strategies for minimizing problems in dealing with customers and maximizing customer satisfaction (for example, through customer partnering arrangements).

Part Two reviews the new project management skill sets. Chapter Six looks at people management skills that project personnel should develop. In particular, it deals with the development of the political skills that project professionals need to survive and thrive in a typical project environment. It also looks at techniques for building authority and managing managers.

Chapter Seven offers practical advice on how to build team spirit in the matrix environment. Matrix management entails the employment of borrowed human resources. The problem with this is that project workers find they have little or no authority in their dealings with these people. The chapter includes a checklist of things to do to build team spirit even when the resources are borrowed.

Chapter Eight looks at decision making on projects. Rational decision making is fundamentally a process of creating priorities. This chapter shows various techniques for making rational decisions, ranging from benefit-cost analysis to the murder board. These techniques have particular relevance for the selection of projects. They can also be used to select project personnel and vendors.

Chapter Nine focuses on improving the quality of estimates made by project staff in the areas of costs, schedules, and resource requirements. Too often, schedule slippages and cost overruns are not caused by poor project execution but rather are consequences of excessively optimistic time and cost estimates made at the outset. This chapter shows techniques for improving the quality of project estimates, thus lowering the likelihood of schedule slippages and cost overruns.

Chapter Ten examines a rapidly growing phenomenon in today's business environment. Increasingly, work is being handled by outsiders—contractors over whom the project organization has marginal authority. The chapter examines some principles of contracting as they relate to projects and offers suggestions for operating effectively in an outsource environment.

Chapter Eleven draws attention to the fact that effective project control requires simultaneous review of both cost and schedule performance. A simple graphical approach to integrated cost/schedule control is provided, followed by a treatment of the sophisticated earned-value cost-accounting technique. The earned-value methodology is rightfully one of the hot growth areas of contemporary project management.

Chapter Twelve examines how accountability can be increased on projects. A major shortcoming of managing with borrowed resources is that accountability becomes diffuse. The constructive use of evaluation allows for the sharpening of accountability. This chapter discusses some of the pitfalls inherent in evaluation and describes an example of a user-friendly evaluation methodology—IBM's structured walk-through.

For evaluation to be effective, organizations must develop meaningful metrics of performance. Chapter Thirteen describes how this can be done.

Finally, Chapter Fourteen offers conclusions about the evolving direction of project management and changes in the project manager's role.

Acknowledgments

A number of people helped make this book possible. I would like to thank Erik Winslow, chairman of the Management Science Department, for his constant support of my writing and research efforts. The sabbatical that enabled me to gain a global perspective on project management and gave me the time to write was made possible through his intervention. I would also like to thank Edwin Phelps and James Duncan of the Educational Services Institute (ESI) for their support. Because of their efforts, I have been able to meet thousands of project workers both in the United States and abroad. Special thanks go to Cedric Crocker, developmental editor for the management series at Jossey-Bass, who occasionally employed a soft-toed boot to motivate me out of my writer's block. Finally—as always—I give thanks to thirteen-year-old Katherine Adele Frame, whose skeptical reception of all my ideas and words keeps me on my toes.

Washington, D.C.   J. Davidson Frame
March 1994

The Author

J. **Davidson Frame** is professor of Management Science at the School of Business and Public Management (SBPM) at the George Washington University in Washington, D.C. He teaches graduate-level courses in project management, international science and technology, and statistics. He has served as director of SBPM's Program on Science, Technology, and Innovation, and as chairman of the Management Science Department. Since 1990, he has also served as Director of the Project Management Certification Program at the Project Management Institute. Prior to entering academia, he was vice president of Computer Horizons, Inc., and manager of its Washington office. While there, he managed some twenty-five information-age projects. Since 1983, he has conducted project management seminars throughout the United States and abroad. About six thousand project professionals have attended these seminars.

Frame has a B.A. degree (1967) in history from the College of Wooster, and an M.A. degree (1969) and Ph.D. degree (1976) in international relations from the American University, focusing primarily on econometrics and economic development. In recent years, Frame's research has concentrated on how needs and requirements are specified effectively. He has authored about forty articles and two books, including *Managing Projects in Organizations* (Jossey-Bass, 1987).

The New
Project Management

Chapter One

The New
Business Environment
and the Need for a
New Project Management

People have been conducting projects for millennia. The pyramids, the Great Wall of China, and the Roman aqueducts bear witness to the sophistication of some of these projects. For the most part, the method of carrying them out entailed more art than science. It was not until recent times that we began to approach the project management effort systematically and to tip the scales in favor of science over art.

Project management as it is practiced today came into being in the post–World War II era. It was the product of a number of forces at work at the time. The development of operations research brought with it the realization that decision tools could be fashioned to allow humans to conduct their affairs in optimal ways. The growth of systems analysis led to an appreciation of the interconnectedness of events and the inherent complexity of modern systems. Its focus on flowcharts also presaged PERT/CPM scheduling techniques. The cold war led to the support of mammoth projects of unprecedented size and complexity, projects that needed

1

new management tools if they were to be carried out effectively. The burgeoning global economy, with its emphasis on large infrastructure projects, led to a similar search for new management tools.

Together these forces shaped project management for the next four decades. The principal instigators of developments in project management during that time were people in the construction and defense industries. They tended to work on large, complex, capital-intensive projects. They held an engineering perspective and gave project management the look and feel of an engineering discipline. Project management knowledge focused on core skills in the areas of budgeting, scheduling, and resource allocation. To a large extent, project management became inextricably linked to its key tools, such as Gantt charts, scheduling networks, and resource-loading charts.

The New Business Environment

New forces have arisen on the world scene in recent times. During the 1980s there was a major realigning of global business forces. The economic position of the Pacific Rim countries strengthened dramatically. They became fearsome competitors and challenged the hegemony of the traditional Western players. Their competitiveness was not simply based on their traditional advantage of cheap labor. It was also rooted in their ability to embed high levels of quality into their products. To put it simply, they produced cheaper and better products than their Western counterparts.

During that time, global markets and production capabilities opened up, and the concept of national economies began to wane. Strange business anomalies arose, such as the discovery that Honda cars manufactured in the United States had more American-made parts than Chrysler products. The collapse of communism added to the globalization of the world economy. Suddenly, major new markets of more than three hundred million people were opened to world business transactions. Global competition increased since the formerly communist countries of Eastern Europe possessed large quantities of low-wage workers who were highly skilled and well educated.

This new business environment forced corporations to rethink how they should do business. Competition became the new watchword. For companies to be competitive, they had to reduce their costs, speed up product development, and focus attention on satisfying their customers. A key to customer satisfaction lay in quality improvements and an increased emphasis on customer service.

The look of companies changed dramatically at this time. To be competitive, they instituted radical transformations in their modes of operation. Such transformations are still being undertaken under the rubric of *reengineering*. They include such actions as downsizing, flattening, empowering employees, and outsourcing.

Downsizing

For companies to be competitive, they must be lean and mean. Large payrolls, which once reflected the power and success of corporations, have now become a liability. Consequently, the 1980s experienced major shrinkages in the work forces of big companies. New hiring was frozen, early retirements were encouraged, entire operations were shut down, and personnel were selectively fired. Middle managers became particularly vulnerable since they were perceived to add little value to operations and merely to contribute to the swelling of bureaucracies.

Flattening

In order to be quick on their feet, companies are restructuring their work forces to eliminate the many levels of bureaucracy that separate the CEO from the floor sweeper. In such flattened organizations, chains of command often disappear. Increasingly, employees find themselves dealing less with clearly defined bosses and subordinates and more with colleagues over whom they have no direct control. Decisions typically have to be achieved through consensus rather than by fiat.

Empowering Employees

The simultaneous need for speedy decision making and customer satisfaction has led to the empowerment of employees who have not traditionally had much clout. Empowerment has taken many forms. One key approach has been to provide employees with decision-making authority in their dealings with customers. For example, if a customer wants to change the configuration of a piece of equipment, the employee is given authority to grant the change if it appears to be reasonable. Previously, the employee would have had to get permission from higher levels.

An interesting outcome of employee empowerment has been the change in the role of "manager" from that of *director* of activities to one of *support*. That is, the role of managers is to do what is necessary to enable their employees to operate as effectively as possible. This situation is called the *inverted pyramid*, a 180-degree reversal of the traditional relationship where employees served their managers.

Outsourcing

The drive for cost saving has led companies to depend more heavily on outsiders to help them in their work. Even as companies downsize, they may increase their business activity. This apparent contradiction is made possible by the outsourcing of services and production. The benefits of outsourcing are reduced cost of investment in new equipment and facilities, lowered pension and health insurance burdens, and a declining need to hire and fire employees in response to business cycles. Thus outsourcing has shifted many of the burdens of doing business from companies onto their contractors.

Interestingly, project management is ideally matched to the new business environment. Project managers are experienced in "thriving on chaos" (Peters, 1987), "managing in turbulent times" (Drucker, 1980), "white water rafting" (Vaill, 1989), "upside-down thinking" (Handy, 1989), and "influence without authority" (Cohen and Bradford, 1990). They are accustomed to working in organizationally flat environments, where bosses do not have direct control over human and material resources but rather are influencers. Outsourcing is not new to them. For decades they have used it as an important mechanism for acquiring products and services on projects.

Still, even though project management is well suited to help organizations manage their efforts in these dynamic times, it too must undergo radical change. The relevance of project management to the needs of our changing world will rapidly disappear without major changes in how we look at and carry out our projects.

The Problem with the Traditional Approach to Project Management

Traditional project management has enabled humans to do some incredible things. For example, it provided the U.S. National Aeronautics and Space Administration (NASA) with the management capability to put men on the moon. It makes possible the construction of oil-drilling platforms in the North Sea. It provides airplane manufacturers with the discipline to design and build complex commercial aircraft. Traditional project management has served us well, so why talk about changing it? If something isn't broken, why fix it?

The problem is that traditional project management *is* broken. One deficiency is its inattention to the importance of customers. Customer satisfaction is often treated as an afterthought. Most energy is directed toward satisfying the famous triple constraints of time, budget, and specifications. Success and failure are typically assessed against meeting schedules, budgets, and specifications, *not* against achieving full customer satisfaction.

One might argue that a focus on the triple constraints is fully consistent with customer satisfaction since the third constraint—specifications—should have customer needs and wants embedded in it. In theory, this is a correct assessment. In practice, however, the specifications often do not take adequate account of customer needs and wants because they are created by "experts" who lack the skills and training to work with customers, who don't understand the customers' business, and who design and build products that are of personal interest to them. They are often driven to build things that will gain them the admiration of their fellow experts. With such an approach, customer satisfaction is a secondary consideration.

Another problem with the traditional approach to project management is its single-minded focus on a fixed set of tools for dealing with scheduling, budgeting, and resource allocation. These tools are well known. In scheduling, they are, chiefly, Gantt charts and PERT/CPM networks. In budgeting, they are S-shaped budget curves. In resource allocation, they are responsibility matrixes, loading charts, and resource Gantts. There are countless additional subsidiary tools and concepts that fill the project manager's toolbox. As stated in the preface, project management is so closely tied to this set of tools that when someone asks, "Do you know project management?" they are really asking whether you know how to do such things as create PERT/CPM networks and S-curves.

There is nothing inherently wrong with tool mastery. All of us can benefit by increasing our skills in using tools. A problem arises, however, when an excessive concern with tools diverts attention from other important matters, such as managing and satisfying customer needs and wants, motivating employees, and acquiring political skills. A reality of project management is that projects seldom fail because a PERT/CPM system crashes. However, they frequently fail for nontechnical reasons such as lack of commitment on the part of staff, political gaffes, and the inability to communicate ideas effectively.

A final problem with traditional project management is its narrow definition of what it should be concerned with. This is seen in two areas. First, traditional project management often limits the project life cycle to four phases: concept, planning, execution, and closeout. This seems to be a reasonable arrangement on the surface. However, in the new competitive global environment, where customer satisfaction is paramount, such a restrictive definition of the life cycle is deficient. With such a life cycle, the project team members can wash their hands of the deliverable after it is turned over to the customer. They are given an opportunity to bail out at the moment of truth. If problems arise in the postproject phase, they can take the attitude, "That's not my problem—see the maintenance people."

For customer satisfaction to be achieved, the life cycle must be extended to encompass one more phase: operations and maintenance. The project team members must be made to realize that their job is not simply to build something but also to assure that it works in a satisfactory way after it is delivered.

Traditional project management also takes a narrow view of

its domain in a second sense: it holds a constricted view of what project managers should be able to do. It sees them primarily as implementers. Someone makes decisions about which projects should be supported. After the nature of the work has been scoped out, it is handed over to the project manager, whose charge is to do the job within scope. A survey I recently conducted of 113 project managers showed that only 29 percent of them played a direct role in choosing the projects on which they worked. The survey showed other deficiencies in the power of project managers: less than a third reported having profit and loss responsibilities. Indeed, most reported that they did not even have adequate budget data to take on meaningful cost responsibilities. A majority also indicated that they worked on only a portion of the project life cycle—no cradle-to-grave responsibility here!

This book argues that such a limited view of what lies in the project manager's domain creates an environment in which it is difficult for project managers to serve their customers effectively. If customer satisfaction is an important ultimate goal of project management, the project manager's role must be redefined to allow it to be achieved.

Over the years, traditional project management has served us well. The time has come, however, for it to change some of its ways in order to adjust to powerful global competitive forces. Specifically, it must adapt to the new conditions facing organizations today: an obsession with customer satisfaction, downsizing, flattening, empowerment, and outsourcing.

The New Project Management

This book examines how project management can most effectively be employed in the new business environment. Its purpose is not to reject traditional project management. It recognizes that most of its features are still relevant today. Rather, it aims to enhance the traditional approach by bringing it more in line with the new business realities.

Three arguments are central to the new project management: (1) project management must become more customer focused; (2) it must explore the use of new management tools; and (3) it must redefine the role of project managers, giving them more power to operate effectively. Each of these arguments will be discussed in turn.

The Need for a Customer Focus

Project managers traditionally measure success and failure in the context of the triple constraints. Failure occurs when a project encounters schedule slippages or cost overruns and/or produces deliverables that do not meet the specs. This traditional outlook is undergoing rapid adjustment. Increasingly, professionals involved with project management recognize that the worst kind of failure you can have is carrying out projects that do not satisfy the customer.

This point is clearly illustrated if we consider the project to build the opera house in Sydney, Australia. This project encountered horrific schedule slippages and cost overruns. By the traditional yardstick of the triple constraints, it was a failed project. However, once built, the opera house became Australia's number one object of civic pride. It is hard to find an Australian tourist poster that does not have a photo of the opera house somewhere on it. Soon after its construction, the citizens of Australia considered it a rousing success. What we see here is success rooted in customer satisfaction, even when the triple constraints are not met.

Customer satisfaction, then, is the key. Ultimately, satisfaction is defined by whether customers actually use the deliverables emerging from projects. Our track record in this respect has not been great. How many deliverables have been created and then placed on the shelf to gather dust? Consider the findings of one study. In 1989, the U.S. Government Accounting Office (GAO), a congressional watchdog agency, investigated 163 software deliverables for nine contracts (U.S. General Accounting Office, 1989). They found that only 2 percent of the deliverables were usable as delivered. Another 3 percent were usable after modest modification, and 19 percent were usable after extensive modification. In all, 76 percent of the paid-for deliverables were never used. As a watchdog agency, the GAO is looking for trouble, so the sample of 163 deliverables does not represent a typical cross section of projects. Still, the magnitude of the problem reflected in the GAO study gives us some food for thought.

Why should we worry about a customer focus? There are a number of compelling answers to this question.

First, in recent times, customers have come to expect good products and services. The Japanese have played a major role in developing such customer expectations. They have been able to trounce their more complacent competitors in the marketplace by focusing on customer satisfaction. We saw a dramatic example of this in the automobile industry. Their emphasis on quality, on fully equipping automobiles with what American companies sold as options, and on solid postsales servicing won the Japanese dominant shares in the market.

Second, a strong customer focus increases the likelihood of repeat business. If the project staff do all they can to achieve customer satisfaction, their efforts will be appreciated by the customer, who may well repay the attention by doing repeat business with the project team.

Third, customer satisfaction means we can wrap up our projects more rapidly. Anyone who has had project experience has encountered the situation where customers refuse to sign off on the deliverable because they believe something is amiss. For example, they may feel that the deliverable does not contain all its promised features or that it has deficiencies in quality. The result of this impasse is an extension of the project. Final payments are delayed and extra expenses are incurred. Greater attentiveness to customer sensibilities decreases the frequency of such occurrences.

The Need to Acquire Nontraditional Project Management Skills

Traditional project management emphasizes acquiring basic skills in scheduling, budgeting, and allocating human and material resources. These are the primary tools of project managers who are mere implementers. They are essentially the tools of technicians.

In their expanded role, project managers need a different set of skills to be effective. Project staff should be proficient in such "hard" skills as the basics of contracting, business finance, integrated cost/schedule control, measuring work performance, monitoring quality, and conducting risk analyses. They should also be adept at such "soft" skills as negotiating, managing change, being politically astute, and understanding the needs and wants of the people they deal with (including customers, peers, staff, and their own managers).

Redefining the Role of Project Managers

As stated earlier, in traditional project management, project managers are seen primarily as *implementers*. Their job is to make things happen. Projects are selected—frequently with no input from project managers, who are then assigned to run them. Plans are developed—sometimes with input from project managers, sometimes without—and then project managers are charged to execute them. Project managers are very much like noncommissioned military officers. The general develops the grand strategies, the major works out the mid-range strategies, the captain develops the tactics, and the sergeants are responsible for executing the tactics in the field.

This approach works well in a stable environment where goals can be clearly defined and there is little competitive pressure. Today's business environment, however, is neither stable nor free from competitive pressure. Old assumptions no longer hold true. A new paradigm must emerge that provides guidance on the roles and responsibilities of the new project managers.

Project Managers Must Become Customer Focused. To the extent that project managers are mere implementers of established plans, they do not have much reason to worry about customer satisfaction. Presumably, the people who sold the system, working with those who authorized and designed it, have taken into account customer needs and wants. In such an environment, project managers behave like good soldiers. "Just point me in the right direction," they say, "and I'll march."

In today's dynamic and competitive business world, this approach no longer works. Consider, for example, projects that are funded through contracts with customers. With such projects, it is not clear that the salespeople, authorizing managers, and designers are doing their jobs properly. A constant complaint heard by project staff is that salespeople, eager to make a sale, are promising customers systems that project staff cannot build, at least not within the constraints of time and budget facing all organizations. Managers are authorizing these commitments because they are anxious to increase business. Unfortunately, they often do not fully understand the project implications of such commitments. Designers, who in most organizations are several steps removed from customers, find themselves trying to design systems that will meet promises made to the customers. In doing so, they frequently interpret customer requirements to match their own design proclivities, which may or may not reflect true customer needs and wants. Clearly, customer satisfaction will not be achieved readily in this all-too-common situation. Today's dynamic business environment requires project managers to be strongly customer focused.

Project Managers Must Be Empowered to Operate Effectively. We hear much talk these days about empowering the work force. Unfortunately, it is not always clear what is meant by the term *empowerment*. In this book, employees are viewed as empowered when they possess the following characteristics:

- *The majority of their decisions can be made independently without having to pass through the chain of command.* A key component of customer satisfaction is quick response time. When customers ask a question or suggest a change, they want to see results quickly. They do not want to sit around waiting while a trivial change request has to get approval from five levels of management. One way to speed response time is to give project workers the power to respond directly and meaningfully to customer inquiries and requests.
- *They possess substantial profit and loss responsibilities.* In modern business activity, the ultimate arbiter of effectiveness is the bottom line. Business operations that lose money are undesirable, whereas those that make money are attractive. This is an obvious truth. In addition, experience shows that people who are held financially accountable for their actions consistently

outperform those who are not. Given these truths, it seems logical to insist that project employees be given profit and loss responsibilities for their projects. In the mid 1990s, we are a long way from this situation. The survey of 113 project managers I mentioned earlier suggests that *fewer than a third of them even have reliable basic cost data to enable them to make rational decisions!*

- *They see themselves largely as independent businessmen and women running their own business.* One of the most effective projects in modern business history, the project to build the IBM personal computer in 1980 to 1981, was carried out as an independent business entity. The project manager was, in effect, the CEO of a small company. He had the same decision-making authority as an independent business person. This means that he had the authority to hire and fire. In addition, his decisions were not constantly monitored by a higher power. In the final analysis, his performance was to be measured by the bottom line. IBM's experience with the PC has been repeated many times in organizations throughout the world. The new business environment demands that project managers see themselves as something more than mere technical implementers. They are, first and foremost, businesspeople whose job is to satisfy their customers while conducting a profitable operation.

- *They possess the business skills and knowledge needed to operate effectively in the new business environment.* Empowerment is very much rooted in competency. Managers who lack basic business and technical skills are not truly empowered to be effective. Traditionally, project management stressed the need to nurture technical skills. As mere implementers of solutions, project staff did not need to possess business knowledge. Today, their role has expanded beyond that of implementer. Customers are demanding that managers help them in developing business solutions as well, and this requires that they possess the business skills to meet this demand.

Traits of the New Project Manager

Over the years, I have conducted an informal survey of hundreds of project managers, asking them to identify what they perceive to be the traits of an ideal project manager. The following list enumerates general traits that emerged from this survey.

The ideal project manager should

- have a thorough understanding of the project goals
- be capable of understanding staff needs
- have a good head for details
- have a strong commitment to the project—that is, be willing to put in long hours on the project
- be able to cope with setbacks and disappointments—any discipline whose guiding principles are governed by Murphy's Law is going to be anxiety ridden!
- possess good negotiation skills since a large part of project life will be spent trying to acquire resources
- be results oriented and practical
- be cost conscious and possess basic business skills
- be politically savvy—that is, be aware of what *not to do* as well as what *to do*
- have a high tolerance for ambiguity—little is clear on most projects

This last point is particularly important. Project managers should have an appreciation for what the Chinese call *yin-yang*. This concept addresses the inherent duality of life and nature: hot versus cold, light versus dark, good versus bad, male versus female, young versus old. Projects are filled with *yin-yang* duality. Following are some common dualities project managers face.

Seeing the big picture versus paying attention to the details. Project managers must constantly balance the big picture against the details. They need to have a grasp of the whole project: why is the project being carried out? What are its most fundamental goals? Are they being achieved? Thus project managers must be able to see the forest. At the same time, they cannot ignore the details. Deadlines have to be met, specifications achieved, resources allocated, expenditures tracked. In short, they must also see the trees. In Jungian terms, they must possess sensation and intuition capabilities simultaneously (Keirsey and Bates, 1978, pp. 16–19).

Maintaining firmness versus being flexible. Projects operate according to firm deadline dates, fixed budgets, and carefully conceived specifications. These things cannot be taken lightly. A major goal of project managers is to get the job done on time, within budget, and according to specs. Any forces that cause the project to drift from the achievement of this goal are strongly resisted. On the other hand, projects are filled with uncertainty. For example, new developments arise that cannot be ignored: competitors produce products that make our goods obsolete, a key customer changes, budget cutbacks occur. Given the inevitability of these changes, project managers must know when and how to behave flexibly.

Being hard versus being soft in dealing with people. A highly successful project manager once told me that a key to his good performance was his ability to wield a "velvet-covered brick." Project environments often seem to be Darwinian laboratories, where only the fittest survive. In such environments, project managers must encase themselves in the toughest armor, like armadillos, in order to endure. At the same time, they need to be responsive to people's needs and wants. They must possess a strong measure of sensitivity. A good example of the velvet-covered brick in action is when a project manager can turn down a request from a supplicant in such a way that the supplicant feels good about the rejection.

Possessing analytical skills versus trusting one's instincts. Projects can be complex business undertakings. I argue strongly in this book that effective project managers must possess good analytical skills in order to understand what is happening on their projects. They should know how to schedule their efforts, using such tools as PERT/CPM, Gantt charts, and earned value; how to develop and track budgets, employing standard financial tools such as present value, internal rate of return, and sunk costs; how to allocate resources with resource histograms, responsibility charts, and resource Gantt charts; and so on. But there are also times when the analytical tools are insufficient. Accomplished project managers learn to pay attention to their gut feeling. This feeling is an outcome of absorbing good and bad experiences over a period of years.

The Increased Value of Project Managers

A review of the traits of the ideal project manager demonstrates that great demands are placed on project managers. Consider the following fact: we do not even expect the CEOs of our great corporations to possess them! Of course, no project manager scores strongly on all the desirable traits listed here. I suspect that the great majority of them are quite weak on most of these traits, and this contributes to the problems encountered on so many projects. But the more desirable traits project managers possess, the more effective they will be.

An interesting thing happened in the 1980s. The outside world came to realize that the key traits necessary to manage the work efforts of modern enterprises are the very ones that project managers have possessed for decades (or millennia, if you want to include the pyramids, the Great Wall, and Hadrian's Wall). The effective managers described in Drucker's *Managing in Turbulent Times* (1980), Peters' *Thriving on Chaos* (1987) and *Liberation Management* (1992), Vaill's *Managing as a Performing Art* (1987), Handy's *The Age of Unreason* (1989), and Reich's *The Work of Nations* (1991) are precisely what we describe here as project managers! These people are coming to occupy center stage in their organizations. If this is true, then the laws of economics suggest that the salaries of effective project managers should rise substantially. These are the scarce people who can *make things happen,* thereby adding tremendous value to their organizations.

Currently, project manager salaries are not particularly elevated, but this is changing. To see this, consider the following incident that occurred in the early 1990s. A large corporation found itself saddled with a major defense project that was in serious trouble and was incurring substantial losses. News of the problems leaked to the business press. The news stories portrayed a company whose management capabilities were mediocre. Ultimately, the failures of this defense project contributed to a decline in the stock price of the company, which reduced the value of the company by a large amount.

A project manager with a good track record was brought into the project to turn it around. Within six months, the losses stopped. By the ninth month, the project was actually making money and the clients were delighted with the deliverables they were receiving. The business press reported the turnaround and pictured the company as a can-do organization that was in firm control of its operations. The company's stock price increased.

Economic theory tells us that people's wages should be tied to the contribution they make to their firm's value. (This is called the *value marginal product*.) If through his actions the successful project manager described here contributed $1,000,000,000 to the value of his company, then theoretically he could be paid $999,999,999 and the company would still be better off having hired him than not! This particular project manager was paid considerably less than a billion dollars. However, shortly after his successes were reported in the press, a competing company offered him a job with a salary in the six-figure range. They recognized that whatever high salary they paid this fellow would be more than offset by the financial gains he would generate for the company.

The experience described here is not unique. In recent times, I have been asked by a number of companies if I could recommend someone to fill senior project management positions in their organizations. In each case, the salary being offered was greater than $100,000 per year.

Conclusions

The world is rapidly changing. In all areas of business, what served us well in the past is only marginally pertinent today. The area of project management is no exception. During the four decades following World War II, its outlook and required skills remained rather static. In the late 1950s, there was a flurry of creative developments that moved project management forward, but from then until the late 1980s, not much changed. One has the feeling that project managers in 1962 would have been comfortable with the project management of 1987.

The turmoil of the 1980s and 1990s changed all that. The desire for survival required that organizations do their work differently. It is this new perspective on project management and the role of project staff that is central to this book.

Part One

Managing

in the New

Business Environment

Part One of this book deals with some key issues that affect project professionals. These issues have received little attention in traditional approaches to project management. In retrospect, they have always been important, even though they have not received the interest they deserve. Today, however, they possess a compelling urgency that is forcing us to place them at the center of our management concerns.

As Chapter One suggests, a hallmark of today's business environment is its chaotic nature. This chaos is rooted in unprecedented rates of change and high levels of complexity. In turn, rapid change and complexity create an environment of high risk in which decision makers possess little certainty about what the future holds. They perceive events through opaque lenses and base their decisions on large measures of speculation and only small doses of certainty.

Complicating things further is the brutally competitive environment that has arisen with the emergence of the economies of the Pacific Rim countries. This competitive environment has

17

stimulated an obsession with winning the hearts and minds of customers. In today's business climate, customer satisfaction lies at the
heart of most business activity.

Part One examines the new business realities and their implications for the management of projects. Chapter Two investigates the pervasiveness of complexity in today's world. It examines
the roots of complexity, identifies its impacts on organizations, and
suggests mechanisms for dealing with it.

The old maxim that "the only constant is change" is no
longer a clever statement of contradiction but a dominant reality of
business life today. Unharnessed change is a leading contributor to
project failure. Changes in personnel, markets, budgets, regulations, and technology stimulate changes in project needs and requirements. Project staff find themselves working with "rubber
baselines." Chapter Three examines the nature and pervasiveness of
change and suggests approaches to dealing with it.

Risk management is perhaps the fastest growing area of interest in project management. Projects face a plethora of risks: technological, financial, social, regulatory, market, and so on. Chapter
Four looks at the increase of risk on projects in recent times and
examines a number of methodologies for identifying and mitigat-
ing risk.

Finally, Chapter Five examines the role of customers in the
new project management. It suggests that project staff increasingly
must develop customer-relations skills. It also offers guidance on
how to work effectively with customers.

The sequencing of these chapters is to a certain extent arbitrary. Each has been written to stand on its own merits so that
readers can read them in whatever sequence is of interest to them.

Chapter Two

Managing Complexity:
Techniques for Fashioning
Order Out of Chaos

The level of complexity we face in our daily lives today is overwhelming. Sometimes I wonder if life really is more complex now than in previous times or whether the sense of complexity is an illusion. But whenever I begin believing it is an illusion, I think back forty years to some mundane affairs and contrast them with comparable affairs today. Then I see how complex life is today.

For example, when I was a boy, in the 1950s, the investment opportunities my father faced were limited: as a middle-class general practitioner, he made a comfortable living in medicine and could place his money in an interest-bearing savings account or put it into U.S. government savings bonds. There were other investment options, of course—for example, he could play the stock market— but these were rather risky and would involve a nontrivial amount of his personal attention.

Forty years later, the investment options for risk-averse middle class citizens are overwhelming: tax-free municipals, no-load mutual funds, commission-based mutuals, treasury bills, savings bonds, money market funds, and certificates of deposit are just a small sampling of offerings that ordinary folk chat about during backyard barbecues. Furthermore, in order to make wise investment decisions, middle-class investors need to be rather astute about the tax law. Beyond this, they should be conversant with the assortment of insurance options available to them (for example, term versus whole life policies), mortgage options (fixed versus adjustable rates), and pension plan alternatives (defined benefit versus money purchase plans). My sense is that my friends and acquaintances today are far more savvy about investment issues than professional investors were back in the 1950s.

My dad's life was simpler in many other ways as well. When he took us kids out to get a bit of ice cream, the flavors we could select were chocolate, vanilla, and strawberry. Today, my daughter must choose among thirty-one flavors when we visit the local Baskin-Robbins. If my dad wanted to purchase a writing implement in 1950, he could choose between a ballpoint pen, a fountain pen, a mechanical pencil, or a wooden pencil. Today, when I go to the stationers I face an overwhelming variety of choices, ranging from quality fountain pens to disposable fountain pens, ballpoints, roller-ball ink pens, vinyl-tipped pens, 0.5mm mechanical pencils, 0.7mm pencils, and so on.

These examples demonstrate that life today is far more complex than it was for our parents and grandparents. One does not need to have an astronomical IQ to speculate that life will be even more complex in the future.

Complexity is a fact of life we cannot escape. It overwhelms us in our personal lives. It is also an aspect of the workplace. Today's literate managers are expected to know how to use personal computers, to understand finance, to have marketing know-how, to be psychologists in their dealings with customers, and so on.

This chapter examines some aspects of complexity that have a bearing on project management. It first investigates the nature of complexity. Why is complexity such a dominant reality today—perhaps *the* dominant reality that organizations and individuals must cope with? It then examines the experiences of organizations that so far have managed to cope with complexity with a fair degree of success. It concludes by enumerating approaches that organizations take to dealing with complexity.

Chaos and Complexity

If just a few years ago you were a physics student, you would be taught that the world is an orderly place. Consider the most famous equation in science: $E = MC^2$. It contains only two variables (E, energy, and M, mass) and two constants (C, the speed of light, and the power of 2), and yet it describes one of the most fundamental physical relationships in nature.

The elegance and precision of physics have long been the envy of life scientists, social scientists, business people, and ordinary, literate citizens. Physics has served as the model of how knowledge should be handled. A major goal of social scientists over the past four decades has been to emulate the methods of physics. This is seen most clearly in economics, where a typical research paper is so filled with mathematical symbols that in reviewing it one would think one was reading a physics paper.

Despite noble efforts to achieve the cleanliness and parsimony of physics, nonphysics disciplines have been caught up in messiness. Biologists and medical researchers find that living systems are inherently messy. Social scientists, whose attentions focus on people, find that humans defy consistently predictable behavior.

Today we recognize that even physics is far messier than popularly conceived. "Clean" physics was the product of the Newtonian era, when clockworks served as the model of physical systems. At first, the parsimonious approach to explaining physical reality worked quite well: relatively simple equations described complex phenomena such as gravitational attraction, the wave properties of light, motion, force, and the properties of heat. But as the easy problems were solved and better techniques of measurement evolved, it became evident that the physical world displayed some characteristics of messiness that were hard to explain.

Albert Einstein, the scientist who gave us the superelegant equation $E = MC^2$, won recognition for his 1906 explanation of Brownian motion. In this work, he showed that some physical processes—the messy ones—are best described statistically rather than according to tight mathematical equations. Similarly, the Heisenberg uncertainty principle (1927) suggested that some physical processes are inherently messy. There was a hint here that physics might share some things with a dice game.

More recently, physicists and mathematicians have recognized the messiness of physical processes by devising new approaches to dealing with them. In the 1970s, fuzzy set theory grew prominent. This approach suggested that in classifying things, we often do not know what group a particular item may belong to at a given point in time. We can only predict its membership in a group probabilistically. In the 1970s, the work of Réné Thom led to the development of catastrophe theory, which postulated that many phenomena, such as the snapping of a steel rod under pressure or the collapse of an economy, are characterized more by discontinuities than by the continuities favored in conventional physics.

The most publicized exploration of messiness is chaos theory, which emerged in the 1980s. The reading public was so fascinated by its precepts that James Gleick's book *Chaos* (1987) became a *New York Times* bestseller for months. Chaos theory emphasized the lack of predictability of basic events. A well-known example of this is what is called the butterfly effect, which holds that the flapping of the wings of a butterfly in one corner of the earth can change weather patterns in another. Thus the most simple events can, through a steady compounding process, result in highly complex consequences that defy prediction.

Concern with chaos led to a growing interest in complexity. The chaos perspective holds that many common phenomena such as weather patterns and economic activity are inherently complex and that traditional linear thinking will not help much in understanding them. In the mid 1980s, the Sante Fe Institute was established with the expressed purpose of understanding complexity in all of its aspects.

Consensus is emerging that complexity is closely tied to the adaptive behavior of systems. For example, a species of insect that falls prey to a certain kind of predator must either alter its physical form or behavior (for example, by camouflage or burrowing) or become extinct. Through this process of adaptation, the system becomes increasingly flexible *and* complex. The rule seems to be that flexible, sophisticated systems have the edge in this competitive world. Consequently, the general drift is toward the increased complexity of systems in both the physical and social world.

In the management arena, the concept of messiness is nothing new to those who practice project management. Whereas traditional management focused on things like chains of command and tying authority to responsibility, project management has centered its attention on getting the job done in an environment where authority is lacking, goals are subject to multiple interpretations, and rules of behavior are ill defined. In project management, Murphy's Law dominates: if things can go wrong, they will. Project management has operated in a management environment of chaos and complexity for decades.

Facets of Complexity

Complexity is a difficult concept to define. In dealing with it, we are tempted to say, "I know it when I see it, but don't ask me to define it." Our problems in defining it stem from its having several facets. For example, complexity is associated with size: large things with many components tend to be more complex than smaller ones with few components. It is also associated with variety: decisions entailing many options are more complex than those with few. It is further associated with difficulty: the *New York Times* crossword puzzle is more complex than the puzzles found in tabloids. In this section, we explore these and additional facets of complexity.

Complexity and Size

In general, large things with many components tend to be considered more complex than smaller ones with few components. In software, a program containing one million lines of code is clearly more complex than one containing a thousand lines. A fighter aircraft is more complex than an automobile. A nuclear power plant is more complex than a coal-fired plant.

Volume-related complexity—what Peter Senge calls *detail complexity* in his book *The Fifth Discipline* (1990)—has two components to it. First, large things with many components have many connections that must be maintained between the components. These connections can grow explosively even as a system's components grow arithmetically. This can be seen in Figure 2.1, which shows what happens as a team gets larger. On a two-person team, only one connection must be maintained in order to coordinate the efforts of the team members. On a three-person team, the number of connections grows to three. With four people it grows to six. With five people it grows to ten. In general, the upper limit of the number of connections that can exist between the components of some entity is $n(n - 1)/2$, or $(n^2 - n)/2$.

Second, the sheer size of something makes it difficult to comprehend. The typical human brain can handle only seven to ten pieces of information simultaneously, so as the volume of information increases, the brain's capacity to deal with it concretely grows increasingly deficient. Those who doubt this assertion can perform a small experiment on themselves. Have a friend create five "random" numbers, the first one seven digits long, the next one eight digits long, and so on. Then have the friend read you the numbers, one at a time. Your job is to write each number down after hearing it once. Most people begin making mistakes with numbers that are nine digits long.

The projects we encounter today often entail manipulating far larger volumes of information than in the past. This fact is obvious to anyone who has been working with personal computers since the early 1980s. The first word processing software packages (really nothing more than text editors) could comfortably fit onto a 360-kilobyte floppy disk. Ten years later, standard word processing packages often occupied 9,000,000 bytes of hard disk space.

The larger volume of information we encounter today is a consequence of at least two factors. For one thing, knowledge is cumulative. This was highlighted in the 1960s by Derek Price in his classic work *Little Science, Big Science* (1963), which demonstrated empirically that the growth of scientific knowledge is exponential. As a consequence, more knowledge is generated in one year than in the previous several years combined. Something like 90 percent of the scientists who ever lived are alive today.

For another thing, we now possess the technology to store

Figure 2.1. The Relationship Between Team Size
and Communications Channels.

Two people, one connection   Three people, three connections

Four people, six connections   Five people, ten connections

and access huge amounts of information cheaply. Anyone with a personal computer can tie into data bases containing billions upon billions of bytes of data covering every conceivable topic. Of course, this situation has led to information overload, so that even the brightest people feel overwhelmed with the amount of information they need to contend with.

Complexity and Variety

The proliferation of options facing us in our lives is overwhelming. I recently encountered this fact at my university when a graduate student informed me that the number of decision support systems employed in operations research had become so large that he was in the process of creating a "meta"-decision support system whose function was to offer its users guidance on what decision support systems to use on different kinds of problems. In effect, he was creating a decision support system of decision support systems. This is not a unique situation. We now have an Association of Associations and an Index of Indexes.

The plethora of options is apparent in project management as well. In 1992, I carried out a survey that identified 372 distinct commercially available project-scheduling software packages. How does one choose from among all the variety?

A large part of the complexity of today's projects is tied to the variety of options facing all project players, from project managers to team members to customers. These options cover all aspects of projects. For example, consider the options associated with the purchase of a single product, component, or service. Virtually any product, component, or service to be employed on a project has multiple suppliers, each with its special features. In buying a laptop computer, should I choose Product A, which is exceedingly lightweight, or Product B, which comes bundled with large amounts of RAM, or Product C, which has a color screen? Decision making was a lot easier in the old days, when the range of options was severely limited.

The dilemma of excessive options that project managers and staff face is obvious. They must constantly make choices from among a plethora of different vendors, employees, designs, proposed solutions, promise dates, and so on. The fact that their projects tend to be unique confounds them because the lessons learned from sorting through options on a previous project are often irrelevant to the current one.

Customers are overwhelmed with options as well. In choosing a product or service, they must decide what fundamental features they want in a deliverable, what bells and whistles can be added, how much they are willing to pay, and what vendors to work with. If they grow overwhelmed by the variety of options, they may freeze up and feel incapable of making a decision (we call this paralysis through analysis), or they may develop cold feet once they make a decision and change their minds. Project staff should be sensitive to this dilemma. An important part of their jobs is to guide customers through the decision process, helping them navigate in unknown waters. One approach to doing this is to simplify the inherently complex decisions customers must make.

Complexity and Difficulty

Complexity is often associated with difficulty. Something that is hard to do is generally viewed as more complex than something that is easy. Integral calculus is more complex than arithmetic. The *New York Times* crossword puzzle is more complex than one appearing in a tabloid.

Complexity rooted in difficulty is generally handled through mastery. For someone learning how to ride a bicycle, the effort appears quite complex at first. The same holds true for someone learning how to touch-type. At the outset, the effort appears daunting. There is so much to learn. But with practice there is mastery, and with mastery what seems complex one day may seem quite simple the next.

To people who are new to a project, grasping its totality may seem impossible. Consider what they must know: the Project Management Institute's Project Management Body of Knowledge stipulates that the competent project manager should have some degree of mastery over time management, cost management, scope management, human resource management, risk management, quality management, contract management, and communication management. Beyond this, project workers are expected to have the technical competence to understand the specific content of their projects. There is much to master even on relatively simple projects.

One solution to the problem of mastery is experience and education. Careful study and hands-on experiences enable project staff to function comfortably in their complex environments. Projects are seldom easy. But experienced and knowledgeable project

managers learn how to cut through the complexity and to focus on
the essentials.

Complexity and Change

The rapid change we face in today's world contributes measurably
to complexity. One way it does this is by creating moving targets.
This is seen clearly in our attempts to define needs and requirements. Even as we think we finally understand the customers' needs,
they are changing. Sources of change include changing technology,
the changing position of competitors, changing economic forces
(for example, the growth of inflation), changing players, and
changing budgets. As any duck would tell you (if only ducks could
speak), it is simpler to be shot as a sitting duck than as a duck on
the wing.

Change also contributes to two facets of complexity discussed
earlier. First, it leads to increases in the volume of information that
must be dealt with. Knowledge grows over time, and today it is
growing exponentially. Second, change increases the options we
face. If the product life cycle for a gizmo is five years, then in a five-
year period we encounter the one gizmo. If, however, the life cycle
has shrunk to one year, then in a five-year period we effectively
encounter five separate products, contributing to a proliferation of
options facing us. Somehow this change must be controlled.

Experience with Project Complexity

Complex projects are not new. Many organizations routinely operate in highly complex environments. Today the greatest master of
managing complex undertakings is the United States Department
of Defense (DoD). Major defense programs, such as the Stealth
bomber (B-2), the cruise missile, fighter aircraft, and Star Wars
dwarf virtually all other human activities when viewed from the
perspective of complexity. Even DoD "business" activities are far
more complex than what private enterprises undertake. The challenges of automating materials management, personnel assignments, and contracting procedures are overwhelming in an
organization having the size and complexity of DoD.

In the private sector, complex projects are most apparent in the software industry. Software programs of over a million lines of code are no longer oddities. Consider the complexity inherent in programs where a single error in a single line of code can cause the whole program to malfunction. Today's complex software routines must function perfectly.

So how do experienced players such as the DoD and software houses manage complexity?

In a nutshell, the DoD manages complexity through *discipline*. It has established an elaborate set of methods and procedures for acquiring, developing, implementing, controlling, and maintaining systems. These methods and procedures reside in documents with the titles *Military Standards* (Mil Standards), *Military Specifications* (Mil Specs), and *DOD Instructions* (DODI). They provide detailed guidance on how to buy, build, and maintain systems. In the search for management discipline, DoD has invented tools that have become project management standards. PERT, earned value analysis, and configuration management are well-known examples of DoD management innovations.

The price of this discipline has been a high level of documentation and bureaucratization. The famous Kelly Johnson, father of Lockheed's Skunkworks, conducted a study that showed that more than half the life cycle costs of major government systems were tied to chasing paper. A recent study conducted by Captain Patrick O'Connell of the U.S. Navy (1990) found that 70 percent of the action items pursued on a major weapons systems program involved administrative actions rather than directly productive activities. The specifications describing something as simple as a police whistle may run sixteen pages.

The DoD has been subjected to a large amount of ridicule for its labyrinthine procedures. Ultimately, such procedures make possible the purchase of $10 hammers for more than $400! Yet in the final analysis, the DoD builds the most complex systems on earth, and its successes are tied closely to the discipline it employs. This fact is not lost on individuals who work on large, complex projects. I once encountered a group of Japanese project managers who worked on $100,000,000 projects and who told me that they were dependent on U.S. Defense Department regulations to guide them in the building of their systems.

Whereas DoD manages complexity through brute force discipline, private sector software houses take a more subtle approach. They too see the need for discipline through documentation, but they strive to handle this through automated procedures of self-documentation. Such procedures are commonly built into CASE (computer aided systems engineering) tools. Ideally, automated self-documentation relieves project staff of the burden of maintaining a paper trail.

Software shops also try to manage complexity by modularizing software. This tactic was employed decades ago by the use of reusable subroutines. It was supplemented by the structured programming methodology, which attempted to minimize unnecessary cross-links between different parts of a program (for example, by forbidding the use of "goto" statements). In more recent times, modularization is found in object-oriented programming and the conscious development of reusable code.

But even with their efforts to "work smart," software shops find that managing complexity entails a large amount of drudge work. For example, a key component of systems integration is testing. Scores of tests may have to be carried out to ascertain whether the different components of an integrated system function together properly. Proper testing requires the maintenance of meticulous records on test procedures and results. Another example: whereas automated self-documentation can keep track of changes to software code, changes to requirements must still be handled by labor-intensive configuration management procedures. Change requests must be screened through a change control board, approved changes lead to revisions of baselines, a configuration management library must be maintained to document the whole requirements management process, and so forth.

A review of experiences in managing complexity at DoD and in software shops leads to an unhappy conclusion: given our current capabilities in dealing with complexity, its management appears to require a high degree of drudge work. With complex projects, project staff should expect to spend a substantial portion of their time creating and maintaining an administrative infrastructure that enables complex efforts to be carried out effectively.

In his book *The Fifth Discipline* (1990), Peter Senge is critical of this approach to managing complexity, although he admits it is useful in such efforts as "mixing many ingredients in a stew . . . [and] following a complex set of instructions to assemble a machine" (p.71). He argues that rather than focusing on *detail complexity* (predictable, linear), managers should come to grips with managing *dynamic complexity* (nonpredictable, nonlinear). He suggests that *systems dynamics* offers the tools to handling dynamic complexity.

Senge is correct in asking us to rethink how we manage complexity. However, at present we must make do with what we've got, and what seems to work is the imposition of a high degree of discipline—an old school approach to handling complexity.

How to Manage Complexity

Organizations can take various steps to manage complexity. This section examines some of the more commonly employed approaches.

Methods and Procedures

As we have seen, the implementation of rigorous methods and procedures lies at the heart of the DoD approach to managing complexity. These methods and procedures evolve over time and are fashioned from experience. Thus there is a strong trial and error aspect to this approach. For example, an investigation triggered by a jet fighter crash might show that the aircraft failed because a wire snapped loose from a critical circuit board. This discovery might lead to revised guidance on how to solder a wire to a circuit board. The new guidance will be issued through a new Mil Spec. This process of experiencing, learning, revising, and promulgating is repeated countless times throughout the Defense community and leads to an expanding body of knowledge on how to build and maintain complex systems (Petroski, 1985).

The key to implementing effective methods and procedures

is captured in the sequence: experience, learn, revise, and promulgate. Any organization that hopes to strengthen its capabilities in managing complexity must consciously work to develop each of these steps carefully. Petroski (1985) has shown that this painstaking learning process lies behind the achievements of our greatest engineering efforts.

Experience. People in the organization must be encouraged to recognize and report experiences that can have a measurable impact on operations. For example, a data entry clerk might notice that he is required to enter the same part number for a component in two locations on a single data form. The second entry is redundant and time consuming and increases the likelihood of data entry error.

The data entry clerk must recognize that what he faces is not just an amusing anomaly, but something that should be fixed. Procedures should exist to enable him to report this problem to someone who can initiate actions to fix it. Incentives might be established to reward suggestions that improve productivity. Quality circles and suggestion boxes are common approaches to capturing the experiences of employees.

Learn. When a problem has been identified, an attempt should be made to understand both its immediate and its broader implications. In the data entry example, important questions that might be addressed include: What can be done to fix the problem on this data form (immediate issue)? What are the costs of data redundancy (broader issue)? Is the problem of data redundancy a common one that exists on other forms employed by the organization (broader issue)?

Revise. Once the full implications of the problem are understood, procedures for dealing with it now and in the future should be established. This will lead to a revision in the way business is conducted. It is important that the write-up of the new procedures be clear and easily understood. It is also important that previous procedures that are now obsolete be expunged.

Promulgate. If the new insights are tucked away in a dark vault out of the reach of project staff, they are useless. Clearly, they must be promulgated so that staff are made aware of their existence. For one thing, they should be incorporated into a master methods and procedures file that captures all of the official rules governing steps that should be carried out on the project. For another, all the individuals directly affected by the rule changes should be personally notified—through fliers, E-mail, or meetings—of the new procedures.

The importance of well-defined methods and procedures for the management of complexity is indisputable. It is a hallmark of all the organizations that demonstrate competence in successfully conducting complex undertakings. However, methods and procedures have their downside as well. Two problems stand out: they add to bureaucracy and they stifle creativity.

The connection between methods and procedures and bureaucracy is obvious. Rules must be documented and files maintained. Project actions must be continually checked and rechecked to ascertain whether they are in conformance with the rules. Lists of methods and procedures tend to become bloated as marginal rules are included and obsolete rules are not removed. Ultimately, the lists may become an impenetrable thicket that hampers progress rather than expediting it.

Methods and procedures stifle creative solutions in at least two ways. First, they interrupt the flow of creative ideas. More energy is spent trying to follow the rules than coming up with new ideas. Second, they reflect the accumulation of past experiences whose pertinence may no longer be relevant. Constantly focusing attention on how things have worked in the past constrains the imagination from visualizing how things might be in the future.

Accent on Simplification

An obvious approach to managing complexity is to keep things as simple as possible. Scientists do this all the time when, for example, they assume a frictionless world. Consider how complex an equation would be that attempted to define fully the action of a body falling on the earth's surface. The ideal equation would account for such factors as the effects of gravity (of both the earth and other celestial bodies), the friction generated by the body passing through air, the effects of air turbulence, the level of humidity, and so forth. In practice, the behavior of a falling body is adequately explained by a simple equation where gravity is the key parameter: $s = 1/2gt^2$, where s is the distance the body falls, g is the pull of gravity (about thirty-two feet per second per second), and t is the amount of time that has passed.

An important way to simplify complexity on projects is through *heuristics*. Heuristics are rules of thumb that provide rough guidance on actions and their consequences. A famous example of a heuristic is Pareto's eighty-twenty rule. Its use can be illustrated with an example from the arena of quality control. Experience shows that roughly 80 percent of the quality problems we encounter can be attributed to 20 percent of all possible causes. Let's say that we find twenty sources of problems in a particular production process. The eighty-twenty rule suggests that if we direct our attention to working on the four key sources (20 percent of the total), 80 percent of our problems will be resolved.

Another way to simplify complexity on projects is to make heavy use of simple test cases. The idea here is to avoid becoming overwhelmed with all the detailed aspects of a problem and to focus on solving smaller, manageable pieces of it one at a time. This is a commonly employed technique in software development. For example, in the top-down design of a complex accounting system, data entered into early test versions of the system might be directed to "stubs" that simply indicate that the data have reached their targets. As the system evolves, the stubs gradually take on increasingly complex functionality. In the end, they evolve into fully functioning modules.

User-Friendliness: Simplicity
Through Increased Complexity

One of the paradoxes of complexity is that the price we frequently pay to make something look simple is increased complexity. This is commonly seen in software applications. Using just a few lines of code, I can write a software routine that computes $2y + 6$ for different values of y. Since I wrote the routine, I personally would have no problem using it. However, if I wanted to turn the routine into a user-friendly application that any computer-literate person could employ, I would have to write hundreds—perhaps even thousands—of lines of code that would create pull-down menus, data entry forms, help functions, and mouse capabilities. If I wanted the routine to print nice-looking hard copy output, large amounts of additional code would have to be written. Note that this additional complexity would not have the slightest impact on the core computation $2y + 6$. The sole function of the added complexity would be to increase the simplicity of using the application.

What user-friendliness does is to reduce the need for the mastery of complex concepts and processes. Someone wishing to use my simple software routine might have to spend considerable time learning the rudiments of programming in C++ language so that they could figure out how my routine functions. With user-friendliness built into the routine, mastery of C++ is unnecessary.

We see examples of simplicity through complexity all around us. Not long ago, typical automobile mechanics had a thorough knowledge of the workings of a car engine so that when one broke down, they would be able to diagnose and fix the problem based on their own knowledge of engines. With the introduction of integrated circuitry into car engines, engines became too complex for mechanics to master fully. Problems now were diagnosed using highly sophisticated computerized engine analyzers, which are in fact expert systems. From the perspective of the mechanics, diagnosis became very simple: one merely had to hook up the computerized analyzer to the engine and read the printout.

Other examples include simplification of the cockpit panels of airplanes (pilots today complain that they have become glorified babysitters), computer-aided design (CAD), and automated medical analyzers. In each of these cases, simplification has been achieved through a significant escalation of hidden complexity.

Expert Systems and Artificial Intelligence

Much of the simplicity through complexity described above is being achieved through expert systems. Using artificial intelligence support tools, these expert systems attempt to emulate the thinking and decision processes of experts. In theory, the computer replaces the need for an expert. Much of the early work in expert systems was carried out in medicine, where it was hoped that a medical doctor in an office could survey a patient's symptoms, feed the information into a computer (which would be tied to an enormous data base covering all known physical ailments), and then read the diagnosis off a computer screen.

In practice, the achievements of expert systems have been disappointing. Problems have arisen primarily in two areas. First, today's expert systems do not capture the subtleties of the fuzzy logic of humans. Many of the most important decisions we make in life—at work or at home—contain a large subjective component that expert systems have not yet been able to emulate. Second, many expert systems are limited by the knowledge base they access. Knowledge is enormously dynamic, changing from minute to minute. Given our resource limitations, how can we continually upgrade the knowledge base of our expert system to maintain its relevance to the real world? Even if we had substantial resources to do this, what kind of knowledge would we have to include in the knowledge base?

It is apparent that at the present time expert systems are most viable in highly structured, rule-based environments. This is good news to people who are dependent upon methods and procedures to assist them in managing large complex projects. These methods and procedures are precisely the kind of application in which expert systems are most appropriate.

In view of the DoD's focus on rules, it is not surprising that it is leading attempts to apply expert systems to the management of complex projects. Expert systems already exist to do such things as process travel orders for project staff, track adherence to Mil Specs, and design and cut sheet metal parts in metal fabrication processes. Given the rule-based nature of important project management techniques such as configuration management (see Chapter Three) and cost/schedule control (see Chapter Eleven), it would seem that expert systems can allow many of the housekeeping chores of project management to be carried out in an automated fashion. If this is true, the enormous administrative costs associated with managing large, complex programs can drop from current rates of 50 to 65 percent of total costs to a much smaller percentage.

Modularization and Reusable Components

The industrial revolution was pushed forward by the use of interchangeable parts. Interchangeability made mass production possible. An early leader in mass production was the armaments factory in Harper's Ferry, West Virginia. By standardizing production of rifle barrels, gun stocks, triggers, hammers, and the like, the factory was able to assemble rifles for the U.S. military at unprecedented levels of output. Prior to this focus on standardization and interchangeability, the stock of each rifle had to be custom carved to fit each unique gun barrel, a long and tedious process. These developments in Harper's Ferry in the mid 1800s ultimately had a major impact on how American companies carried out their manufacturing operations.

Today's modularization is the contemporary variation of interchangeable parts. With modularization, a system is constructed in such a way that its individual parts can stand alone. For example, the system known as a house is today made up of many distinct modularized components (for example, bath and shower units in many homes are prefabricated at the factory). In software, code is modularized by breaking it into stand-alone pieces (for example, one piece may carry out sorts, another may format output).

Modularization reduces complexity in at least two ways. First, it reduces the number of links between different components of the system. Each module is relatively self-contained. Within the module there may be a great many links holding the module together, but cross-module links are minimized. This feature has important implications for fixing problems and enhancing the system. If a part of the system breaks down, one need merely replace the module in which the break has occurred. Or one can work to repair the break without worrying about the systemwide impacts of the repair. Similarly, with modularization, a system can be upgraded one module at a time.

Modularization reduces complexity in a second way: it reduces the requirement for system mastery. If modules are designed in such a way that they can be easily fit to each other or easily swapped, then people working with a system need merely be familiar with the modules' broad capabilities rather than with their details. For example, in the old days of radio repair, electricians might have had to rewire an electrical connection to fix a problem. They had to have a mastery of the circuitry so that they would not make a change that would cause more problems than it solved. Today, electronic devices are built in such a way that repairs are made simply by swapping components. No knowledge of the workings of the components is needed.

Modeling

PERT networks are a well-known example of modeling in project management. By showing how tasks are linked together, the PERT network allows project staff to examine alternative scheduling scenarios. They can address questions such as: What will happen to project duration if a noncritical task slips by three weeks? How effectively will the duration be compressed if several key tasks are carried out in parallel? If Task A slips, what impact will this have on the scheduling of Task B? With modern PERT/CPM software, fully integrated modeling can be carried out, showing the interconnections between schedule, budget, and resource allocations.

With the construction of a good model, it is not necessary to understand all the details defining a process in order to appreciate the consequences of certain actions. For example, we don't need to understand the mathematics of turbulence to appreciate its effect on the performance of an aircraft. We need only create a physical model of the aircraft and examine its response to various types of airflow through simulations conducted in a wind tunnel.

Thus models contribute to the management of complexity by reducing the requirement for understanding a process in all of its details. They permit people to focus on the consequences of actions without having to understand their intricacies. (The employment of models in project management is discussed in Chapter Four.)

Systems Analysis and Cybernetics

Systems analysis emerged in the 1950s as a means to get a handle on complexity. It recognized that many objects and processes can be described as systems, where *system* can be defined as a whole made up of interrelated parts. Because of the interconnectedness of the parts, it turns out that even a system with relatively few parts can possess an enormous number of connections between them. For example, a system with 10 parts possesses up to 45 connections, a system with 20 parts up to 190 connections, and a system with 100 parts up to 4,950 connections. Thus complexity is built into all but the most trivial systems.

The early systems analysts identified a number of core concepts that still dominate systems thinking today. At the heart of their model is the *system* itself. It can be a hardware system, software system, political system, economic system, or human system. (Systems analysis poses generic precepts, so the specific nature of the system is unimportant.) Surrounding the system is its *environment*. An important issue in systems analysis is identifying the *boundary* separating the system from its environment. The system receives *inputs* from the environment, which it processes in some fashion. It then issues *outputs*, its response to the inputs. The appropriateness of the response is determined through an analysis of *feedback*. This feedback leads to the creation of new inputs and outputs. The purpose of feedback is to aid the system in achieving some sort of balance. The rudiments of a system are pictured in Figure 2.2.

Figure 2.2. Rudiments of a System.

This abstract treatment of a system is better understood through a concrete example. Consider the human body as a system. When the body enters into a hot room (environment), its sensory receptors perceive an uncomfortably high temperature (input). The body reacts by instructing the eccrine glands to perspire (output). The effect of the perspiration is to cool the body. If the body continues to feel overheated (feedback), it persists in perspiring. If the evaporation of the sweat occurs very rapidly, leading to a drop of skin temperature (feedback), perspiration will cease.

Systems analysts capture the actions of the pieces of the system upon each other through diagrams. The most basic diagrams are called *flowcharts*. They detail the steps by which a sequence of actions is carried out. Very often, portraying a system by means of a flowchart is an essential action carried out in the early stages of system development. A simple flowchart is shown in Figure 2.3. By allowing us to track the details of a system, flowcharts enable us to handle what Senge calls *detail complexity*, that is, complexity that derives from the sheer volume of things to be handled.

More sophisticated diagrams are called *systems diagrams*. They focus on how feedback (both positive and negative) affects the functioning of the system. A simple circular systems diagram is shown in Figure 2.4. Complex systems interactions can be portrayed effectively by linking together clusters of these circular diagrams. This type of diagramming allows us to capture what Senge calls *dynamic complexity*. That is, they keep us from getting bogged down in details and enable us to see high-level patterns. Various dynamic simulation tools have emerged based on these systems diagrams (for example, Dynamo) that permit sophisticated modeling of complex situations.

Conclusions

Complexity is a fact of modern life. Our lives today are far more complex than they were just a few years ago. They will be more complex tomorrow than today. One of the great challenges facing organizations and individuals is learning how to manage complexity. It is precisely project management's track record in successfully coping with complexity that gives it its strong appeal to contem-

Figure 2.3. A Simple Flowchart.

porary management thinkers. They see in it a ready-made approach to handling the complexity that is overwhelming modern organizations. However, despite its past successes in managing complexity, project management is reaching the limits of what it can do in a cost-effective way. Unfortunately, those of us who think about how projects can best be carried out have not come up with any breakthrough ideas on how to manage complex undertakings more effectively. At present, the only guidance we can offer is to continue

Figure 2.4. A Simple Circular Systems Diagram.

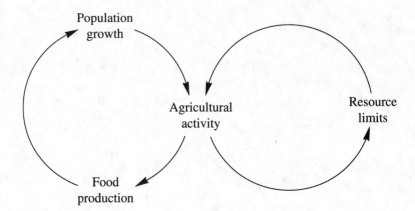

using the approaches that have worked in the past—to focus on maintaining rigorous project discipline through the development and maintenance of detailed methods and procedures, the development and testing of models of project activities, the close scrutiny of time and cost data, and the implementation of strong change management procedures. In the final analysis, all of these approaches amount to working hard, not working smart. As a consequence, we find ourselves in a situation where between 50 and 65 percent of our project budgets is dedicated to chasing paper.

The big question we now face is: are we willing to dedicate so many of our resources to what amounts to housekeeping chores? The increased sophistication of expert systems offers one possible resolution to some of our problems. Expert systems are most effective in dealing with housekeeping chores and might enable administrative budgets to drop dramatically. Beyond this, we must devote a substantial portion of our thinking to conceptual blockbusting so that we can develop new approaches to managing complexity.

Chapter Three

Engaging Change:

Knowing When to Embrace,

Accept, or Challenge

During a corporate reorganization, the western region division of an industrial products company gets a new head. She sends a memo to all employees telling them of her vision of the division's future. The exciting challenge, she says, is to break out of the old mold and to blaze new trails.

After a progress review of a new control system being developed by an engineering firm, its customers are so stimulated by what they have seen that they ask the firm to add some new features to it even before the design is complete.

Owing to incompatibility of word processing software in the purchasing department of a government agency, the agency information resource manager requires that everyone use a single standard word processing system. This means that the majority of employees must be retrained to use the new software.

At the halfway point on a project, the lead contact in the customer organization moves on to another job and is replaced by someone who is lukewarm about the importance of the project. Consequently, the project is put on the back burner, and its very survival is in jeopardy.

Three months before the rollout of a new product, a company's principal competitor places its own product into the market, and this makes the new product obsolete. The company's development group scrambles to see if the new product can be resuscitated by means of some design changes. The never-launched advertising campaign for the new product is put onto the scrap heap.

There is nothing extraordinary about these stories. They reflect the typical fare encountered by typical project workers in typical organizations today. The common theme of each story is, of course, *change.* In today's chaotic world, change is the one thing people can count on, leading us to quip that *the only constant is change.*

I have been so impressed by the volume of change in the workplace in recent years that I conducted an informal survey of several hundred project managers, asking them a series of questions about the change they experience in their work environments. When asked, "Have you encountered some kind of reorganization in your department during the past twelve months?" about three-quarters of the respondents answered yes. When asked, "Have you experienced some kind of meaningful change in your own job responsibilities during the past twelve months?" about 80 percent answered yes. Over half reported that a change in customer personnel in the previous year had had a measurable impact on project progress (generally a negative impact).

Consider the implications of these findings: if they reflect the experiences of typical project workers, they indicate that projects are being carried out in an environment of astounding turmoil. Such turmoil leads to fluctuating priorities, blurred visions of goals, and "rubber baselines." Ultimately, it contributes to schedule slippages, cost overruns, poorly specified requirements, and reduced customer satisfaction.

Clearly, an important management challenge facing project

managers is the management of change. In a stable world, change management is a nonissue: we carefully develop a plan and then stick to it. But in a chaotic world, we must come to grips with the inevitability of change. The idea of developing a plan and sticking to it is absurd in a wildly fluctuating world. Change will happen. The big question is: are we prepared to deal with it?

Sources of Change

Change on projects stems from a broad array of sources. Some key sources include the following.

Changing Players

A dominant feature of the 1990s is the constant shifting of players in organizations. Much of this is a consequence of chronic institutional reorganization that began in the 1980s. Companies and government agencies are constantly adjusting their organization charts in an attempt to develop a formula that will enable them to function effectively in a chaotic world. In the 1990s this effort carried the exotic name of corporate "reengineering."

A significant problem with this juggling of players is the shifting of priorities it engenders. Every time managers take over a new position, they view it as their prerogative to change the rules. Their rationale is, "If I am going to be judged for my actions, then I do not want to inherit someone else's problems; I want to start with a clean slate." Although this outlook is understandable, it leads to the situation where previous commitments are abandoned each time a new manager takes over a position.

Budgetary Instability

A 1989 study conducted by the U.S. General Accounting Office (GAO) found that the most frequently cited problem associated with cost and schedule overruns on major projects is "budgetary instability." Funds available to conduct project efforts at one moment are gone in the next moment. They may be put back into the budget a little later, only to be taken out again at some future time.

Rational planning becomes problematic in such an environment. On federal government projects, the key culprit in this game is Congress, which whimsically adds and removes funds from project budgets as part of its annual budget cycle.

Budgetary instability is not unique to government. Increases in global competition put enormous pressure on companies to watch their spending. Consequently, project workers in private companies often find that the budgets they were promised have been pared back.

Changing Technology

Technology is changing at an ever-faster pace. Such change has dramatic implications for conducting project work. In an era when the life expectancy of a new technology is extremely short, any project that has a time horizon greater than six months must grapple with changing technology. Common questions facing project staff include: Is a particular solution that we recommend going to be relevant next year in view of changes in technology? How does technological change affect the way we conduct our operations internally? (For example, Should we be communicating with each other through electronic mail? Should we be storing documents electronically?)

Changing Competitive Environment

In a competitive world, the actions of our competitors can have large impacts on how we do our work. If they offer an attractive new product or service, we may find ourselves dropping whatever we are working on to develop a competing product or service. The sudden shift of work priorities produced by this reactive strategy is likely to disrupt ongoing work. Resources dedicated to a long-term project may be siphoned away to support our short-term response.

People Changing Their Minds

A ubiquitous source of change on projects is key people changing their minds. As projects evolve, we can count on our customers, managers, and technical staff to alter their views of what they need and want. This is a natural occurrence. At the earliest stages of a project, their vision of the deliverable is vague and requirements are largely an abstraction. As the deliverable becomes more tangible and people see what they really will get, they ask for change. If they like what they see, they often ask for enhancements even before the deliverable is complete. If they don't like what they see, they request changes to make the deliverable more responsive to their needs and wants.

Changing Macroeconomic Forces

Changing macroeconomic forces can create enormous pressure for change on our projects. For example, a sudden surge of inflation can invalidate cost estimates for projects. This occurred on a large scale in the United States in the late 1970s when the inflation rate climbed to 17 percent per year. Economic recession can result in dramatic cutbacks in project budgets and staffing. Recession-induced layoffs of skilled workers are particularly devastating since they represent the loss of years of experience that is difficult to replace. One frustrating feature of changing macroeconomic conditions is that they lie completely out of the control of project organizations. All project staff can do is develop contingency plans to deal with these uncontrollable forces.

Change Management Strategies

This chapter offers a three-point strategy for coping with change. First, organizations and individuals must develop a pro-change mind-set. They must appreciate the inevitability of change and see it as something positive, something that offers them opportunities for growth. This is not easy to do because organizations and people naturally resist change.

Second, organizations and individuals must learn how and when to "go with the flow." There are times when resistance to change can break them, just as a dry twig can be easily snapped with little pressure. Occasionally, it is appropriate to use change's own momentum to direct it into desired channels. A promising approach to going with the flow is rapid prototyping. This methodology entails involving customers in defining requirements by having them react to tangible prototypes. The prototyping process will be outlined and its strengths and weaknesses highlighted later in this chapter.

Third, just as there are times when it is appropriate to go with the flow, there are also times when some degree of resistance to change is proper. Not all change is equally important or necessary. In some cases, it may be needed for survival. In others, it may add no value and may be unnecessarily disruptive and destructive. Configuration management, a dominant change management discipline employed heavily in technical organizations, is a methodology that puts the brakes on change. It filters out trivial or damaging change and allows meaningful change to be implemented. The basic principles of configuration management are outlined in this chapter.

Developing a Pro-Change Mind-Set

To a large extent, history can be viewed as a struggle between the forces of change and the forces of reaction. The essence of this struggle was captured by the ancient Greeks in the compelling story of Prometheus, the man who stole fire from the gods and presented it as a gift to humans. His act greatly displeased the gods because it gave humans the capacity to innovate and be rebellious, something that did not serve the interests of the gods. To show their displeasure, they punished him severely.

Punishing innovators seems to have been a favorite pastime of reactionaries throughout human history. Galileo was forced by the Church to recant some of his scientific views because they challenged the status quo. In 1925, the state of Tennessee tried to stop a high school teacher from teaching Darwinian evolution because these teachings violated biblical dogma. In much of the Middle East today, fundamentalists are attempting to turn back the clock and return to the old ways. (The irony here is that beginning in the eighth century, Islam itself offered a radical viewpoint that challenged traditional perspectives and led to the flowering of science, the arts, and literature.)

In the end, the forces of change consistently beat the forces of reaction. But the gains are often achieved through bitter struggle and are often short-lived because today's revolutionary becomes tomorrow's reactionary. And so the cycle goes—change begets reaction, which begets change, which begets reaction, and so on.

Most humans are not great fans of change. They tend to resist it, at both the individual and group level. The origin of some of this resistance is psychological: results of Myers-Briggs psychological typing suggest that only 16 percent of the population are naturally "Promethean"—individuals who, following Prometheus, actively seek out new solutions. The remainder take a more traditional view of life.

Beyond psychological factors, there are external forces that encourage people to stick with the status quo. One force is captured in the expression "If it ain't broke, don't fix it." This view holds that if the current way of doing things is functioning smoothly, we should not tamper with it. At best, our fixes are unnecessary. At worst, they may create more problems than they resolve.

Another force resisting change stems from the investments we have made to maintain the status quo. When these investments are substantial, we are reluctant to walk away from them. In their *Industrial Renaissance* (1983), Abernathy, Clark, and Kantrow argue convincingly that as companies mature, their success rests increasingly on cost-saving investments in specialized equipment and processes, investments that ultimately restrict their options and their ability to support innovation.

Still another force resisting change is our reluctance to abandon formulas that have served us well in the past. Fat margins produced from the sales of mainframes made IBM blind to the precariousness of its dependence on mainframes in an era of powerful desktop computing. Consequently, IBM experienced some gutwrenching adjustments in the 1990s to get it back on track. Similarly, Digital Equipment's enormous success with engineering-oriented minicomputers made it reluctant to join the microcomputer revolution, much to its ultimate disadvantage.

The problem traditionalists face in revolutionary times is that they are crushed beneath the tidal wave of change. Those resisting it are overwhelmed by the change agents. The change agents themselves derive much of their energy from the fact that they do not have a stake in the past. It has been noted many times that innovation within an industry often comes from the outside. (This is the key message of the classic work by John Jewkes, David Sawers, and Richard Stillerman, *The Sources of Invention*, 1969.) Even within a given industry, the most vigorous change agents are the desperados, those who are in bad shape and have little or nothing to lose. In the U.S. automobile industry, Chrysler Corporation—which stood on the edge of bankruptcy in the 1980s—became the most innovative American car producer in the 1990s with its production of the LH model car.

Clearly, for organizations to survive and thrive in these turbulent times, they must develop a pro-change mind-set. They must alter their cultures so that change is seen as something desirable, filled with opportunity. Given people's natural resistance to change, the development of a pro-change mind-set is not easily achieved. Some steps organizations can take to create it include the following.

Develop an Appreciation of Change Through Education and Training. Although many people pay lip service to the importance of change, few truly understand its positive nature. One way they can develop a better understanding is through education. For example, they can be taught that without a willingness to accept change, humans would still be roaming the savannahs and forests, picking berries and hunting game. (A common characteristic of aboriginal societies is the total absence of change over thousands of years.) Through historical examples, they can learn that much of what makes our lives comfortable today is the consequence of change that was mightily resisted by our ancestors. Along these lines, they can also see that those who resist change are ultimately crushed by it. In the final analysis, Galileo's views prevailed, and his persecutors are vilified in today's history books. The state of Tennessee failed in its attempts to quash the teaching of evolution as a consequence of the famous Scopes trial. Although Islamic fundamentalism is a powerful force in the Middle East today, it is encountering strong resistance from backers of policies that favor economic growth.

To make the educational experience meaningful in the context of change today, managers should be exposed to current management thinking and trends, which offer a perspective on the role of managers that is radically different from the traditional approach. They should see that empowerment of the work force is not a do-good exercise but rather a requirement that must be implemented if an organization wants to remain competitive. They should understand that their role is no longer to command but to support their staff to do the best job possible. They should be made to appreciate that the most successful business people in recent times—Walmart's Sam Walton and Microsoft's Bill Gates, for example—are those who thrive on "upside-down thinking."

Although education can be used to raise people's consciousness about the benefits of change, training is required to provide them with the skills to implement it. For example, experience shows that a good way to overcome the resistance of peasants to the mechanization of agriculture is to train them to use tractors and combines. Once they have firsthand experience in using machinery, they become converts. Suddenly, those who resisted change become its foremost proponents.

Similarly, we should not expect technical project managers to become comfortable with their new role as general business managers if they lack basic business skills. To become effective general business managers, they should receive training on business fundamentals in such areas as finance, marketing, and human resource management. Further, we should not expect managers to readily accept their new role as coaches and supporters (as opposed to bosses) if they do not possess basic coaching skills to allow them to fill the new role effectively.

The chief drawback to education and training is their expense. Resources must be committed to the development of curricula, the purchase of materials, the cost of travel, and the salaries of trainers. Equally important, enormous costs are incurred as the trainees are taken away from their jobs in order to sit in the classroom. Who will do the work when they are gone? Nevertheless, despite the expense of continual education and training, successful organizations realize that it is difficult to effect the transformation of a corporate culture without it.

Encourage Upside-Down Thinking. In his book *The Age of Unreason* (1989), Charles Handy argues convincingly that the individuals and organizations that thrive in turbulent times are those who are capable of upside-down thinking. They do not seize on obvious solutions. They perceive opportunity where others see threat. They also refuse to be complaisant: they are very nervous with statements like "if it ain't broke, don't fix it" and "it's worked in the past, so it's bound to work in the future."

The key features of upside-down thinking are captured in an old story in which two boys are shown a room full of manure. Upon seeing the room, the first boy (a traditionalist) says, "Augh, that's disgusting. A room full of manure." In contrast, the second boy (an upside-down thinker) jumps into the room and begins digging into the manure, shouting, "With all this manure, there's got to be a pony in here somewhere."

A good example of upside-down thinking is found in Mack Hanon, James J. Cribbin, and Herman C. Heiser's classic book *Consultative Selling* (1970). The book introduced the idea that companies should see themselves as selling solutions rather than hardware. The authors recognized that in many industries hardware had become a commodity. Thus it was difficult to distinguish one box from another. With commodities, products are distinguished primarily according to price. Consequently, in a competitive market, profit margins tend to be low.

However, if salespeople see their job as helping customers solve their problems, then customers perceive them as offering high value. This solutions approach to making a sale makes the customer the vendor's long-term partner (another upside-down concept) and increases profit margins.

This upside-down idea runs contrary to what salespeople have been taught. Even today, salespeople earn their living through commissions and meeting sales targets, and the measure of their success is the amount of hardware they can move. A major challenge facing today's business organizations is to identify means to reward salespeople for promoting the sale of solutions rather than hardware. This is a formidable undertaking. For one thing, solutions are abstract, whereas hardware is concrete. It is always more difficult to deal with abstract things than with tangibles. In addition, the sale of solutions requires a high level of sophistication and competency in sales staff. Anyone can sell boxes. It takes savvy and perceptive people to sell solutions.

The need for upside-down thinking in project management is overwhelming. Following are some contemporary upside-down thoughts that challenge the prevailing wisdom:

Operations and maintenance efforts should be treated as part of the project life cycle. The traditional project management perspective has been that the project life cycle ends once the deliverable has been handed over to the customer. This view is reflected in the position taken by the Project Management Institute, which holds that the life cycle is made up of four phases: concept, development, execution, and closeout.

The problem with this view is that it leads to short-term thinking on the part of the project team. It encourages the following perspective: "Our job is to get the deliverable out the door. What happens to it later is not our concern."

Of course, what happens to the deliverable after it has been delivered to the customer should be of great concern to the project team. If the deliverable is not used, is underused, or is used inappropriately, then some measure of project failure has occurred. In the final analysis, project success and failure is determined by customer satisfaction. Customer satisfaction in turn is determined in the operations and maintenance phase, at which time customers actually use what the project team has produced.

Technical people must be adept at understanding and offering business solutions to problems. I recently ran a seminar for thirty information systems professionals working at a large financial services firm. I asked them to identify the key problems they faced in their project work. The most frequently cited complaint was, "Our customers expect us to come up with business solutions to their problems. This isn't our job. Our job is to develop technical solutions."

These professionals were taking a traditional view of their roles. They saw themselves narrowly as technicians. Although this perspective may have worked in the old days, it does not today. Why *not* take on the role of adviser on business solutions? In an era of massive layoffs of white-collar employees, smart workers are those who identify their value to their customers and who work to increase it. If customers want more than technical solutions to problems, then project staff should develop the capabilities to offer them expanded service. As guides to business solutions, technical people enhance their power. They should not feel threatened by the new challenges.

There is no such thing as "the" customer. There are always multiple customers. The new focus on customer satisfaction on projects is healthy and gratifying. It has arisen because it works. The organizations with the greatest project successes are those that always keep one eye on customers and one on the work at hand. Organizations that treat customer needs and wants as afterthoughts get into serious trouble. Their projects are plagued with confusion and miscommunication. They have difficulty achieving customer acceptance at the end of the project. They produce deliverables that often are not utilized, are underutilized, or are employed inappropriately.

The new focus on customers is reflected in the discussions and pronouncements of project staff and management, who openly define their key objective as "satisfying the customer." This is a worthwhile sentiment. However, the way it is phrased may lead to a distorted view of what customer satisfaction entails. The problem is that *the* customer is a fiction. The phrase implies the existence of a monolithic customer perspective. This implication is picked up in such comments as "What the customer really wants is an information system that accesses data more quickly," or "The customer won't accept that modification to the design."

There is no monolithic customer perspective because all projects have multiple customers. When project staff begin to identify a single individual (or group of individuals) as *the* customer they are inviting trouble. To see this, consider the case of a typical defense procurement. Let us play the role of a defense contractor working on a project to develop an upgrade to an existing fighter aircraft. We are likely to define *the* customer as a powerful general who has great decision-making authority over work on the fighter. From our perspective as a contractor, we are particularly interested in his budget powers.

Note, however, that there are other important players who are also customers. Pilots clearly fall into this category. Their chief concern is the performance of the aircraft on a mission. Maintenance crews are another set of customers. They are primarily interested in having aircraft that are easily maintainable. Purchasing personnel are also customers. They want aircraft that minimize problems in purchasing parts and services. Congress—representative of the public at large—is a customer. It pays the bills and is anxious to get value for the taxpayer dollars expended. Other actors come into play as well. The important thing to observe here is that on this project there are multiple players who possess multiple, possibly conflicting goals.

If the contractor defines the general as the sole customer, it is likely to produce a deliverable that leaves large numbers of other customers dissatisfied. The irony is that in the real world of defense contracting, the general will have moved on to another assignment before the project is finished, putting it at the mercy of his replacement, who has his own particular agenda. This discussion is not merely an academic exercise. In the building of Los Angeles class nuclear submarines, General Dynamics made the mistake of defining Admiral Hyman Rickover as *the* customer. In their obsession to satisfy Rickover, General Dynamics managers caused their company to suffer one of the most notorious cost overruns in history.

A key function of managers is to support their workers, not to direct them. The day of the directing boss who spews out ten orders a minute is past. A key role of managers is to create an environment that enables their team members to do the best job possible.

Use Crises to Shake up Stagnant Attitudes. Quite frequently, my students provide me with insights that dramatically affect my view of how the world functions. A good example of this occurred several years ago when four Japanese graduate students visited my office after class. We had just discussed how project managers can build authority on projects. The students approached me to say that they enjoyed the discussion and found most of the issues we covered to be pertinent to their lives in Japanese companies. They pointed out, however, that an important approach to building authority was not discussed.

"In Japanese organizations, we often create authority by announcing a crisis," said the chief spokesperson of the four students. "When a crisis is identified, we have an obligation to do our best to resolve it."

"You read in the newspapers how Japanese workers routinely work sixty-hour work weeks," offered another student. "We spend so much time at work in order to deal with crises. You don't think we enjoy ignoring our families, do you?"

During a half-hour period, the four students described how the work life of a Japanese manager is filled with never-ending crises. Although these crises motivate Japanese workers to work long weeks, they grow a bit tiring after a while. Each student expressed his distaste for this pressure-cooker environment.

Over the years, I have reflected on what these students told me. I have shared their comments with Japanese colleagues as well as with hundreds of students who have attended my seminars. My colleagues confirm that the experiences of the four students are quite typical. They point out that life in Japan has always been precarious (earthquakes, tsunamis, famine, political chaos, no natural resources), leading the population to view life as a series of never-ending crises that must be dealt with one at a time.

In thinking about the role of crises in Japanese management, I have been mulling over an intriguing question: would this approach work in the United States and other Western countries, which have cultures that differ from Japan's in many respects? My conclusion is a qualified yes. In today's fiercely competitive environment, the crises facing organizations throughout the world are real. In Western countries, cost pressures have resulted in unprecedented payroll cuts as companies seek to do more with less. The work force is very sensitive to the large number of layoffs occurring across a broad range of industries. They also realize that even the best companies are only marginally competitive and must keep a tight lid on escalating costs. Consequently, Western workers are beginning to look more like their Japanese counterparts. Increasingly, they view the world as an unstable and insecure place. They recognize that they may be called upon to work long weeks to help maintain their company's competitive position. They don't balk at the demands being placed on them, because to do so might jeopardize their jobs and their company's well-being.

The implications for project managers of the new crisis-filled work environment are clear: it is acceptable today to use crises to direct the attention of project workers and upper management to key issues. Specifically, crises can be used to change traditional attitudes and to focus people on new ways of doing things. For example, a common problem facing project organizations is that the sales staff give away business in order to make a sale. They either offer project services for less than cost or promise to include features in the deliverable that project staff cannot produce. If this behavior leads to a number of clearly defined disasters, project managers can use the emerging crisis to revamp the way sales staff do business. "Look at the mess the old approach to doing business has created," they can argue. "We must revamp our approach to selling our project services if we want to stay viable."

Here is another example that I recently encountered. I was asked by the training director of a Fortune 500 company to carry out a management seminar at a large factory in the Southwest. "I have one peculiar request to make, however," said the training director. "Is it possible to conduct the class from 7 A.M. to 1 P.M. with no lunch break?" I responded that I saw no problem with such a time frame.

I was curious about these hours, so I asked the training director why he was requesting them. He explained that headquarters was debating whether to close down the factory. During the past two years, half the employees had been laid off. The factory workers were gravely concerned that soon they would all be out of a job. They felt that to function more productively, they needed management training. Yet they didn't dare take too much time off from their work to obtain training in view of the precarious state of their operation. So they decided to do a double job: they would receive management training from 7 A.M. until 1 P.M. Then they would go to their jobs on the factory floor from 1 P.M. until 6 P.M.. This made for a long day. Since such a long workday violated union work rules, they voted to suspend the work rules temporarily. Such an action would have been unthinkable a decade earlier. The point here is that crisis can be employed as a vehicle to initiate radical change.

Although I haven't conducted a scientific study of the employment of crisis management in Western organizations, my impression—based on working with many project workers throughout the world—is that it is growing. Workers are being asked to work longer days and over weekends in order to respond to crises that arise with increasing frequency. The 1970s dream of thirty-hour work weeks and two-month vacations is a thing of the past.

The dangers of reliance on crises to motivate the work force are plain. Most obvious is the danger of burnout. How energetic and creative can we expect our work force to be if they spend sixty hours a week on the job and eschew vacations? What impact does this have on their family lives?

Another danger is that the continual announcements of crises can wear thin. In the West, crisis management has traditionally been associated with loss of control. The crisis manager is seen to be a reactive "firefighter" who responds to events rather than initiating them. Western workers may ultimately reject the precept that perpetual crisis is a natural state of affairs.

Going with the Flow with Rapid Prototyping

One way to manage change is to harness its momentum and direct it in desired directions. An appropriate analogy is a canoeist trying to negotiate his or her canoe down rapids. Ninety-five percent of the canoe's downstream progress is determined by the force of water rushing around boulders and over falls. Perhaps 5 percent is directed by the canoeist, who by means of controlled paddling can move the canoe laterally, allowing it to proceed along one channel rather than another and enabling it to avoid collisions with rocks. Attempts to go against the powerful current lead to frustration and failure. Success is based on going with the flow in a controlled manner.

Rapid prototyping is a methodology that arose in the 1980s that manages change by going with the flow. Its origins lie in software development, but today its applications extend across a broad range of activities. Its basic premise is that in a rapidly changing world, it is often impossible to prespecify requirements precisely. Even when possible, it may be undesirable to do so.

Proponents of rapid prototyping recognize that a major

problem of project staff in specifying requirements is that the customers they attempt to serve don't know their needs or wants. Furthermore, customers are incapable of determining whether the requirements presented to them by project staff early in the project life cycle truly represent their interests because at this stage these interests are rather abstract and difficult to visualize. Consequently, as a deliverable gradually emerges and they see what they are actually getting, they begin demanding changes to the requirements. If they like what they see, they may very well request enhancements to the evolving deliverable. ("What you're producing is fantastic! Now can you add the following bells and whistles to make it superlative?") If they don't like what they see, they will request changes to make it right. The point is, there *will* be change no matter what.

The rapid prototyping perspective sees this phenomenon not as a problem but rather as an opportunity. Why not obtain customers' involvement in developing requirements by having them react to prototypes that are presented to them from time to time? Because the prototypes represent a tangible deliverable, customers can respond to them more meaningfully than they can to abstract statements.

The Rapid Prototyping Procedure

The rapid prototyping methodology is summarized in Figure 3.1. The first steps in the process represent classic systems analysis. Project staff interview customers to identify their needs and wants. They then try to determine whether these needs and wants can be satisfied in view of budget, schedule, and technical constraints. They also review how these needs and wants are being addressed by current procedures. As a result of this process, they formulate their view of what the customer requirements should be.

With classic systems development, these requirements serve as the basis for developing a new system. The requirements are used to formulate a design. Then the design is employed to actually build a deliverable. For this approach to result in a deliverable that meets customer needs and wants, the original requirements must be on target. The problem is that they often are not.

Figure 3.1. The Rapid Prototyping Life Cycle.

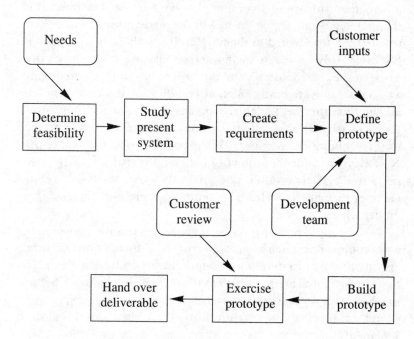

With rapid prototyping, the requirements emerging from systems analysis are viewed as just the first step in the development of customer-focused requirements. They are used to build a prototype so that customers can see what they will get. In software development, the prototype vehicle is computer screen images. For example, in a project to develop a simple management information system (MIS), three sets of prototypes might be used. One would be screen images illustrating data entry forms. Another would be screen images of data retrieval forms. The third would be help menus.

When the first prototype is ready, the development team arranges to meet with a panel of customers. The composition of this panel is crucial to the success of the project. Panel members must accurately reflect the interests of the full range of customers. For example, in our MIS example, the panel should reflect the perspective of data entry clerks, data retrieval personnel, and a set of the people who use the data to help them in their decision making. If the wrong panel members are chosen, the resulting requirements will not be relevant to customer needs and wants.

The first meeting between customers and developers is a classic kickoff meeting. Developers introduce themselves and the prototyping process. They show the customer panel the prototype they have developed. At this point, the prototype is nothing more than screen images. There is no depth behind them. Still, they serve a valuable function because customers see what they will get. At this kickoff meeting, they are generally delighted to find that they are working with something that has the "look and feel" of the final product. They may immediately begin offering suggestions for improving the prototype.

After the first meeting, developers go off for several weeks and begin adding muscle and sinews to the prototype skeleton. They are careful not to add too much detail. (This process is called top-down design.) Their objective at this point is to produce as quickly as possible a prototype that customers can work with to give them an accurate sense of what they are getting. Once this revised prototype is ready, they hand it to the panel of customers for their review. The panel then "exercises" the prototype. For example, if it is well developed, they may be able to enter sample data into the data entry forms. Because the prototype is just a shell at this point, it is incapable of doing anything meaningful with the entered data. Nonetheless, this data entry exercise is important because it may bring to the surface issues that might otherwise be ignored ("Look, the employee identification number is too short. Two more digits should be added to it.")

On small systems, the prototype-exercising process can be undertaken very quickly—in a matter of hours. On larger systems, it will consume substantially more time.

As a consequence of hands-on experience with the emerging product, the customer panel is prepared to offer useful guidance to the development team on further development of the product. Once the prototype exercise process is complete, the customer panel meets with the developers to present their reactions. In our MIS example, they may find that the design of the data retrieval forms is a bit cumbersome. Some data fields can be eliminated, others added.

They may also complain that the help menus use arcane terminology that they do not understand. The development team assesses these comments and determines which can be accommodated and which cannot. They then go off and add more detail to the still skimpy prototype.

The whole process is repeated over and over again until a satisfactory product emerges.

In the early days of prototyping, there was a great deal of concern that refinements of the prototype could go on indefinitely. Experience with prototyping suggests that this is not really a problem. Three very simple rules have emerged for stopping the process. First, the process can cease when a target date has been reached. Second, it can stop when the budget has been fully expended. Third, it can stop when there is general agreement between the customer panel and developers that enough has been done. Actually, with prototyping you can stop the process at almost any time and still have viable requirements. (Remember: the process *began* with a set of requirements established through conventional systems analysis.)

At this point in the cycle, rapid prototyping can travel down one of two roads. With small, simple projects, it is possible that the prototype has gradually evolved into a usable product. If this is the case, the development team may hand over the prototype to the customers and end the whole process. Rapid-prototyping purists do not like this approach. They argue that the product that emerges through the prototyping process is poorly designed since it was put together in a piecemeal fashion. The chief problem with poorly designed systems is that they are difficult to maintain. When they break, they are hard to fix. When enhancements are desired, they may be impossible to develop.

The second road that rapid prototyping can take is called the "throwaway model" approach. With this approach, the prototype that emerges from the process is given to the development group's requirements experts. They study it to see what features the customers find valuable. As a consequence of this study, they write up detailed requirements that are ultimately used as the core of a highly disciplined development process. Once the detailed requirements have been created, the prototype is thrown away.

Strengths of Rapid Prototyping

A key advantage of rapid prototyping is that it leads to unprecedented levels of customer acceptance of deliverables. High customer acceptance occurs because customers are actively and meaningfully involved in defining their requirements. The serious problem of setting unrealistic customer expectations—a common problem in project management—disappears with rapid prototyping since customers see exactly what they will get. Another familiar difficulty—developers who ignore customer sensibilities—fades away because developers are forced to listen to what customers have to say.

Some of the greatest benefits of rapid prototyping are tied to the customers' exercising of the prototype. This effort has a number of salubrious effects. First, it entails constant testing of the evolving product. It exposes bugs early and offers developers an opportunity to deal with them while they are still manageable.

Second, it gets customers actively involved in developing requirements. They now become part of the development team. In fact, rapid prototyping is a customer partnering methodology. To the extent that their suggestions are incorporated into the final requirements, customers are committed to living with the solutions the developer-customer team offers.

Third, exercising the prototype is a form of training. In order to exercise the prototype, customers must learn how to work the system. The more they exercise the prototype, the more comfortable they will be in using the final product.

Pitfalls of Rapid Prototyping

Although rapid prototyping has led to astonishing levels of customer satisfaction, it is not a panacea. Over the last few years, I have interviewed customers and developers associated with more than fifty prototyped projects in order to learn of their experiences. The people I interviewed—both customers and developers—overwhelmingly supported the prototyping process. However, they also warned me of some of the pitfalls they encountered. Following are the pitfalls they described.

The Development Team Is Not Equipped to Deal with Customers Effectively. The most serious complaints I heard about rapid prototyping center on the toll it takes on the development team. "It's killing my technical people," complained the director of data processing of a large international organization. He explained that his technical staff possessed neither the training nor the inclination to deal effectively with customers. They did not become programmers and analysts because they enjoyed dealing with people. So when they were directly exposed to customers they encountered a number of frustrations. For example, their customers had difficulty distinguishing between prototypes and the real thing. As the prototype became more sophisticated, customers didn't understand why the developers didn't simply turn it over to them as the final product. They did not fully appreciate that the prototypes they were exercising had no real depth.

A number of approaches have been implemented to deal with this problem. One is to appoint someone to the development team who has both people skills and knowledge of the technology. This individual serves as the main point of contact between the customer panel and the development team, playing the role of buffer. The problem inherent in this solution is that an additional communications layer has been placed between customers and developers, increasing the likelihood of some measure of miscommunication.

A second approach is to put one or two educated customers on the development team. If they grasp the technological issues involved in the development process, they can interact productively with the development team members. Two potential problems can arise with this approach: (1) the customers on the development team can start changing requirements at whim, aggravating difficulties of rubber baselines—I call this the Trojan Horse effect; (2) the customers can become captivated by the technology and lose touch with their customer base so that after a while, they no longer represent customer interests.

A third approach is to improve the human relations skills of the members of the development team through training.

The Prototype Platform Is Different from the Platform on Which the System Will Actually Run. The single most frequent piece of advice I received from system developers during my interviews was:

never prototype a system on a platform that is different from the platform on which the built system will function. I heard many horror stories of teams that developed prototypes of mainframe systems on personal computers, employing user-friendly fourth-generation language report generators (4GLs) as the prototyping vehicle. Customers became accustomed to working with prototypes that were flexible, colorful, and easy to adjust. Upon delivery of the real system, customers were horrified to see that it had the cumbersomeness of a mainframe system and used monochrome monitors. Even the keyboard was different from what they used in exercising the prototypes. Needless to say, they vented their frustrations upon the development team.

The Prototyping Process Lacks Discipline. A key goal of prototyping is customer involvement in developing requirements in a dynamic environment. For this to work properly, prototypes must be built as quickly as possible. Creative perspectives are emphasized. In all the excitement, it is not surprising that rapid prototyping efforts frequently lack the disciplines of documentation and effective change control. I sometimes quip that rapid prototyping is all heart and no discipline.

Discipline must be built into the prototyping effort. Rules must be established that each round of the prototyping process be fully documented. Key decisions and actions should be written down. In addition, changes should not be made in a haphazard, free-flow fashion. A change control board made up of representatives of key stakeholders might be established to review change requests that have a measurable impact on schedule, budget, and specifications.

Rapid Prototyping on Nonsoftware Projects

It might seem that rapid prototyping's usefulness is limited to software projects. Actually, it can be employed effectively on a wide range of projects. Two examples of its use on nonsoftware projects are offered here.

Smithsonian Institution's Natural History Museum. One evening, after I presented a lecture on rapid prototyping to my graduate project management students at George Washington University, a student who worked at the Smithsonian Institution approached me. She was a curator at the Natural History Museum.

"The prototyping process you described is precisely what I employ when I create a new display at the Natural History Museum," she said. She went on to describe how a display is created at the museum. First, a number of drawings of a possible new display are created. Then a group of people representing the public are brought together and shown the drawings. They are asked to respond to the different drawings and to identify the features that they find most appealing. A handful of drawings are singled out as possible prospects for the display. The ideas represented in these drawings are then embodied in three-dimensional models of the displays.

The group of public representatives are then reassembled, shown the physical models, and asked to respond. Consideration is given to their responses, and one model is selected as the one that will serve as the actual display. This model is rebuilt and refined. The public representatives are assembled for a final time to review and respond to this last model. Their comments are solicited, and, based on them and other considerations, the actual display is built.

Seattle's Woodland Park Zoo. The designers of recent improvements to Seattle's Woodland Park Zoo used computer-aided design software to create three-dimensional images of animal habitats and landscapes that they proposed to build. These images allowed the viewer to "stroll" through the zoo and to see different displays from different angles. The designers showed these images to key zoo personnel to get their responses to the proposed habitats. These reviews resulted in important insights that led to significant alterations in the proposed designs. For example, some reviewers pointed out that various obstructions, such as tree branches and shrubs, would block a clear view of the animals in their habitats.

Resisting Change with Configuration Management

Just as rapid prototyping is all heart and no discipline, configuration management (CM) is all discipline and no heart. CM is a methodology whose chief tenet is to treat specifications like a contract.

Customers should get nothing more or less than a deliverable that meets the specs. No deviations from the specs are accepted unless changes to the specs have gone through a rigorous screening process and have been approved by the proper authorities. Such a contractual approach protects customers from developers and implementers digressing from the specs. It also protects project staff from whimsical customer changes to the requirements.

Note that the underlying philosophy of such an approach is to satisfy the specifications (that is, the contract), not to satisfy the customer. This may seem out of touch with the current focus on customer satisfaction, but it really is not. The key to making CM customer focused is to make sure that the specifications truly respond to customer needs and wants.

CM's origins date to the U.S. defense contracting community in the 1950s. At that time, it became obvious that building weapons systems had become too complex to be done in a traditional ad hoc fashion. In particular, a consensus emerged that all changes to a complex system should be fully documented and tracked by a sophisticated tracking system. Without proper documentation of changes, it becomes nearly impossible to fix or enhance complex systems. CM was the proposed solution to this problem. Beginning in the mid 1950s, builders of complex defense systems were required to employ CM to document and track changes on all their larger projects. Today, employment of CM has gone beyond hardware development to software projects as well. A well-known software variant of CM is called *version control*.

Basic Steps in Developing a System with Configuration Management

In developing or modifying a system with CM, every attempt is made to resist incidental change. What customers sign off on is what customers get—not an iota more or an iota less. The following development process allows CM to minimize specious change.

Step 1: Develop Detailed Specifications

With CM, the development process begins with the creation of detailed specifications. Traditionally, these specifications would be generated through classic systems analytical procedures. That is, systems analysts would go out with clipboard in hand, review existing technologies and procedures, interview key people, identify future needs, and then develop system specifications. The problem with this approach is that it often leads to the generation of specifications that are not truly responsive to customer needs and wants. Today, customer-focused specifications are increasingly being generated by means of rapid prototyping.

Once the detailed specifications have been created, then they must be approved by pertinent authorities in both the customer and developer organizations. After they have signed off on the specs, the specs become a *baseline*.

Step 2: Develop a General Design

Guidance on developing the general design comes from the baseline (that is, the specifications) and only the baseline. As the general design takes form, it is frequently tested against the baseline for *traceability*. That is, every element of the general design must be tied to a specification. A *forward trace* starts with a specification and attempts to find a corresponding general design element. If no such element exists, it must be added. A *backward trace* starts with a general design element and attempts to find a corresponding specification. If none is found, the general design element is eliminated since it represents an addition to the design that is out of line with the specifications.

After a satisfactory general design has been developed and approved by pertinent authorities in both the customer and developer organizations, it becomes the new baseline. The specifications can be put away for a while. This is not a problem since they are actually embedded in the general design.

Step 3: Develop a Detailed Design

The detailed design is built according to the new baseline (that is, the general design) and only the baseline. As in Step 2, care is taken to maintain traceability. When the detailed design is nearly finished, it may be subjected to a *functional configuration audit*. That is, independent experts may be asked to review the design and to offer their opinion as to whether the system that emerges from it will function in the prescribed fashion. After the detailed design has been approved by pertinent authorities in both the customer and developer organizations, it becomes the new baseline.

Step 4: Build and Test the System

The system is built in accordance with the last baseline (that is, the detailed design). As it takes form, it should be tested periodically against the latest version of approved specifications. When the system is fully built, it may be subjected to a *physical configuration audit*, a full-scale test to ascertain whether the actual system behaves properly in accordance with the specifications. At the end of this step, the development effort is complete.

Change Control

Change on projects is inevitable. Even as the development process proceeds in a disciplined way, change will occur and configuration management must be prepared to deal with it. For example, during the general design stage it may become obvious that some of the specifications defined earlier are not realistic and must be modified. Or during the building stage the project team may find that an important component needed in the emerging deliverable is no longer produced and that a substitute must be found.

Configuration management deals with change through careful screening of change requests, meticulous documentation, and controlled updates incorporating changes. Each of these elements of change control in CM will be discussed briefly.

Screening of Change Requests

Screening of change requests focuses on determining which change requests have merit and which do not. The process generally begins when someone (for example, a customer, a manager, or a member of the technical staff) submits a change request to the project manager on a form. Different organizations have different names for these forms: *request-for-change forms, mods* (modification requests), or *engineering change proposals* (the term commonly used on defense projects).

Upon receiving the change request, the project manager must make an important classification decision. Is this a Category A change (one with a major impact on schedule, budget, or quality) or a Category B change (a low-impact change)? If it is a Category B change, the project manager may make a decision on the spot as to whether the change should be effected. If it is a Category A change, the screening process will be more deliberate. The change request will be turned over to a change control board (CCB) for careful review.

The CCB is primarily interested in the management impacts of a change. In reviewing a change request, the board members want to know its effect on the project budget, schedule, and specifications. Only after conducting a managerial review of this sort is the CCB prepared to weigh the costs against the benefits of a change.

The CCB is typically made up of a small number of people representing different stakeholders in the organization. Ideally, representation comes from technical, financial, marketing, and production groups. With such an interdisciplinary composition, the team is unlikely to view change requests from an overly narrow perspective.

Many organizations subject change requests to technical scrutiny as well as managerial scrutiny. To do this, they establish an engineering review board (ERB) that operates in parallel with the CCB. The chief objective of the ERB is to determine whether change requests have technical merit. In organizations that have both a CCB and an ERB, if both boards approve a change it will be granted. If both disapprove of a change, it will be denied. If there is a mixed verdict, the two groups will work together to establish a consensus about future action.

The principal strength of this rigorous screening process is that it discourages trivial change. "Scope creep" is not likely to occur if individual change requests are subjected to rigorous scrutiny. Another strength is that the CCB can act collectively to resist harmful change requests from powerful players within or outside the organization. A properly constituted CCB—operating as a col-

lective unit representing a broad range of organizational interests—
is empowered to say no to even the most commanding individuals.
As such, CCBs can serve as project managers' friends, enabling them
to say no to unreasonable change requests through indirect means.

An obvious problem with the CCB is its potential as a bot-
tleneck. If the CCB spends too much time reviewing change requests, progress on the project may grind to a halt. Effective
employment of the CCB entails a balancing act: on the one hand,
scrutiny of change requests must be rigorous; on the other, the best
interests of the project require that the review process occur as
quickly as possible.

Documenting Change

Very small projects do not need elaborate documentation. When
you change the washer of a leaky faucet, it doesn't make sense to
document the process in detail. However, as projects become larger
and more complex, documentation takes on increasing importance.
Following are some functions of documentation:

- It enables the project team to maintain an audit trail of their
  actions. If at some point a customer complains that the team did
  not undertake certain crucial steps on the project, the team can
  pull out the pertinent documentation to support their position.
- It records information that is beyond the capability of people to
  retain in their heads.
- It serves as a tool for coordinating the actions of different sets
  of team players. When someone new arrives on the scene, the
  quickest way he or she can get up to speed is to review documentation on what has transpired on the project so far.
- It is necessary for debugging and enhancing systems. For example, if a building experiences an electrical problem, the first step
  taken to fix the problem should be to acquire a wiring diagram.
  Without such a diagram, the repair job will be heavily dependent upon trial and error fixes.

In CM, careful documentation of change requests and actions is important. Effective CM systems have CM data bases, librar-

ies, and librarians to maintain the documentation. This, of course, means that CM systems involve a large amount of paperwork.

The CM process is heavily bureaucratic. Today, the term *bureaucracy* has negative connotations. This was not always so. As Max Weber showed in his work, bureaucracies arise for a purpose. They are natural organizational responses to dealing with complexity. It is a fundamental premise of CM that bureaucracy is the price we must be willing to pay in order to manage complexity.

Updating Change

As changes are accepted and incorporated, the project must be revised to reflect their presence. Baselines must be revised. People downstream must be warned, "Change is on the way!" A key component of CM is updating change in an orderly fashion. The updating process is closely tied to the documentation effort since a major element of updating is revision of the documentation.

Conclusions

One of the great frustrations project staff face on their projects is constant change. The people they deal with constantly change. New bosses, new customers, new vendors, and new technical staff must be dealt with. Each time new people come on the scene, they bring with them a set of priorities different from their predecessors. Thus priorities are always changing. Other common sources of change include technology, budgets, regulations, and resources.

It is easy to view change as an impediment to progress on projects. When change occurs unchecked, it is indeed a hindrance. However, change is inevitable. Ranting against it is as ineffective as King Canute's imprecations against the ocean's incoming tide. To deal with change constructively, project staff must accept its inevitability. Then they must begin developing strategies to deal with it. A good first step is to recognize that change is not inherently bad—in fact, it creates opportunity.

Strategies for dealing with change basically fall into two categories. One is to go with the flow. This approach recognizes that change can be constructive. It is particularly effective in dealing with high-flux situations, such as defining customer needs and requirements.

A second strategy is to resist change. Not all change is good. Whimsical change that reflects capricious fluctuations in mood is an example. Such change leads to cost and schedule overruns and possibly degraded product quality without adding anything to the project effort.

Effective project management requires that project staff be able to distinguish between good and detrimental change. It also demands that project staff be prepared to deal with change in the most effective manner possible.

Chapter Four

Managing Risk:
Identifying, Analyzing,
and Planning Responses

From the beginnings of human existence, life has been chancy. During the days of hunting and gathering, humans never knew for sure whether a hunting expedition would end successfully. In order to increase the likelihood of success, they would act out the hunt through paintings on the walls of their caves. Today we see the beautiful results of their efforts in the caves of Lascaux in the Périgord region of France.

As humans settled on the land and shifted their focus from hunting to cultivation, the production of food stabilized. Still, some years were better than others; drought, floods, and pestilence could drastically lower the food supply. Some people believed that these disasters were inflicted by angry gods and therefore made various offerings to appease them—including human sacrifice. The Egyptians took a more effective approach to managing the swings of nature. As the biblical story of Joseph shows us, they developed an inventory management system for grain production, using stores of grain accrued during the fat years to cover the shortages of the lean years.

What the experience of our forebears teaches us is that humans have been engaged in the management of risk for millennia. Some of their approaches were more efficacious than others. The Egyptian case tells us that a fundamental cornerstone of risk management—contingency planning—was being employed on a large scale four thousand years ago.

In recent years, there has been a growing awareness of the presence of risk on projects and the need to manage it consciously. The existence of risk is reflected in *the* fundamental law of project management: Murphy's Law, which states that if something can go wrong, it will.

Projects are particularly susceptible to risk because each project is unique in some measure. The degree of uniqueness can vary dramatically. Thus a state of the art semiconductor research project will have more unique features than a project to carry out the one-thousandth installation of a small telephone switch. This uniqueness means that the past is an imperfect guide to the future. We are never completely sure what the future holds. There is always a risk that things will not go as planned.

Official recognition of risk as a special concern of project management came in the late 1980s, when the Project Management Institute declared risk management a part of its core Project Management Body of Knowledge (PMBOK).

Perspectives on Risk

It seems as if everyone is involved in risk management these days. In business school, students learn how to measure the risk of a stock portfolio. A low-risk portfolio is one whose performance analysts can predict with a high degree of certainty. A high-risk portfolio is one whose performance can fluctuate dramatically.

Civil engineers look at risk from the perspective of system failure. On many civil engineering projects, system failure can have dramatic consequences. A bridge that collapses, a nuclear power plant that experiences a meltdown, or a building that cannot withstand a 7.5 Richter scale earthquake presents risks that have both economic and safety implications.

Insurance companies have been in the business of risk analysis for centuries. They insure clients against losses. In effect, they allow their clients to deflect risk by transferring responsibility for losses from the clients onto themselves. They stay in business by estimating the likelihood that their clients will suffer losses and weighing this against income generated through insurance premiums.

Definitions of acceptable risk are different for stockholders, civil engineers, and insurers, reflecting the varied consequences of undesirable outcomes. Although a 10 percent probability of a downside loss is acceptable in a business context, it is totally unacceptable in the building of a nuclear power plant, where a nuclear accident can lead to the loss of thousands of lives.

Risk and Variability

Ultimately, what ties the different perspectives on risk together is the concept of variability. Risk is fundamentally a measure of the extent to which a given outcome might deviate from what is expected or desired. Consider the performance of two stocks over a period of a year. Stock A's price averages $20.00 a share. During the year, its lowest price is $19.50 per share, and its highest reaches $20.50 per share. Stock B's price also averages $20.00 per share. However, it hits a low of $10.00 per share and a high of $30.00 per share. The variability of its price is substantially larger than that of Stock A. From an investment perspective, Stock B presents a greater investment risk than Stock A.

In many cases, variability can be measured quite precisely. It is known that many phenomena, such as body weight, height, the volume of soda distributed by a bottling machine, and IQ, are distributed normally (that is, according to a bell-shaped curve). Events that occur rarely can often be described by a Poisson distribution. Statisticians are thoroughly familiar with the properties of a plethora of distributions, including uniform, beta, gamma, hypergeometric, and binomial distributions. If we know the statistical distribution of some phenomenon, we can make probabilistic guesses about the occurrence of a specific event.

The usefulness of distributions in predicting outcomes has been applied in project management for decades and is embedded

**Figure 4.1. Using the Triangular Distribution to
Estimate Expected Task Duration.**

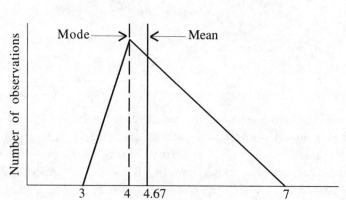

Number of hours for paint to dry

in its best-known technique: PERT (Program Evaluation and Review Technique, developed by the navy in 1957). The people who created the PERT scheduling technique realized that any estimate of the duration of a proposed task is subject to uncertainty.

This can be illustrated in a numerical example. Suppose we are trying to estimate the amount of time it will take for paint to dry on a newly painted chair. Historical evidence tells us that on warm, dry days, the paint may dry in as little as three hours. On cool, humid days, however, it may dry in seven hours. Most typically, it dries in four hours. These three data points can describe critical points in a triangular distribution. The three-hour estimate is our optimistic estimate, the seven-hour estimate our pessimistic estimate, and the four-hour estimate what is most likely to occur. The triangular distribution associated with paint drying on our chairs is pictured in Figure 4.1.

Given this array of possible outcomes, how long does it take the paint on an average chair to dry? PERT allows us to estimate the expected value (that is, the average duration) of paint drying on many chairs. The formula for computing this expected value is:

Expected duration = [optimistic duration
                     + most likely duration
                     + pessimistic duration]/3

In our example, we have

Expected duration = [3 + 4 + 7]/3 = 14/3 = 4.67

That is, given that the paint may dry in as little as three hours, as much as seven hours, and most likely in four hours, it will, on the average, take 4.67 hours to dry. This value is a *point estimate*. This one number summarizes what is likely to happen after accounting for the variability of the outcome. However, realistically, we know that there is a range of possible outcomes. We acknowledge this in everyday life when we make a statement such as "It will take you three hours to reach Los Angeles, give or take a half hour." What we want to know is how to compute this "give or take" figure.

In statistics, the "give or take" of an estimate is often computed as *standard deviation*. Over the years, I have taught business statistics to hundreds of MBA students and have seen the beads of sweat form on their upper lips as we discussed the implications of standard deviation. To many of them, standard deviation is an arcane concept that is as easy to understand as the equations describing the Second Law of Thermodynamics. Actually, standard deviation is a simple, user-friendly concept. It is basically a measure of the "slop"—or variability—of our estimate. In the example of paint drying on our chairs, a rough estimate of the standard deviation of our triangular distribution can be obtained with the following equation (Duncan and Nevison, 1994):

Standard deviation = [optimistic duration
                      – pessimistic duration]/5

Substituting our paint-drying data into this equation, we have:

Standard deviation = [7 – 3]/5 = 4/5 = 0.80

Thus we can say that typically the paint on our chairs dries in 4.67 hours, plus or minus four-fifths of an hour.

The concept of standard deviation is important in risk analysis. Standard deviation measures the variability of an estimate. Risk is concerned with variability. Thus standard deviation can be taken to be a measure of risk. The larger the standard deviation of an estimate, the greater its variability and concomitant risk. For example, experience may show us that Task A costs $10,000 to carry out, with a standard deviation of $1,000. Task B also typically costs $10,000, but its associated standard deviation is $3,000. The precision of our estimate of the cost of Task B is weaker than for our estimate of the cost of Task A. Thus the risk associated with Task B is greater than that associated with Task A.

Range of Risks

The concept of risk is closely tied to the concept of information. When information is lacking, uncertainty increases, which leads to greater risk. When pertinent information is bountiful, uncertainty decreases, leading to a parallel decrease in risk. Clearly, a key strategy for managing risk is to increase the amount of information we can feed into the decision process. More will be said about this later.

To appreciate the range of risk facing us on our projects, we can picture a continuum ranging from total uncertainty to total certainty. With total uncertainty, everything is unknown. We lack data, either because we have never collected it or because the data are inherently difficult to compute. Here risk is high because there may be a great variation in the outcomes that can occur. We are just not sure what these outcomes might be.

With total certainty, everything is known. We can predict the consequences of actions with 100 percent accuracy. Here risk is zero since there is no variability in outcomes.

Of course, in most decision-making situations, the uncertainty we face lies somewhere between the two extremes. On tasks that we have carried out many times, we know from experience what the range of outcomes will be. In the chair-painting example given above, data from past experiences tell us that it might take the paint as long as seven hours to dry or as little as three hours, and that most typically it dries in four hours. Although we do not know with 100 percent certainty how long it will take for the paint to dry, we nonetheless have a good idea of what to expect.

In contrast, we also encounter surprise situations, which can be labeled "unknown unknowns." For example, a competitor can produce a major advance in an integrated circuit design that makes our technology obsolete. Or a war in the Middle East may cause oil shortages that invalidate all our project material cost estimates.

In general, to get a better handle on risk, we should strive to reduce the unknowns.

Sources of Risk on Projects

In project management, a little paranoia is healthy. We don't just suspect that risk lurks behind every shrub, pillar, and door. It really does! Risk is everywhere. The only time we do not encounter risk is when we make decisions with total certainty, and such decisions are rare.

Our principal concern is to learn how to categorize the risks we encounter. One useful categorization is the distinction between risks that arise in the environment and those that arise internally. Sources of risk coming from outside our organization include changes in government regulations, the introduction of new competitor products, and major technological breakthroughs made at a university lab. Environmental risk sources coming from within our organization (but outside our work unit) include such things as the appointment of a new vice president in charge of our division, budget cuts associated with declining corporate profitability, and the assignment of resources to our project coming from other work units.

A major feature of environmental risks is that they are largely uncontrollable. At best, we strive to identify them so that we can be prepared to deal with them.

Sources of internal risk include unreliability of worker performance, office politics, and unchecked expenditures. We often have some measure of control over such risks. For example, good human resource management practices will help reduce problems of worker unreliability, awareness of political agendas will mitigate the impacts of office politics, and close monitoring of expenditures will reduce the likelihood of cost overruns.

Of course, risks can be categorized in other ways as well. A common approach is to categorize them functionally. *Technical risk* comprises the risk factors associated with the development or operation of the deliverable. Our concern here is with "bugs" and "glitches." Software modules that ran beautifully when tested independently fail when we try to run them as an integrated product. A soldered electrical connection won't hold because of the vibration of a motor. A chemical compound we have spent millions of dollars to develop becomes unstable at temperatures above 35 degrees Celsius.

Technical risk is highest when our projects tread new terrain or when they entail working with highly complex systems. Basic research and systems integration projects are notorious for their technical surprises. Risk is lowest when we revisit familiar ground.

Market risk is the risk that the product or service we develop will fail in the marketplace. Business history is replete with tales of products that overcame enormous technical obstacles, only to fail commercially. The best known example is DuPont's Corfam, a synthetic leather that cost a fortune to develop but that ultimately was rejected by consumers.

Financial risk comprises risks having to do with cash flow and profitability. Many companies with excellent products have gone out of business simply because they ran out of cash to pay the bills. Cash shortages can result if accounts receivable are not collected promptly, if a key customer disappears, if money is tied up in equipment, or if financial reserves are limited. Similarly, a company will not stay in business long unless it achieves profits. There are countless ways for companies to fail to achieve their profit objectives.

Human risk arises from the fact that the human players in projects—project staff, managers, customers, vendors—are complex, marginally predictable beings. Projects are constantly plagued with problems of human resource reliability, competence, and availability. They are further buffeted by the consequences of political struggles, the turnover of key players, and the fickleness of customers. If one were to create a detailed list of risk factors affecting a specific project, the list of human risks would surely be the longest.

Risk-Reward Trade-Offs

We are willing to assume risks because we anticipate that the rewards of our venture will more than offset the losses. The higher the potential rewards, the greater the risks we are willing to incur. This is a well-established principle of business, and we see evidence of it everywhere. Investment in over the counter start-up companies can return us eighty cents on the dollar in a year; it can also lead to massive losses of our investment capital if the companies perform poorly. In contrast, we can be reasonably sure that an investment in stable blue chip stocks will not result in major losses; by the same token, we should not expect to make a killing on them.

The risk-reward trade-off is also seen on our projects. Companies typically set higher hurdle rates (that is, required return) for high-risk projects than low-risk ones. In recent years, the business press has been filled with laments that the risk aversion of American companies has led them to abandon support of long-term, state of the art research and development projects that, while risky, could lead to major breakthroughs that would keep American companies in a leadership position in global markets.

Management science has developed a relatively simple tool for weighing the risks of failure against the opportunity for success. It is called *expected monetary value*. I will illustrate this approach with a simple example and will leave it to the readers' imaginations to see how more sophisticated variations on the basic principles can provide them with powerful insights into the risk-reward trade-off.

Suppose a company's marketing experts estimate that a project to develop Product X may ultimately generate $1,000,000 in net revenue. After taking into account such things as technical risks, market risks, and financial risks, they calculate that the overall probability of developing a successful product is 70 percent. Meanwhile, the company's costing experts estimate that all costs associated with bringing the product to market, including project costs, tool-up expenses, production expenses, and marketing costs, will be $300,000.

If we were to envision this project occurring millions of times, we could say that the expected value of the company's gains would be $1,000,000 (potential gain) times 0.7 (probability of achieving these gains). Thus the expected value of gains would be $700,000. The expected value of losses would be $300,000 (investment outlay) times 0.3 (probability of not achieving gains). That is, expected losses would be $90,000.

The expected value of *net gains* (expected gains minus expected losses) is $700,000 minus $90,000, or $610,000. This tells us that given the probabilities of gains and losses, coupled with estimates of the dollar value of anticipated gains and losses, it appears that we have a winner.

Risk and Time Horizons

In general, there is a positive correlation between level of risk and projected time horizon. That is, the further off an event is in the future, the less certain we are of its exact composition, and the higher the probability that some unanticipated action will affect it adversely. We encounter this reality in our daily lives. We have a precise sense of what we will be doing one hour from now. We are less sure of what we will be doing one week from now, and even less sure of our activities one year into the future.

On our projects, the highest level of risk is found at the very outset, when we face a long and uncertain future. As the project proceeds and we begin achieving our milestones and gaining experience, the risks associated with completing the project generally decrease. In the last hours of the project, after the deliverable has been built and fully tested, the risks of not completing the work become very low indeed.

Even as risks are decreasing, there is a countervailing force at work: as time goes by and we commit human and material resources to the project, our *stake* in it increases. In the earliest stages, we have invested little in the project, so that if we walk away from it, we have lost little. However, if we walk away from a project when we are far into the life cycle, we stand to lose a great deal.

The interplay of risk and stake is pictured in Figure 4.2.

Figure 4.2. Risk Versus Stake.

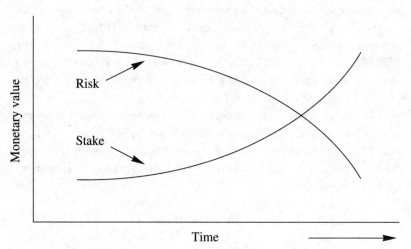

Risk Exposure

Clearly, the size of the investment requirement for a project has a bearing on whether it will be supported. From the perspective of risk, the chief concern is: how much do we have at stake in the project? The size of the stake is called *risk exposure*. The larger the risk exposure, the more we will lose if things go wrong. In general, we would like to maximize benefits while minimizing exposure to risk.

Table 4.1 shows the kind of risk-reward dilemma we often face in making decisions about how to proceed on our projects. To keep the example simple, we will assume that the dollar values portrayed represent real value (that is, the cost of capital is zero and there is no time value of money). Project B is clearly more profitable than Project A ($1,100 versus $800).

Note that risk exposure is greater in Project A than in Project B in the early years. In the first year, Project A requires outlays of $700 compared to outlays of $300 for Project B. In the second through fourth years, Project B's total outlays are larger than Project A's. If there is a reasonable probability of failure in the early stages of these projects, Project B has the lower risk exposure. In Year 4, the risk balance begins to shift. Although the total outlays

Table 4.1. Comparing Variability of Risk over Time.

Table 4.1a. Project A

	Outlays	Income	Profit	Cumulative profit
Year 1	700	0	-700	-700
Year 2	200	0	-200	-900
Year 3	100	700	600	-300
Year 4	0	600	600	300
Year 5	0	500	500	800
Total	1,000	1,800	800	800

Table 4.1b. Project B

	Outlays	Income	Profit	Cumulative profit
Year 1	300	0	-300	-300
Year 2	300	0	-300	-600
Year 3	300	600	300	-300
Year 4	300	800	500	200
Year 5	0	900	900	1,100
Total	1,200	2,300	1,100	1,100

for Project A ($1,000) are lower than for Project B ($1,200), the cash inflows offset outlays better in Project B than Project A. From a five-year perspective, it is clear that over the life of the projects, the overall risk exposure of Project A is lower than that of Project B.

Risk Management

When project professionals encounter risk on their projects, what can they do about it? An obvious answer to this question is: they should *manage* it. Risk management is a broad concept. Wideman (1992) has divided it into four parts: risk identification, risk assessment, risk response planning, and documentation.

Risk identification is a process of uncovering potential risk events in order to avoid unpleasant surprises. It should be undertaken systematically. It can focus on both internal and external risks; those that are predictable versus those that are unpredictable; those over which we have a measure of control versus those that are largely uncontrollable; and those that are technical versus those that are nontechnical.

As organizations gain experience in identifying risks, they should document their findings. At a minimum, they should develop a checklist of risk factors that must be dealt with on typical projects. If possible, different risk factors should be weighted according to their importance. An example of some risk factors and their associated weights for a data processing project is shown in Exhibit 4.1. The actual document from which these risk factors were taken contains a total of seventy-five risk factors, so what is seen here is just the tip of the iceberg.

Risk assessment attempts to identify the nature of risk events and to anticipate their impacts on the project. Although the assessment process frequently involves subjective judgments, it is desirable to quantify the risks to as great an extent as possible. Included here are attempts to determine the probabilities of outcomes. If the organization has a good historical record of project data, it may be possible to use these data to generate probabilities. Otherwise, the probabilities will be based on subjective guesses.

Modeling the project can provide good insights into the project's dynamics and the consequences of risk events. Project scheduling software can offer risk analysts a computerized modeling tool. The software has scheduling, budgeting, and resource management capabilities built into it so that it is possible to develop comprehensive "what if" scenarios. Models of pieces of the projects can also be investigated. For example, best case, worst case, and most likely budget scenarios can be investigated. Once again, the existence of powerful software tools—in particular, electronic spreadsheets—can greatly aid the modeling process. More will be said about modeling below.

Risk response planning is concerned with developing strategies to cope with risk events. Whereas risk identification and assessment provide us with an understanding of what can happen on the project, response planning furnishes us with actions we can take to either avoid a risk event or dampen its impacts. It generally focuses on three risk-coping strategies: developing and following system standards, acquiring insurance, and developing planning alternatives.

The development of and adherence to *system standards* can

**Exhibit 4.1. Typical Items Appearing in a Listing of Risk Factors
for a Data Processing Project.**

What is the status of the project team training plan? (Weight = 2)

a.	No training plan required	N/A - 0
b.	Complete plan in place	Low - 1
c.	Plan under development	Medium - 2
d.	No plan available	High - 3

What is the documentation approach for the proposed/existing system?
(Weight = 3)

a.	Excellent standards closely adhered to and carried out as an integral part of system and program development	Low - 1
b.	Adequate practices, but not uniformly adhered to	Medium - 2
c.	Poor or no standards; where standards exist, minimal adherence	High - 3

How much is the development affected by external systems? (Weight = 5)

a.	All critical intersystem communications are controlled through Interface Control Documents; standard protocols are utilized; interfaces are stable	Low - 1
b.	All critical intersystem communications are controlled through Interface Control Documents; some protocols may be nonstandard; interfaces change infrequently	Medium - 2
c.	Not all critical intersystem communications are controlled through Interface Control Documents; some protocols may be nonstandard; some interfaces change infrequently	High - 3

How many output reports are projected? (Weight = 1)

a.	Less than 10	Low - 1
b.	10 to 20	Medium - 2
c.	More than 20	High - 3

help us both to avoid problems and to deal with them effectively
once they arise. As an instrument of risk avoidance, standards keep
us from taking missteps. They are analogous to a detailed recipe in
a cookbook. If we follow an established recipe closely, we should

encounter few surprises and should produce a product that looks and tastes the way it is supposed to. Without the recipe, our dash of salt here and pinch of oregano there may lead to a culinary monstrosity.

Standards can also be created to deal with untoward events. We continually encounter such standards (often in the form of procedures) in our everyday lives: "In repairing the computer, unplug it from the electrical outlet before opening the chassis"; "If mixing the red and yellow dyes results in an orange that is too intense, add a little blue to subdue the color"; or "If it appears that the front tires have excessive wear on your front-wheel drive car, swap them with the rear tires."

The employment of *insurance* is a risk deflection strategy. When we purchase insurance, we are effectively transferring the risk from our shoulders onto those of the insurer. In project work, insurance typically focuses on direct property damage, legal liability, indirect consequential loss, and personnel issues (including health and life insurance).

Finally, the development of *planning alternatives* offers us a risk response strategy. The best known approach is contingency planning. With this approach, we map out different courses of action that should be undertaken, given different contingencies. In serious project work, where the consequences of failure may be disastrous, the contingency plans may be very detailed. A looser approach is to establish a contingency fund to cope with unforeseen events. How the funds are expended and the problem fixed are not defined in detail but are left up to the discretion of the project staff who are wrestling with the problem.

The fourth component of risk management is *documentation*. The importance of effective documentation cannot be overstated. Most organizations sit on a mountain of data that can provide them with valuable insights as to how they are doing their jobs. They have schedule and budget data embedded in their time sheets. They have additional budget data in their monthly budget reports, detailing how money is being spent. Project proposals provide a glimpse of what the organization said it could do in the preproject phase, statements of work detail project obligations, and postmortems describe what actually happened. Technical documentation, including the results of technical testing, generally exists in abundance. Most important, enormous amounts of information reside in the heads of the project participants.

Managers face two problems in dealing with all this data. First, they do not see its inherent value. To them, it is just a bunch of facts and figures cramming the corporate file cabinets. Because they lack sufficient background in data analysis, they find it difficult to picture how the data can be fashioned into something worthwhile.

Second, there are logistical problems in converting all this data into useful information. Who is going to do it? What steps should they take? How will it be reported and incorporated in project management? This second problem is not as intractable as it sounds, even in this era of budget cutbacks. Local colleges and universities are wonderful sources of low-cost, skilled talent. Graduate students in economics, engineering, statistics, and related disciplines are eager to find part-time employment with local organizations. They generally have the skills, discipline, and energy to carry out assignments like this.

Ultimately, the purpose of the documentation is to provide baseline data on what it takes to do a job. If a software writer promises us that she can write her software module in three weeks, we can show her data demonstrating that no one has written such modules in less than eight weeks. If upper management pressures us to shave 20 percent off our cost estimate on a bid, we can employ our historical model to illustrate the budget and schedule consequences of such an action. The important thing is that by collecting and employing historical data, we are creating an environment in which our perceptions of the future are based on informed judgment, rather than on wild seat-of-the-pants guesses.

Modeling

The advent of the personal computer has given project managers the capability to carry out risk analyses that would have been unthinkable just a decade ago. As I mentioned earlier, computerized PERT/CPM software packages allow us to create mathematical models of our projects, integrating schedule, budget, and resource management factors. Once the model has been created, project staff can put it through its paces, playing all manner of "what if" games. What if our budget is cut by 10 percent? What if the testing personnel arrive a week late? What if three additional people are made available to design our software product? Questions such as these can be readily addressed with project scheduling software.

Of particular relevance to risk management is software that allows project analysts to conduct statistical simulations of pertinent budget, schedule, and resource allocation scenarios. Most of these simulations employ the Monte Carlo approach. The use of this approach is best explained through illustrations.

Table 4.2 compares how much time it takes George and Martha to prepare for a picnic. On the average, their performance is identical: both typically take ten minutes to prepare sandwiches, six minutes to gather equipment, and four minutes to pack the car. Thus, on the average, each takes twenty minutes to prepare for the picnic. However, experience shows that George's performance on these tasks is less predictable than Martha's. This is reflected in the larger standard deviation values George possesses for each of the tasks.

Let us assume that the variability of both George's and Martha's performance can be described by the bell-shaped curve. The only difference between their curves is the standard deviation. With Monte Carlo simulation, the values for each of the activities can be allowed to fluctuate randomly according to their respective bell-shaped curves. Because of the larger standard deviations associated with his efforts, George's durations will fluctuate more wildly than Martha's.

In Table 4.2, we generated one thousand possible scenarios, assuming random fluctuations in duration generated by the bell-shaped curve. The results of this "experiment" are reported at the bottom of the table.

Owing to the high level of variability in George's performance, we see that it may take him as much as 31.6 minutes to prepare for the picnic or as few as 9.4 minutes. On the average it will take him 20 minutes. Martha, in contrast, performs in a more predictable manner: it may take her as much as 23.1 minutes or as little as 16.8 minutes to make her preparations. On the average, it

Table 4.2. A Schedule Simulation.

	George		Martha	
	Estimated duration	*Standard deviation*	*Estimated duration*	*Standard deviation*
Make sandwiches	10 min	3 min	10 min	1 min
Gather equipment	6 min	2 min	6 min	0.5 min
Pack car	4 min	2 min	4 min	0.5 min
TOTAL DURATION	20 min		20 min	
Maximum duration (simulated)	31.6 min		23.1 min	
Minimum duration (simulated)	9.4 min		16.8 min	
Standard deviation of total duration	4.3 min		1.3 min	
25% chance that value lies beyond:	22.6 min		20.7 min	

takes her 20 minutes. Clearly, there is a greater risk in depending on George than on Martha even though their performance is equal on average.

Table 4.3 illustrates the use of Monte Carlo simulation in projecting costs. Let us say that our organization's professional cost estimators base their estimates on the most likely costs of each task. They gather these data by reviewing previous project experiences. Using these data, they determine that the estimated cost for carrying out a project is $354,500.

As the table indicates, there is actually quite a bit of variability associated with each estimate. For example, experience shows us that design might cost as little as $3,200 or as much as $4,500. Most frequently, it costs $3,500. When we have optimistic, pessimistic, and realistic estimates such as this, we can allow Monte Carlo sim-

Table 4.3. Cost Estimation Simulation.

	Estimate (based on "most likely" costs)	Best case costs	Most likely costs	Worst case costs
Design	$3,500	$3,200	$3,500	$4,500
Development	$36,000	$33,000	$36,000	$42,000
Testing	$3,000	$2,800	$3,000	$3,200
Production (# of units × unit cost)	$312,000			
# of units	1,200	1,200	1,200	1,200
Unit cost	$260	$220	$260	$330
Total Cost	$354,500			

Simulation Results, Assuming Numbers Generated Randomly Using a Triangular Distribution

	Best case	Mean value	Worst case
TOTAL COST	$308,114	$367,736	$439,298

Probability that total costs will be greater than $375,000 is 21.6%.

ulations to generate random data according to a triangular distribution. We have done precisely this in Table 4.3. The results of the simulation, involving one thousand iterations, show us that the expected value of costs is higher than originally predicted: $367,736 versus $354,500. Furthermore, the simulation shows us the range of costs we might expect, from a minimum of $308,114 to a maximum of $439,298. The simulation also alerts us to the fact that there is a fair probability that total costs will exceed $375,000 (a 21.6 percent probability). The frequency distribution associated with this simulation is pictured in Figure 4.3.

Conclusions

Risk is ubiquitous. It is part of the natural order of things. Although projects have been facing risks and their consequences for

Figure 4.3. Frequency Distribution of Project Costs Derived from Monte Carlo Simulation.

Values are in thousands of dollars

millennia, only in recent years has risk management become a widespread concern of business and government. Some of the newly found interest in risk is a consequence of the chaotic management environment that has developed recently. Global competition is keen, product life cycles are shortening, consumer loyalty is gone, large companies are undergoing massive downsizing—nothing is certain. In such an environment, it is natural for people to strive to generate order out of chaos.

I believe the interest in risk management has also been piqued by advances in information technology. Progress in information storage and retrieval gives ordinary citizens access to massive quantities of previously inaccessible data (for example, through compact disks and low-cost data services such as Prodigy). When used effectively, such data increase the information we need to make informed judgments. In so doing, they reduce risk.

Software developments have also stimulated interest in risk management. Project-scheduling software now enables ordinary project managers to create sophisticated models of their projects on their PCs; this previously required the power of mainframes and battalions of programmers. Once the project is modeled, it can be used to explore the full range of consequences arising from different actions.

As we have seen, statistical simulation software brings the power of Monte Carlo risk analysis within reach of ordinary project staff. As a point of interest, it should be noted that the software that ran the Monte Carlo simulations described in this chapter cost $50 and required one hour of study to learn to use.

Whatever the origins of the current interest in risk management, it is clear that risk analysis is here to stay. A solid understanding of risk, its implications, and management is now a required item in the project manager's toolbox.

Chapter Five

Satisfying Customers:

Knowing Who They Are,

What They Want, and When

They Are Right or Wrong

A key to surviving and thriving in these competitive times is to win customers and then keep them. Obsession with customer satisfaction is what is driving management change today. It underlies the total quality management (TQM) movement, the speed-to-market effort, and attempts at corporate reengineering.

This obsession with customer satisfaction is leading to great improvements in standards of living and quality of life. Goods and services are better than ever—and cheaper to boot! However, there is a cost associated with achieving customer satisfaction. Organizations must rethink how they do business. As customers move from the periphery to center stage, old ways of doing business no longer work. The organization's shift toward a customer focus may lead to discomfort among the work force as they adjust to new ways of operating. It may lead to high levels of anxiety since customer-focused organizations tend to be lean and jobs may have to be pared.

Obsession with customer satisfaction is part of the new project management. Evidence of this is seen in the explosive growth of customer-developer teaming arrangements. A move in this direction was presaged by Hanon, Cribbin, and Heiser in their classic 1970 work *Consultative Selling*. This book pioneered the ideas that high-value organizations are in the business of selling solutions, not hardware, and that customer satisfaction is best achieved through partnering arrangements. It was not until the late 1980s that organizations began adopting these ideas on a grand scale.

Customer satisfaction will not happen by accident. Exhortations to do our best and to keep the customer smiling will not do the trick. Customer satisfaction will occur only through conscious efforts to alter the way we approach our work. There must be not only a change in attitudes but also a change in the way we organize our efforts. This chapter explores some steps that can be taken to increase the likelihood of customer satisfaction on projects.

Who Are Our Customers?

An important first step toward achieving customer satisfaction is to raise the question, Who are our customers? Note that there is a world of difference between this question and the one that is most frequently raised: Who *is* our customer? The point is, on our projects we always deal with multiple customers.

Consider, for example, a project to install point-of-entry terminals at a chain of thirty retail stores. These terminals allow sales staff to enter sales data directly into the company's central computer as sales are being made. The project team—that is, employees of the seller of the hardware, software, and services—faces a plethora of customers in the buying organizations. The managers and salespeople at each of the thirty retail stores are one set of customers, as are the information systems department, the finance department, the accounting department, the purchasing department, the human resource management department, the facilities management group, and upper management at headquarters.

Note that each of the customers enumerated here has a different set of interests. Salespeople want ease of use, the accountants are most interested in how sales data can be consolidated, human resources is interested in how personnel will be trained to use the new system, and so on. There are few shared interests among the different sets of customers. There may in fact be substantial differences. For example, the information systems group is likely to be most interested in functionality ("Let's make sure it's state of the art"), whereas salespeople are concerned with usability. Anyone who has worked with computer systems recognizes that there is often a strong tension between functionality and usability.

The project team often faces the difficult task of sorting through the contending needs of different customers in order to define customer needs and requirements. Needless to say, this can be a challenging undertaking. Satisfaction of one set of needs may generate hostility from customers with opposing interests. The needs definition process must be filled with compromise and balance. For needs to be defined effectively, the project team members must possess well-developed people management capabilities and must thoroughly understand the business of the customer organization. These skills have not been prized in project management until quite recently.

Identifying customers is complicated by the fact that we often must deal with internal customers as well as external ones. If I am developing a new financial reporting system for my company, the principal customer organization with which I will deal is the finance department, an internal customer. In most of my project actions—whether for projects with external or internal customers—I am also concerned with satisfying a broad array of internal players whom I identify as my customer, including my boss, the functional managers with whom I must work, and higher levels of management.

The point here is that project staff need to recognize that there is nothing obvious or trivial about identifying who the customers are. Identification of the customers entails careful study. If project staff do not realize this truth, they are likely to encounter some nasty surprises.

Meeting Customer Expectations

Before we organize our efforts to better satisfy both our internal and external customers, we must have an understanding of what leads to customer satisfaction. In particular, we must recognize that customer satisfaction is tied to customer expectations. If we fall short of these expectations, we will have unhappy customers. So what are these expectations?

First, customers expect that the product or service that they receive is usable. For example, an end user receiving a new computer expects that the computer will function as a useful device when set up according to the instructions. This end user's expectations will not be met if after he or she stokes up the computer for its first run an error message appears on the monitor stating that the system won't run because of a chip failure on the motherboard. In this state, the computer is unusable and the customer will be dissatisfied.

Similarly, in a project to write user documentation for a new hardware product, copyeditors (an internal customer) may expect that the chapters they receive for editing are complete—that there is no missing text. They certainly do not wish to begin work only to find out when they are nearly done that they have to redo the job because crucial information was missing in the original package submitted to them.

Second, customers expect us to keep our promises. If we say we will deliver a product or service by March 15, they will have that date etched into their memories. A March 16 delivery will fall short of their expectations. If we say that the product or service will cost them a certain amount, that is what they plan to pay for it. They will not sympathize with us when we tell them that we have to charge them a 20 percent surcharge because of unanticipated delays in the delivery of a crucial part. If we say that the product or service will meet certain minimum performance standards, they will hold us to these standards. Anything that falls short of these standards will disappoint them.

Third, customers expect us to serve them competently and graciously. They expect that those assigned to do a job know what they are doing. It does not always work this way. We have all experienced the repairman who spends countless hours diagnosing a problem in our equipment by endlessly swapping parts, when all that was wrong with the equipment was that it was not plugged into the electrical outlet. Customers also expect that those providing them with products or services behave in a friendly, well-mannered fashion. Surly behavior does nothing to improve project performance. Its predictable outcome is to generate customer unhappiness.

Finally, customers expect us to understand their needs and wants and to address these effectively. This means that we must understand the environment in which they function, the constraints they face, and the solutions they seek. We must sympathize with their struggles. Much of our energy must be directed at satisfying their needs and wants.

In the final analysis, what customers expect is that we will alleviate their problems, not add to them. They want things to go smoothly and according to plan. To a large extent, customer satisfaction is as much rooted in the avoidance of hassles and surprises as in the achievement of specific goals. Customers want to see positive results. They don't want to listen to a litany of our problems and hear excuses for poor performance.

Understanding Customers' Needs and Requirements

The importance of doing a good job of identifying needs and specifying requirements cannot be overstated. To appreciate this, we must recognize that needs definitions start off a series of events that ultimately results in the production of a deliverable designed to satisfy the needs. It is needs that get the project ball rolling. Requirements, in turn, are developed from our understanding of needs. They serve as the basis of the project plan, which is built around them. A major function of the plan is to provide us with step-by-step insights into what it takes to satisfy the requirements.

If we do a bad job at the earliest stages of the project life cycle, this will have ripple effects throughout the project's life. No matter how detailed and carefully contrived the plan may be, it will be a bad plan if it addresses misunderstood needs or poorly specified requirements. Similarly, project control efforts will come to naught if the needs and requirements analyses are poorly done. If the plan is no good, who cares if the variance between plan and actuals is nearly zero? It should be apparent that the success of a project hinges on the quality of the needs and requirements analyses.

Perhaps the single most important step we can take to assure the proper identification of customers' needs is to hire competent needs analysts. There are many pitfalls in defining needs. Inexperienced project personnel are likely to fall into a majority of them, causing customer unhappiness and jeopardizing the project. In hiring competent needs analysts, what should we look for? The following section examines the traits of the most effective needs analysts.

Traits of Effective Needs Analysts

In reviewing candidates for the job of needs analyst, one should choose individuals who possess the following six characteristics.

First, because the project is directed at meeting customer needs, the analysts must have a strong ability to deal with customers and extract from them a sense of what they truly need. They must be in part psychologists so that they understand what makes the customers tick, and in part sociologists who can discern the social milieu in which the customers function.

Second, they must have good political skills. This means they must recognize that all customers are not equal in a political sense. Some are more significant to the success of the project than others. They must also recognize that some needs and requirements, no matter how compelling, may not be addressable for political reasons. For example, a needs and requirements analysis of a production process at Alpha Computer Corporation may determine that certain manufacturing efficiencies could be realized by using a Beta Computer Corporation computer to drive a machine tool, but such a solution—which suggests dependence on a competitor's product—may be politically unacceptable in Alpha's environment.

Third, they must be technically competent. They should be able to match customers' ill-defined needs to possible solutions. This requires a solid grounding in the technical aspects of the problems being addressed. Good human relations skills by themselves are insufficient for properly defining needs and specifying requirements.

Fourth, they must be open-minded and possess a good imagination. Open-mindedness is necessary so that they do not close off possible solutions to problems because of a narrow outlook. A good imagination is important for a number of reasons. For example, with a good imagination, they can anticipate different problems that might arise given alternative ways of positing project needs and requirements. In addition, a good imagination will help to develop creative solutions to problems.

Fifth, they must have a high tolerance for ambiguity. Because customers do not generally know what they need or want, they will provide the needs analysts with mixed signals. This can be frustrating for the needs analysts, who may begin to develop the impression that customers are not terribly bright and that they are hell-bent on making life difficult. Without a high tolerance for ambiguity and an appreciation of the difficulties customers have in articulating their needs, project staff may develop a paranoid streak ("The customers are out to get me!") and may begin to view them with a certain disdain ("How can I be expected to respect people who don't have the foggiest notion of what they want?").

Finally, they must be articulate. That is, they should be able to take fuzzy suggestions and insights offered by customers and forge them into clear statements of needs, which in turn can be translated into clear and useful requirements.

The traits listed here are certainly desirable in project staff members charged with defining needs and specifying requirements. Unfortunately, they are not commonly found in most project staff members, who tend to view needs definition and requirements specification narrowly through a technical prism. They do this because their project-related training typically has been technically oriented. The needs analysis for an avionics project may be carried out by an electrical engineer, for a financial data base project by an accountant, or for an office automation project by a computer scientist.

These individuals generally have little in their background or personality to enable them to satisfy most of the desirable traits in our list. Their technical background has done little to provide them with human relations skills, political skills, or communication skills that can make them more articulate. On the contrary, their rigorous "hard" background often encourages them to view "soft" skills with disdain. As a result, they often lack the sensitivity necessary to define needs and specify requirements that will satisfy customers operating in the real world, where technical fixes seldom

work as intended. Following are some common outcomes emerging
from needs-requirements analyses carried out by project staff
lacking the basic skills necessary for doing a good job.

Gold-plating of needs. Here the needs analysts serve up a
Mercedes Benz, although what customers really need is a Hyundai.
The technical perfectionist may find it difficult to suggest simple
and direct solutions to needs when this provides customers with less
functionality than they could have with more sophisticated
solutions.

In part, gold-plating is rooted in professional pride. Technically competent systems analysts are understandably reluctant to
waste their abilities on mundane solutions to problems. In part, it
is also a consequence of the training technically competent needs
analysts have received. In this training, they are constantly exposed
to state of the art developments and have little or no experience with
humbler solutions to problems. They develop an outlook that non-
state-of-the-art solutions are second-rate.

Selective filtering of needs. The essence of selective filtering
of needs is captured in the old adage that states, "To a four-year-old
boy with a hammer, all the world is a nail." What we have here are
people defining things narrowly in the context of their particular
experiences, values, and expertise. We encounter this frequently in
our lives. A psychologist might think that the world's problems
could be solved if world leaders underwent a bit of psychotherapy.
To a Marxist economist, the world's problems could be solved by
putting the means of production into the hands of the proletariat.
A Protestant minister might argue that the world's problems could
be resolved through a reconciliation of sinners and God. And so on.

In the case of projects, it is easy for needs analysts to fall into
a trap of defining customers needs according to their particular
areas of expertise. If they are an authority on relational data bases,
they may see this as a solution to all problems. They then interpret
customer needs and requirements from the perspective of relational
data bases even though this might not be appropriate. What they
are doing here is replacing the customers' true needs with their own
needs to employ their expertise.

Operating in a patronizing fashion. Working with customers
can be enormously frustrating for project staff. Because customers

typically only have the remotest sense of what they need, they may behave in ways that project staff perceive as fickle, ignorant, illogical, and spiteful. For project staff lacking good human relations skills, a coping strategy to deal with customer foibles might be summed up as, "These people obviously don't have the slightest idea of what they need. Also, the technology we're dealing with here is over their heads. Since I am the expert, I'll call the shots and give them what I know they need, even if they disagree with my judgments." The problem with this approach is that it may result in customer rejection of the final deliverable since customers perceive their needs differently from the expert.

Steps for Improving Needs Definition

Given the problems inherent in defining needs effectively, it is evident that defining needs properly is not easy. This section examines some steps that project personnel can take to improve the likelihood that they will define the real needs of customers rather than some distortion of those needs.

Step 1: Understand the Present
System in Its Total Context

Most works that offer guidance on how to design and implement hardware and software systems suggest that the first step systems analysts should take is to study the existing system. This includes doing such things as gaining a detailed understanding of the functions performed by the current system, identifying information flows within the system, listing inputs into the system, listing outputs emerging from the system, and so on. The rationale for this effort is that we must understand how things are being done now if we wish to understand how they can be done better.

This is good advice as far as it goes. The problem is that it does not go far enough. The approach tends to put blinders on project staff, forcing them to focus only on the technical dimensions of the problem facing them.

What is being suggested in Step 1 goes beyond conventional systems analysis advice. Understanding the technical dimensions of the current system is of course vital to understanding why customers feel that the system should be replaced with something better suited to meeting their needs.

However, needs analysts must go beyond purely technical investigations of problems. They should strive to understand the present system in its total context. What is the organizational milieu in which the system functions? Who are the relevant actors? What is the political environment like? What is the hidden agenda? Without a thorough grounding in these broader issues, needs analysts will have only a myopic view of what is really needed to satisfy customers.

Step 2: Identify Multiple Customers and Prioritize Their Needs

Step 1 should provide the needs analysts with a good idea of who is affected by the project and who has an interest in its outcome—these are customers in the broadest sense of the term. They include different players in the customer organization as well as individuals in the project organization. Since there are always multiple customers, needs analysts performing Step 1 should be able to generate a list of several individuals.

In Step 2, the analysts refine the list of interested parties and strive to determine the nature of their interests. Actors who are only peripherally involved with the project can be dropped from the list. Of those remaining, analysts should focus especially on individuals whose actions (or inactions) will have a measurable impact on the project and its deliverable. Their stake in the project should be identified. Furthermore, recognizing that the relevant actors have different interests—interests that may in fact be at cross-purposes—needs analysts should try to sort out these interests and develop a rough sense of how they should be prioritized.

If the project deliverable is something that will be sold commercially in the open market (for example, a toaster or a piece of software), Step 2 includes conducting a market research study that examines the preferences of consumers in detail.

Step 3: Put Together a Needs-Defining Task Force

As a result of undertaking Steps 1 and 2, the needs analyst has a rough idea of the technical dimensions of the problem, who the customers are, and what their interests are. This information is gathered through interviews, observation, and a review of organizational procedures. In most needs analyses, the analysts are now deemed ready to define the needs carefully, enabling them to serve as the basis of functional requirements.

Unfortunately, careful needs definition at this point is probably premature. Since a major objective of project management is to produce deliverables that satisfy customers, it is now time to involve customers actively in the needs analysis. This can be done effectively by creating a needs-defining task force representing the different sets of customers. For example, an office automation task force may be composed of representatives from key constituencies, such as secretaries, management, professional workers, and the information technology group.

The task force can strengthen the needs analysis in at least three ways. First, since it is made up of representatives of different constituencies, it allows for the cross-fertilization of ideas. The resulting suggestions as to what customer needs are will therefore be more robust than if needs were identified by only one or two people.

Second, the task force allows the different customer groups to develop a consensus about their needs through give-and-take interaction. This shifts the burden of making some hard decisions from the needs analysts to the customers themselves. Furthermore, whatever priorities emerge through this process are likely to be less arbitrary than if determined by a single individual.

Third, because relevant customer constituencies play an active role in defining their needs, they have, in effect, "bought into" the project. Later on, they will be more likely to cooperate with project staff as the project develops and more likely to be satisfied with the final deliverable than they would have been if a statement of needs had been foisted on them by an outsider.

The customer partnering technique of rapid prototyping (see

Chapter Three) in effect employs task forces in this way to develop customer-focused requirements.

Step 4: Educate the Customers

Customers generally do not know what they need with any degree of precision. A major function of needs analysts is to work closely with customers to help them develop a more precise sense of their needs. An important step can be taken in this direction by educating customers. Most obviously, they should be given some understanding of the technical issues involved. What are these issues? What kind of deliverables can be developed to address them? What are the capabilities of the deliverables? What are their limitations?

It would also be useful to educate customers on some of the rudiments of project management so that they can gain a better appreciation of the practical aspects of what it takes to address their needs. In particular, the needs analysts should explain to them that their needs inevitably will be shifting and that such shifts put a tremendous burden on keeping the project on track. By recognizing that it is natural to have shifting needs, and by further understanding that this causes problems in the execution of projects, customers are likely to be more careful in how they formulate their needs in order to minimize the most serious kinds of disruptions.

Customers' Responsibilities in Defining Their Needs

The responsibility for putting together a good statement of needs does not rest solely on the needs analysts. A good statement of needs is the product of a partnership between the needs analysts and the customers. For their part, customers must do their share to maximize the likelihood that the needs statement does indeed meet their needs. Customers can do many specific things to help out in the needs definition effort. For example, they can write down the problems they are facing as they see them, they can compose brief statements of what they perceive their needs to be, and they can document how they currently carry out their work.

Although their specific contributions may vary from situation to situation, customers should be aware of at least two universal realities. First, they should recognize their limitations and realize that such limitations are natural and do not reflect deficiencies. The extent of their ignorance can be substantial. In general, they do not really know what they need and do not have the skills necessary to uncover these needs precisely. They do not possess expert knowledge of the technologies embodied in possible solutions to their problems. They are unaware of alternative solutions and their respective consequences. They do not know what it takes to design, build, install, and maintain an effective deliverable. If they insist that they know exactly what their needs are at the outset of the needs definition effort, and if the needs analysts take them at their word, there is a good chance that needs/requirements-related problems will arise later in the project.

Second, customers should recognize that the project management process is a grand exercise in compromise, from defining needs all the way up to writing the final documentation at the conclusion of the project. Their needs are not going to be satisfied perfectly. Because there are multiple customers involved in projects, their needs must be reconciled with the often-conflicting needs of fellow customers. Because all projects operate under resource and time constraints, the articulation of customers' needs will be tempered by budget and schedule realities. Customers should also reconcile themselves to the inevitability of compromise if they want a workable needs statement to emerge from the needs definition process.

Organizing to Achieve Customer Satisfaction

The achievement of customer satisfaction requires constant and conscious effort. It will not happen by accident. It entails commitment on the part of the whole organization to make it work. For example, a customer-support environment must be created, enabling project staff to respond quickly and incisively to customer concerns. Top management must be willing to share decision-making authority with project workers. Accounting systems must be created to support the efforts of grassroots decision makers. And so on.

We now examine a five-pronged approach to organizing for

customer satisfaction. First, the corporate culture must be changed to support a customer-focused approach. In some organizations, this may be tantamount to calling for a revolution. Old ways must be abandoned and new ones adopted. In this process of changing the corporate culture, we must never forget that change involves more than just adjustments in attitudes. It requires nothing less than a restructuring of the way the organization does its business so that a customer-support system can be effectively developed and maintained. It also requires a shift of the power locus. Project managers and other project staff—the frontline troops encountering customers on a daily basis—must be empowered to do what it takes to assure customer satisfaction.

Second, every effort must be made to develop projects as islands of stability in a sea of change. A primary feature of life today is breakneck change. Product life cycles are measured in months, currency exchange rates vary from minute to minute, worker mobility is ever-increasing, and so on. Unbridled change is one of the greatest threats to project success. Sources of change on projects include customers changing their minds about what they want; management turnovers that lead to shifts in priorities; competitors introducing products that make our efforts obsolete; and reinterpretations of requirements as the deliverable makes its way through marketing, design, prototyping, production, the handover, and finally the postproduction stage.

Third, the organization must adopt a total life cycle outlook on its project efforts. This means that projects should be viewed from a cradle-to-grave perspective. The process begins with the identification of customer needs and wants. The primary objective of the project should be to satisfy these needs and wants. With the life cycle approach, we recognize that the process does not end with the handover of the deliverable to the customer. The customer must be able to operate the deliverable and to maintain it as well. Consequently, project staff must do their work with one eye always focused on the operations and maintenance of the final product. The life cycle does not end with the handover but rather extends to the time period beyond.

Fourth, mechanisms must be established to assure customer satisfaction. This translates into the development of methods and procedures that ensure that customer sensibilities will not be violated by oversights and sloppy procedures. We must strive to create a situation where it is impossible to hear the comment, "Oops. That poor fellow was not served properly because his case fell between the cracks."

Fifth, everything possible must be done to improve the capabilities of project staff. This requires a new look at their role. As was stated earlier, project staff have traditionally been viewed as mere implementers of the plan. They have played little or no role in actually developing plans. Clearly, the management skills necessary to fulfill this role are not very demanding. Staff simply need basic scheduling knowledge and the technical skills to fulfill the plan. Consequently, traditional project management training focuses intensively on learning how to work with scheduling tools such as Gantt charts and PERT/CPM networks.

With a customer-focused outlook, the role of project staff changes dramatically. They are no longer mere implementers of plans developed by others. They must be able to respond quickly and effectively to customer requirements. To do this, they must be able to operate like independent businessmen and women concerned with both satisfying their customers and maintaining profitability. Consequently, they need to develop a profound appreciation of basic business concepts, such as opportunity costs, the time value of money, and benefit/cost principles.

Each of these five issues will now be discussed in some depth.

Issue 1: Reformulation of the Corporate Culture

The concept of corporate culture is important. Corporate culture effectively defines the limits of what an organization can do. If an organization's underlying culture harks back to past glories and is hostile to new ideas, no amount of restructuring will transform it into an innovator. If the culture cherishes the perquisites of power, it is unlikely to be metamorphosed into a flat organization. If the culture is engineering driven, customer needs and requirements are apt to be overlooked.

In recent years, an enormous amount of attention has been directed toward understanding and transforming corporate cultures. There has been a general outcry to reformulate corporate cultures to allow organizations to operate more effectively in a competitive environment. Advice on what should be done flows from many quarters. Today, the key source of advice comes from proponents of corporate reengineering (see, for example, Hammer and Champy's *Reengineering the Corporation,* 1993). For the most part this advice is good. Although the details for action differ from adviser to adviser, the basic thrust is constant: the corporate culture should encourage flatter, more democratic operations; it should empower employees; it should be obsessed with satisfying customers; it should encourage faster production of products and services; and it should be open to the outside so that the organization can deal effectively with outsourcing and strategic alliances.

Although discussions about the need for reformulating corporate cultures abound in the management literature and the boardrooms of corporations, very little of the dialogue has been directed specifically at project management. What impact does corporate culture have on the way projects are carried out? What cultural postures are most conducive to meeting project needs? The answers to these and related questions call for a corporate culture that shares the following features.

Focus on Value. Value should be a word that appears frequently in the conversations of project employees. In exploring different decision alternatives to further the project's goals, staff should weigh each alternative according to the value it adds to the organization in general and the project in particular. For example, when they are choosing vendors' products that will be used on the project, the question they should address is "Which product offers the most value?" and not "Which product is cheapest?" Similarly, when they are choosing a design or material or function to incorporate into an emerging deliverable, the question for them to answer is "Which alternative offers the customers the greatest value?"

A focus on value requires that decision makers take into account a *range* of factors in making their decisions. Decisions should not be based on price alone, nor should they be based purely on performance. These two factors should be considered together. Other factors should be given consideration as well, including the physical appearance of the deliverable, its overall "sex appeal," and its life expectancy. Ultimately, a focus on value compels organizations to place greater emphasis on quality. Today in many organizations the concepts of value and quality are viewed as interchangeable.

Tolerate and Encourage Upside-Down Thinking. As mentioned in Chapter Three, Charles Handy (1989) talks convincingly about the need for upside-down thinking in organizations today. In a static world, the past serves as an excellent guide to the future. Experience dictates clear solutions to problems. However, in the turbulent world we face today, a prescription to conform and follow the old ways leads to disaster. In such a world, people have to be able to break out of the mold occasionally. Otherwise, the organization will find itself in a rut. Upside-down thinking allows different ideas to compete with each other. It creates an environment that the best professionals find stimulating and challenging and allows the organization to rejuvenate itself continually.

Share Power Throughout the Organization. All employees should be viewed as decision makers. They are *not* cogs in a machine. The traditional hierarchical organization does not operate effectively in a world characterized by constant dramatic change. Investing all power in the hands of top management implies that top management has the solutions to all problems. In a static world, top management may indeed know most of the solutions. In a turbulent world, though, no one grasps more than a small fraction of the answers. Interestingly, rank-and-file employees are often better informed than their "superiors" in such circumstances since they have firsthand knowledge of a rapidly evolving situation. By the time managers in the rarefied heights of the hierarchy receive information on what is happening, circumstances have changed.

The need to empower project managers is particularly acute. Currently, they possess large amounts of responsibility without corresponding authority. One reason for this situation is that they do not own the resources they need to employ in their work. Their resources are borrowed from different functional groups. Information systems consultants come from the data processing organization, design engineers from the engineering division, editors from the media department, and so on. Other problems include the frequent requirement that they run projects that they had no role in selecting or planning, lack of profit and loss responsibilities, lack of skills and information needed to do a good job, and frequent rotation of assignments.

Take a Long-Term View. When there is rapid change, there is a temptation to take a short-term view of life. Change, after all, leads to uncertainty. There is less uncertainty in the short run than in the long run. We can be pretty sure that whatever long-term guesses we make will be wrong. So, the argument goes, let us focus on the short term.

Unfortunately, most worthwhile achievements are carried out in the long run and consequently require a long-term outlook. A simple landscaping project requires a five- to ten-year time horizon (trees and shrubs do not develop fully overnight). An urban renewal project may require a ten- to twenty-year outlook. When in 1961 President Kennedy announced a project to send humans to the moon, he set the target date to be the end of the decade.

On projects, many forces reinforce a short-term perspective. For example, account executives are concerned with making a sale. Once a project contract is signed, they turn their attention to other opportunities. If they made promises to the customer that project staff cannot fulfill, they are not held accountable. The constant turnover of personnel in U.S. organizations encourages a short-term outlook as well. On most projects you can be certain that at least one key player (the project manager, the project champion, the CEO, the procurement head, or key members of the client organization) will be gone within six to nine months. Their departure often leads to painful changes in the project requirements, which in turn are important contributors to time and cost overruns. In this situation, long-term considerations are sacrificed to short-term exigencies.

The corporate culture must extol the virtues of a long-term outlook. It must cast a cold eye on all undertakings that encourage short-term results. It must also convey the attitude that short-term setbacks are tolerable when they lead ultimately to long-term gains. The best way to let people know the importance of this outlook to the organization is to create incentive systems that reward long-term behavior and to develop organizational structures that make it difficult to be a short-termer.

Assume a Total Customer Focus. Clearly, a significant organizational requirement leading to customer-focused project management is the nurturing of a culture that is obsessed with customer satisfaction. Customers must be seen as kings and queens. Customer satisfaction must be touted as the highest goal. All decisions must be assessed according to their impacts on customers.

Given such a focus, project management takes on a new meaning. The traditional view of project success—doing the job on time, within budget, and according to specs—gives way to a new perspective—producing a deliverable that satisfies customers. The traditional orphan stages of the life cycle—concept and closeout—become crucial. Concept is important because it is here that customers' needs are identified. Everything that follows on the project should be geared to addressing these needs. Close-out is important because it is here that the project team prepares to hand over the deliverable to customers. This is the moment of truth, when the team learns whether in the final analysis it has indeed satisfied customers.

A customer-focused culture requires a new attitude toward customers. They should not be seen as an irritant that gets in the way of doing the job. Their confusion about the technical requirements of the project should not be viewed as a sign of obtuseness. Their inability to define what they want and need should not be interpreted as fickleness. Instead of being seen as antagonists, they should be viewed as *partners* in the project. In the final analysis, they are the "experts" on their needs and requirements. Together, the project team and the customers work to reveal these needs and requirements and to develop a deliverable to satisfy them.

Issue 2: Focus on Stability and Continuity

A recent review of cost and schedule overruns on major federal government projects concluded that a prime cause of these problems was budgetary instability. Although major projects occur over several years, congressional funding is obligated on a year-by-year basis. The problem is that each year things change dramatically, and, as a consequence, congressional priorities shift.

One major source of change, of course, is political elections. Congressmen and women are elected every two years, senators every six, and presidents every four. At each election, there is a possibility that the congressional actors overseeing a project's funding will change. If the actors don't change, there is a strong probability that their outlooks will shift with the latest political winds. If national defense is a political hot button one year, congressmen and women will trip over each other to sponsor costly defense projects. If in the next year defense issues fade into the background and the budget deficit is the key political concern, defense project budgets may suddenly be slashed, forcing contractors to lay off critical workers and to shut down facilities. If in the following year there is an international crisis and defense issues become paramount once again, massive amounts of money may flow to defense contractors again. The costs of rehiring workers and reactivating facilities will, of course, be substantial. The original project schedules will be unachievable. Cost and schedule overruns are effectively hardwired into the system.

To gain a full appreciation of the potential of budgetary instability to create havoc, one should consider what can happen in the federal environment over a five-year period of time. During this time period there may be three congressional and two presidential elections. The opportunities for opening and closing and then reopening the funding spigots for projects are limitless.

Unfortunately, parallel sources of instability exist in the private sector. At the highest levels, CEOs, COOs, divisional vice presidents, CFOs, and other senior executives come and go. With the arrival and departure of each of these actors, major shifts in priorities are likely to occur. At the project level, we encounter a similar shuffling of key players. Project managers are rotated out of jobs, technical personnel leave the company in search of greener pastures elsewhere, reorganizations move projects from one divisional unit to another, some divisions are spun off through leveraged buyouts, and other divisions are brought in through mergers and acquisitions. Note that all this churning is occurring in *both the developer organization and the customer organization.* As in the federal case, this kind of instability leads to time and cost overruns and to the development of patchwork deliverables.

Shifting actors are not the only source of project instability. Many other causes abound. For example, purchasing policies that award contracts to low bidders typically lead to a continual rotation of suppliers as this year's low bidder is replaced by next year's low bidder. Sales commissions awarded once an item is shipped may encourage the shipping of goods at the convenience of the account executives, contrary to the requirements of the plan. Transfer of project responsibility from one group to another as the project works its way through the life cycle opens the door for regular reinterpretation of project requirements. Changes in the environment (for example, inflation, the entry of new competitors into the market, or new technology) may stimulate reinterpretations of the project charter. And so on.

Clearly, effective project management requires that the project team be able to cope with all these forces of instability.

Isssue 3: Assume a Life Cycle Perspective

Many projects get into trouble because of the piecemeal approach taken to executing them. The people who select the project are not the people who design the deliverable. Those who create the project plans are not the individuals who have responsibility to execute them. Those charged with operations and maintenance of the deliverable in the postproject stage generally did not participate in any aspect of its development.

This reality was revealed in the study I mentioned earlier of 113 project professionals. They were asked to describe their degree of involvement in five distinct phases of the project life cycle: concept, planning, execution, closeout, and operations and maintenance. Thirty-two percent of the project managers who responded reported that they most typically worked on only two of the five phases. Only 20 percent worked on all five phases. Furthermore, only 29 percent reported involvement in the concept phase—meaning that they were responsible for carrying out efforts in which they had no inputs during the formative early stage.

These data suggest situations that are natural breeding grounds of discontinuity. There is no integrating force to assure that the project sticks to its goals. In fact, there are many forces of *disintegration*, with different actors pursuing their own agenda as the deliverable makes its way through the life cycle. The consequences of this are dramatic. For one thing, we can be assured that what comes out of the pipeline is not what was initially put into it. The danger here is that what comes out is no longer geared to the customers' wants and needs. In addition, it is likely that the basic design underlying the deliverable will become a patchwork as different actors have the opportunity to tweak it to their own requirements. Thus although we set out to design a horse, we wind up with a camel. Ultimately, problems of discontinuity translate into shifting baselines, which in turn yield cost and schedule overruns.

Effective project management requires a life cycle approach to running the project. Efforts must be taken to assure that at all times the project is seen in its entirety. The implications of such an outlook are substantial: deliverables are now designed to be operable and maintainable, requirements remain steady regardless of life cycle stage, and key actors who work on the project throughout its life develop a commitment to the project in its entirety, not just to pieces of it.

Assumption of a life cycle approach is not easy. As we saw in the preceding section of this chapter, there are many disintegrative forces at work. Personnel replacement, low bid–focused procurement systems, and dynamic environments provide just a partial list of these disintegrative forces.

Issue 4: Establish Methods and Procedures to Assure Customer Satisfaction

Projects are inherently complex undertakings. They are made up of interrelated parts, so that failure of one part may have significant downstream consequences. They are unique, so that past experience is an imperfect guide to the future. They entail the utilization of borrowed resources that may not be available when they are needed. They operate in a management quagmire, where accountability is unclear and key actors who follow their own agenda may operate at cross-purposes with each other.

Such an environment is ideal for dropping the ball and falling through the cracks. In this environment there is a constant lurking threat that the best intentions will go awry, that promises made will not be kept. Consequently customers are likely to be chronically disappointed.

Chaos need not reign supreme on projects. It can be contained to a degree by the implementation of thoughtful methods and procedures. These are commonly embodied in something called an M&P (methods and procedures) document. This document lays out the rules governing the procedures that should be followed in executing a project. Since all actors should abide by these rules, regardless of their skills area or their position in the organization, the rules add an important element of continuity and consistency to the project.

Methods and procedures should focus intensively on making sure that things do not fall through the cracks. For example, they may require that customer walk-throughs be conducted at periodic intervals. Furthermore, they may describe the steps that should be taken to conduct the walk-through. These walk-throughs serve at least two important functions: (1) they assure customers that they are not being ignored, and (2) they protect the project team from accusations that customer views were not solicited.

Another example: methods and procedures should detail how project staff should deal with pressures to change requirements. The M&P document should spell out how change requests should be captured, evaluated, and implemented. Only through such procedures can the inevitable problem of shifting baselines be managed.

The establishment of effective methods and procedures requires that special attention be given to documentation. Projects are filled with documentation. Common documents include the project charter, the statement of work (SOW), the project contract, preliminary design review (PDR) and critical design review (CDR) documents, monthly progress reports, specifications, performance appraisal documents, punch lists, user manuals, and engineering change proposals.

Anyone with substantial project experience recognizes that documentation has the characteristics of both Dr. Jekyll and Mr. Hyde. On the positive side, when documents are tied to critical milestones, they provide project staff with a mechanism for pacing themselves through the life cycle. Furthermore, they supply the project with an audit trail, providing both the project staff and the customer with information on what has been done. Finally, they impose a discipline on the project, requiring project staff to pay attention to crucial management issues and to do their job in a consistent fashion.

On the negative side, an emphasis on documentation—and the whole methods and procedures exercise, for that matter—can lead to excessive bureaucratization. A time may arrive when project staff are spending more hours filling out forms in triplicate than doing their project work. Bureaucratization can discourage staff initiative and encourage managing "by the book." It will lead to a slowing down of project staff response time to various project exigencies and customer requests. Ultimately, excessive bureaucratization will reduce productivity and erode the competitive position of the organization.

Clearly, effective project management necessitates a balance between the need for the discipline of established methods and procedures (and their attendant documentation) and the need for flexibility and responsiveness to customer requirements.

Issue 5: Strengthen Capabilities of Project Staff

Recently I was looking at power tools in a large hardware shopping center. Nearby, a customer was asking some questions of a sales clerk.

"Is this the power drill that was advertised as being on sale in today's newspaper?" the customer asked. He held up a box containing a power drill.

"Yes, it is," the sales clerk answered.

The customer examined the box carefully. "It says on the box that this is Model 5062. Isn't the drill that's on sale Model 5060?"

The sales clerk took the box and read the label. "It does say Model 5062," the clerk said. "I think somebody must have mislabeled the box."

"So this is definitely the drill that's on sale?"

"Uh . . . Yes."

"Now does this drill run at two speeds?"

"That's correct."

"Wait a second. It says on the box that it is only a one-speed drill."

And so the conversation went. It was clear that the sales clerk was a fountain of misinformation. The fact that he did not know what he was talking about never stopped him from proffering incorrect information. Anyone listening to his advice was going to have serious difficulties on his or her home projects. And their anger would be directed not only at him, but at the hardware store that employed him as well.

Customer satisfaction demands that sellers of goods and services—whether sales clerks, project managers, or technical specialists—be highly competent in their work. The perception of incompetence will certainly shake customers and result in lost business.

Until recently, competence in project management meant that project staff possessed the technical skills to do the job and sufficient management skills to work with budgets and schedules. However, today customers are demanding more of project staff. In particular, they see project staff as *business partners*. They expect them to know the customers' business and to possess basic business skills.

Thus project staff increasingly are receiving training in business fundamentals. In particular, they are studying topics such as the rudiments of capital budgeting techniques, contracting basics, decision-making methodologies, forecasting, and reading financial statements.

What to Do When Customers Don't Cooperate

For a period of nine months in 1992 to 1993, I had an opportunity to travel the globe and meet several hundred project professionals from some twenty countries. I was at first surprised and then de-

lighted to find that project workers everywhere—from Buenos Aires
to Birmingham to Sydney to Toronto to Singapore—were sensitive
to the need to adopt the perspective of a new project management.
They were customer focused. They realized that customers expected
them to offer business solutions as well as technical solutions. They
were sensitive to the radical transformations occurring in their own
organizations: downsizing, outsourcing, and flattening.

One of the greatest revelations I had in dealing with these
people was that one of their most common complaints was that
customers were not behaving responsibly on their projects. Specifically, project managers everywhere revealed to me that a prime
cause of schedule slippages and cost overruns on their projects was
customers who did not meet their obligations. They complained
that customers held them tightly to meeting milestone commitments. Yet when it came time for customers to meet their own
obligations, they were lax in doing so.

For example, a frequent complaint was that customers were
slow in responding to inputs coming from the project team. The
team might send the results of a systems test for customers to review
and approve and then find themselves waiting for months for a
customer response. Of course, delays in customer turnaround
caused major schedule slippages on their projects, which were often
blamed on the project team.

Most of the project managers I spoke with attributed these
problems to disorganization in the customer organization. I looked
into some of the complaints in detail and found this diagnosis to
be a bit superficial. My suspicion is that the majority of the delays
in customer turnaround were tied to political problems existing in
the customer organization. It should be recalled that the idea of the
customer—a monolithic entity with a consistent world view—is a
myth. There are always multiple customers who hold conflicting
interests. The power balance among these customers often shifts.
For example, a player from the financial department whose views
prevailed during the project definition phase is promoted to a different division, leaving a power vacuum. The vacuum is filled by
another player from the information technology group whose views
differ dramatically from those of the previous dominant player.

Suddenly, project priorities in the customer organization shift to reflect the new power balance.

Thus the customer organization may be reluctant to respond to system test results because a positive response indicates customer approval of the direction the project is taking. However, shifts in the political winds may give the customer organization second thoughts about the project's goals. The result: decision paralysis.

So what is the project team to do in such a situation? Three possible responses stand out.

First, remind the customer organization of its contractual obligations. Point out to key authorities the schedule and budget consequences of the customers' inaction. Make it clear to them that if they do not abide by the contract, the contractor's obligations become null and void.

Many project managers are reluctant to take this step. They fear that by focusing on the contract, they will alienate their customers and lose future business. I have two responses to this. First, why were they so silly as to enter into a one-sided contract that put all the onus of performance on them? Second, if customer irresponsibility causes them to lose money on their project, why are they worried about losing business with an organization that has forced them to suffer financial losses—and may well maintain this pattern in future business transactions?

Second, emphasize very clearly at the outset of the project the importance to project success of meeting certain key milestones, including those requiring customer inputs. Periodically remind the customers of upcoming obligations. The key point here is to indicate continually to the customer organization that the project team takes its responsibilities seriously and that it expects the customer organization to do the same.

Third, establish a steering committee to oversee project progress. Members should include individuals from the customer organization as well as representatives of the project organization. The members of the steering committee should be quite powerful individuals so that decisions coming from the committee must be taken seriously. If the customer organization fails to meet its commitments, this fact should be raised before the steering committee for action. Hopefully, a powerful steering committee will become an ally of the project team and will pressure pertinent players to meet their obligations.

Conclusions

With the new project management, project success is defined largely by customer satisfaction. Achieving such satisfaction does not come easily. It requires project organizations to abandon their old technical-focused paradigms and to adopt ones that concentrate on customers. It also requires people to recognize that there is no such thing as *the* customer, who possesses a single, consistent view of project requirements. In fact, all projects must address the often conflicting needs of multiple customers.

Part Two

Tools for the New

Project Management

Part Two of this books looks at the skill sets that project management professionals should possess in order to deal with the issues raised in Part One. The skills required of today's project professionals go far beyond the set of skills demanded of them until quite recently. The traditional view of project professionals as implementers required skills development in the areas of budgeting, scheduling, and allocating human and material resources.

In today's business environment, however, project professionals have responsibilities that go beyond mere implementation. To be effective, today's project professionals must be capable in the political arena, able to forge teams in the matrix environment, competent to make independent decisions, qualified to predict future scenarios, able to deal with outsiders through contracts, and so forth.

Part Two comprises eight chapters, each of which deals with an area in which skills mastery should be achieved for effective project management. Chapter Six focuses on political skills. Project managers often possess high levels of responsibility without possessing commensurate levels of authority. This chapter shows how the conscientious cultivation of political awareness and development of whatever authority sources are available can enable project managers to influence outcomes even under these adverse conditions.

Chapter Seven examines one of the most fundamental dilemmas facing the project professional: how can I create a sense of team spirit when the team players assigned to the project are borrowed resources?

Chapter Eight reviews decision-making principles and techniques to help project professionals select projects, staff, material resources, and vendors. Techniques are suggested for better decision making, including benefit-cost analysis, peer review, the murder board, and the poor man's hierarchy.

Chapter Nine focuses on one of the leading causes of project failure: poor estimation of costs, schedules, and specifications. Techniques are offered for improving the quality of project estimates, thus lowering the likelihood of schedule slippages, cost overruns, and the development of poor quality deliverables.

Chapter Ten reviews one of the dominant phenomena of business today: the employment of outsiders to carry out the organization's work. The chapter examines key principles of contracting as they relate to projects and offers suggestions for operating effectively in an outsource environment.

Chapter Eleven examines one of the most sophisticated techniques of project management: the cost/schedule control system, also known as the earned value methodology.

Chapter Twelve reviews attempts to increase accountability on projects. Pitfalls of traditional approaches to evaluation are discussed. The structured walk-through—evaluation with a human face—is highlighted.

Chapter Thirteen examines the measurement of work performance. It shows how the employment of work performance measures enhances project control and increases the likelihood of project success.

As with Part One, the chapters in Part Two have been written as self-contained entities. Consequently they can be read in whatever order the reader finds useful.

Chapter Six

Acquiring
Political Skills
and Building Influence

Practitioners of the new project management recognize that life is often messy. Management practice has a way of deviating sharply from management theory. People do not fit into neat categories and do not behave according to well-known formulas.

One important messy reality is that on projects, politics is inevitable. All project managers will encounter it in some measure. It is futile to fight it. Wise project managers learn to accommodate to it. Although the term *politics* has negative connotations, project managers who master its intricacies come to see its positive qualities. They know that if they are to get the job done, then they will have to develop political skills.

What Is Politics?

The concept of politics is difficult to nail down. Even dictionaries— normally precise in defining terms—are not very helpful here. Their definitions of politics often have an element of circularity to them, as in "the art or science of political government" (*American Heritage Dictionary*, 1978, p. 1015). To the extent that they talk of politics outside the context of government, they portray it in highly negative terms, as in "factional scheming within a group" (*Webster's New World Dictionary*, 1964, p. 1132).

Any practical discussion of politics must come to grips with its negative image because for many people this negative image stands in the way of their developing effective political skills. President John Kennedy caught the spirit of our ambivalence toward politics when he said, "Mothers may still want their favorite sons to grow up to be President, but . . . they do not want them to become politicians in the process" (*American Heritage Dictionary*, 1978, p. 1015). The negative feeling toward politics is captured in adjectives commonly used to describe the politician: conniving, shifty, unprincipled, selfish, corrupt, Machiavellian, amoral. The common theme of these adjectives is the nonadherence of politicians to a clear set of moral principles that guide them in their undertakings.

Although many examples in our daily newspapers appear to confirm this view of politics and the politician, we must recognize that the image of politics as sleaze strongly distorts the true nature of politics. At heart, *politics is the art of influence.* For the most part, politicians do not achieve their goals and the goals of their constituents by virtue of their powerful muscles, their large bank accounts, or their use of military force. Politicians are successful in their work only to the extent that they can effectively *influence* others to do their bidding. For example, elected politicians must first influence the electorate to vote for them. Once elected, they maintain their influence by serving their constituents' needs. To do this, they influence other politicians to back their positions. When politicians lose this ability to influence the outcome of events, they become powerless.

Another feature of politics is that it is the lubricant that allows the wheels of organized human activity to turn without jamming. People are in conflict with each other because they pursue conflicting goals. We see this all around us at all levels of human activity. At the level of the individual, we may find a husband and wife struggling over the household thermostat because one wants the house to be warmer, the other cooler. At the level of the community, we frequently encounter battles between advocates of economic growth and antigrowth forces who want to maintain the aesthetic integrity of the community. At the national level, there are struggles between those who desire strong government social programs and those who champion a laissez-faire role for government. Internationally, of course, the struggle over conflicting goals can have catastrophic consequences resulting in war.

The way conflict is resolved is through accommodation—which is to say, through political efforts. If this does not work, the consequences will be chaos, stalemate, or outright hostile actions. This is what Karl von Clausewitz meant when he said, in his classic book *On War*, "War is the continuation of politics by other means" (1833).

Taking into account these considerations, we can improve upon dictionary definitions of politics by defining it in the following way: *Politics is the process whereby attempts are made to achieve goals through accommodation and the exercise of influence.*

Politics in Projects

Project environments are excellent breeding grounds for rampant politics. An important reason for this is that authority on projects is diffuse. On most projects, managers do not "own" their resources. Staff are borrowed from functional areas, so they "belong" to someone else. A large part of efforts of project managers is devoted to wangling these resources from functional managers. Their lives are complicated by the fact that they are competing against other project managers and functional heads for these scarce resources like five hungry dogs fighting for a single bone. Obtaining needed resources often entails a good deal of horse trading and the occasional issuance of implied or explicit threats.

Players to Contend with in the Project Environment

Authority is diffuse in another sense as well. On most projects, managers find themselves surrounded by many key players who have the power to make or break the project. It behooves project managers to spend some time reflecting on these actors and how they can affect the course of events. Such reflection will identify the many ways that politics creeps into projects. The following are some key players.

Bosses

Project managers work with varying degrees of independence. Some call the shots on budgeting, scheduling, and resource utilization; others are basically baby-sitters. In all cases, they are ultimately accountable to someone above them in the hierarchy. That is, they have bosses.

Bosses can make a big difference in whether project managers have good or bad experiences with their projects. They can affect project performance both materially and psychologically. For example, in an emergency they can supply their project managers with extra human and material resources. On a psychological plane, fear of a bad performance review by the boss can make a project manager so risk-averse that no hard decisions are made on the project.

There is one important political fact that all project managers should bear in mind: their bosses are not neutral in regard to their project. Their bosses are in fact stakeholders in the project. For example, bosses themselves have bosses. Their relations with their bosses may be sensitive to the performance of the project manager. Success of a highly visible project may reflect positively on their management ability and lead to promotions and bonuses, whereas failure may assure them a spot in their organization's gulag.

Bosses are frequently stakeholders in another sense as well: with the acquisition of projects, they can enlarge their turf. Our project may be yet one more tool they can employ to strengthen their position in the organization. Even bosses who are totally devoid of ambition are stakeholders in a very mundane sense: if their project managers should run into trouble, this will create administrative and political hassles for them and make their lives generally unpleasant.

The political implications of bosses being stakeholders are

significant. It means that politically savvy project managers must view their decisions from their boss's perspective. They must know what their boss's goals are in relation to the project. If they do not do this, they may find their decisions being reversed and support for their efforts declining. Ultimately, insensitivity to the boss's goals may lead to poor performance ratings and denial of future managerial responsibilities.

Peers

By the term *peers* we are referring to coworkers who operate at the same level of responsibility as we do. They very likely are project managers themselves. Because they are our equals in the hierarchy, we have no direct control over them. If we want their cooperation, we must obtain this through influence, not fiat.

Our relations with our project peers are often filled with ambiguity. On the one hand, they can be our helpmates. They can provide us with crucial information, share their resources, offer us a shoulder to cry on, serve as a sounding board for ideas, and act as our political allies.

On the other hand, they are our competitors. This is true in two senses. First, they compete with us for scarce resources. As a consequence, they may be involved in all sorts of behind-the-scenes machinations to assure that they can acquire these resources—possibly at our expense. Second, they compete with us for career advancement. As we progress higher in the organizational pyramid, there is more and more competition for fewer job slots. The fact that pyramids are crumbling and organizations are flattening only intensifies competition. If our peers have any ambition at all, we can be sure that they hear a little voice somewhere inside them telling them that our successes may jeopardize their advancement.

Functional Managers Controlling Resources

Because project managers do not own their resources, they must borrow them from functional areas within the organization. Project managers spend a good deal of effort trying to acquire needed resources from the functional managers who control them.

Their chief concerns in acquiring resources revolve around the following questions: Can I acquire resources that satisfy the technical requirements of the project? Will they be of good quality and do what it takes to get the job done? Will I have enough of them? Will I be able to obtain them when I need them? Will I be able to keep them for the time I need them, or will they be pulled off the project to fight fires somewhere else?

Sometimes the acquisition of these resources is straightforward. For example, the project manager may tell the head of data processing that she needs a data base specialist for a two-month period beginning on September 9th. After checking a resource calendar, the DP head may make arrangements guaranteeing her that her request will be satisfied.

However, obtaining resources is generally more complex than this. Project environments are dynamic. Plans change—schedules slip, budgets are cut or augmented, new tasks emerge, people become ill, new staff sign on, and so on. In such an environment, the acquisition of resources becomes a major challenge. Success in getting who we need when we need them may depend more upon our powers of persuasion over managers who control resources than upon our ability to fill out resource request forms properly. That is, in acquiring resources, political skills can be important.

Customers

Not long ago customers played only a peripheral role on projects even though the purpose of these projects was purportedly to produce a deliverable that would satisfy them. The reason for this was confidence in the superior expertise of the project staff. The assumption was that by dint of their education, experience, and high levels of intelligence, project staff knew what was best for customers. This being the case, why muddy the waters with heavy customer involvement in the development of the deliverable?

An important feature of the new project management is the belief that customers are kings. In fact, project success and failure are defined in terms of satisfying customers. A project is said to fail if its deliverables are not used or are underused or misused by customers. In the new project management, the view that the experts know what is best for customers is seen to be paternalistic and self-serving.

As Chapter Five pointed out, close contact with customers carries with it a major consequence that is relatively new to project management: project staff must develop good people skills so that they can interact productively with their clients. They have to become politically astute since they are dealing with players who lie outside of their control and who possess different goals than they do. This means that they must be able to put themselves into their customers' shoes so that they can appreciate their needs more fully. They must also be willing and able to live with compromise since their vision of what is best for the customers will often differ from the customers' perception of what is best.

Unfortunately, the development of good customer relations skills can be stressful for many project staff members, who did not go into computer programming, electrical engineering, or accounting because they had an urge to work closely with people. For the most part, these individuals have little political savvy. Yet to work effectively to produce deliverables that satisfy customers, they must develop it.

Vendors

On the surface, it would appear that there should be few political problems with vendors since project managers have a degree of control over them. After all, if vendors do not deliver, project managers need not pay them.

This view hides a reality that experienced project managers are acutely aware of: getting something out of vendors is a complex process. Common problems in dealing with them include:

- The deliverable arrives late, causing us to incur a schedule slippage.
- The deliverable does not meet the specifications agreed upon, so it is unusable.
- The invoice price of the deliverable is higher than the estimated price originally quoted, contributing to cost overruns.

When these kinds of problems arise, how should they be dealt with? Or better yet, what can be done to avoid them in the first place? The answers to these questions are not obvious and must be worked out in the context of specific circumstances. Frequently the answers involve more than threatening nonpayment for goods, canceling the contract, or instituting a lawsuit for breach of contract. A project staff's primary objective in dealing with vendors is to get the needed goods and services from them in as effective a manner as possible. If vendor problems translate into budget, schedule, or requirements problems for the project, it is small consolation to us that we can withhold payments.

As with so much in project management, dealing with vendors requires political skills. With these skills, project staff can anticipate problems before they arise and identify ways to pressure the vendors to meet their obligations. Without them, project staff are at the mercy of events that lie outside of their control.

Others (Purchasing, Information Resource Management, Contracts, Secretaries)

The list of project players who can be involved in political activity extends beyond what has been listed here. A sampling of other common players includes:

- Purchasing department—for example, their foot-dragging in placing orders can lead to slow deliveries of needed supplies and services.
- Information resource management—for example, their insistence that we buy a computer that meets organizational standards may lead to the procurement of a device that does not fully meet the project's needs.
- Contracts office—for example, their narrow interpretation of contract clauses may not allow for needed changes in the requirements for a deliverable to be supplied by a contractor.
- Secretaries—for example, their lack of commitment to project work may lead to delays in progress and poor quality reports.

Being a Better Politician

Some people seem to be born politicians. They appear to have an instinctive capacity to size up the political dimensions of different situations and to know what to do to have their will prevail. Being politically astute is as natural to them as taking a stroll.

Most of us are not born politicians. Furthermore, our upbringing and education do not prepare us for the political realities of life because our parents and teachers are as politically naive as we are. In fact, given the prevailing view that politics is dirty, we are encouraged to avoid anything that smacks of political maneuvering. As a consequence, when we enter into political situations, we are like lambs being led to slaughter.

Common Political Pitfalls

There are many ways that we can get into trouble politically. Following are some of the more common political pitfalls.

Accepting Things at Face Value. One thing that politics shares with such diverse undertakings as psychoanalysis, the new physics, Oriental religions, and magic is the view that *things aren't as they seem.* Reality occurs at many different levels. Plato captured this in *The Republic* in his allegory of people trapped in a cave who perceive moving shadows on the wall to be reality since that is all they have ever experienced. Behind this reality, of course, there is a deeper reality of three-dimensional objects passing in front of a light, casting the shadows that fall on the wall. *The Republic,* incidentally, is not only a great philosophical work; it is also a political statement. The Greeks—inventors of democracy—did not perceive politics as a shameful thing.

Good politicians are adept at penetrating through the superficial to identify the real issues. For example, the office head says he wants to automate the office to increase productivity. The astute project manager who knows the boss well may recognize that what the boss really wants is a modern-looking facility—an office filled with machines that hum rather than machines that clunk. This knowledge provides the project manager with important insights that increase the probability of project success.

Insensitivity to Political Realities. Some people have the political finesse of a bull in a china shop. Their primary trait is to make waves politically through their actions. To them, concern for the political consequences of their actions is overridden by a philosophy of "Damn the torpedoes, full speed ahead!"

Frequently, these individuals fall into the trap of not making much effort to do needed political spadework before they carry out their undertakings. Consider the case of the project manager who appointed a twenty-three-year-old hotshot as a task leader in charge of a group of people in their forties and fifties. When warned that the age differential between the task leader and the staff might create morale problems for the project team, he responded, "I don't care. These old-timers will be gone in a few years. We've got to give our young blood the chance to learn how to manage effectively." His goal to speed up the professional development of young staff may have been admirable. However, his insensitivity to the views of the older project team members ultimately led to a revolt that made the life of the twenty-three-year-old so miserable that he soon left the company. Had the project manager done a bit of political spadework, he might have softened the team opposition to the young manager, or else he might have seen the futility of putting a youngster in charge of old hands.

The Hyperpolitician. Sometimes project workers can get into trouble by being too political. These individuals thrive on gossip and behind-the-scenes manipulation. They hold no firm views on anything, preferring to bend with the prevailing political currents of the organization. They are, in fact, a cartoon caricature of the weasely politician.

The problem is that in playing the role of the stereotypical politician, they are not being politically effective. Their political machinations are transparent to all. The ultimate goal of effective politicians is to *influence others* to do their bidding, not to engage in backslapping and backstabbing on a large scale. More often than not, the ability to influence others requires subtlety and a quiet appreciation of what others need, want, and feel. Hyperpoliticians lack this subtlety.

Hyperpoliticians can get into trouble in a number of ways. For example, through their blatant political maneuverings, they may lose the respect of their fellow workers, who may perceive them as lacking substance. This will ultimately limit their career development and their ability to get others to cooperate with them. Another common pitfall facing hyperpoliticians is that their political maneuverings may backfire on them. The alliance they make may come apart so that yesterday's ally becomes today's enemy. Furthermore, yesterday's enemy is likely to remain today's enemy as well, leaving them with few friends.

The Hypopolitician. Diametrically opposed to the hyperpolitician is the *hypo*politician. Whereas the former pursues too much of a good thing, the latter underperforms politically. Hypopoliticians eschew politics for a number of reasons. Some see it as an unprincipled undertaking, and they do not want to be sullied by it. Others view it as silly and demeaning and avoid politics for fear of being branded as superficial. Still others who have a natural tendency toward introversion are uncomfortable with the demands for extraverted behavior required of a politician.

The big problem facing hypopoliticians is that they are either avoiding or ignoring something that will definitely affect them. Politics on projects is inevitable owing to the very nature of projects and the environment in which they are carried out. By understanding politics and developing basic political skills, hypopoliticians can improve their project performance. By avoiding politics, they have diminished the degree of control they can exercise over their projects.

A Guide to Action

Up until now, the discussion has concentrated on exploring the general nature of politics on projects. At this point, we turn our attention to a program of action, where we address the question: What do we need to do to become more effective politically? The approach offered here is a four-step undertaking:

- Step 1: Develop a positive attitude toward politics.
- Step 2: Lay a solid foundation for political action by developing a base of authority.
- Step 3: Identify key elements of the environment.
- Step 4: Identify and implement a course of action.

Step 1: Develop a Positive Attitude Toward Politics

A principal theme of this chapter is that politics is inevitable on projects, so we might as well learn to live with it and to use our knowledge to become more effective managers. We must dispel the notion that politics is an inherently sleazy or frivolous activity and should recall that it is fundamentally concerned with *achieving goals through accommodation and influence.* Inasmuch as we rarely have direct control over much of anything on our projects, it behooves us to become masters of accommodation and influence in order to gain some control over our efforts so that we can achieve our objectives.

Step 2: Lay a Solid Foundation for Political Action by Developing a Base of Authority

A fundamental problem facing project managers is that they have responsibility without authority. As we have seen, the reason for the absence of authority is that project managers typically do not own the resources they work with. Instead, their resources are borrowed.

Why is authority important? Because it provides us with the capacity to get others to do our bidding. Without authority we have no clout, no leverage over our staff and colleagues. Without authority, we must depend upon the good will of others to get the job done. We are not really in control of our project.

Clearly, a major objective of effective project managers should be to develop a base of authority. This authority base, coupled with an awareness of the environment in which they operate (discussed in Step 3), will give them the fundamental skills and resources needed to navigate the political waters of the project. There are many different kinds of authority. This chapter focuses on a handful that are relevant to most project situations. These will be discussed in detail later.

So effective political action requires the development of authority. It is authority that gives project managers a measure of influence over their staff, their bosses, and their peers. However, proper use of this authority demands that they have a good appreciation of the environment in which this authority will be applied. This brings us to the third step that must be undertaken to develop good political skills: the development of a good sense of the environment in which we operate.

Step 3: Identify Key Elements of the Environment

In his book *The Politics of Projects* (1983), Robert Block points out that in order to operate effectively as project managers, we must have a solid grasp of the environment in which we work. An important talent possessed by all successful professional politicians is the ability to divine what is happening around them. Accordingly, his book devotes a great deal of attention to describing how to carry out a politically savvy environmental assessment. This can be achieved by addressing three basic questions:

- Who are the players?
- What are their goals?
- Who am I?

Who Are the Players? Politics is a process of people interacting with people, so it makes sense to undertake a systematic survey to identify the players that will be affected by our project and/or will have an effect on it. The important thing about this survey is to create as long a list of potentially relevant players as possible at the outset. In creating a long list, we reduce the likelihood that we have overlooked key players. Later on, we can shrink the list to manageable dimensions by eliminating marginal players.

In deciding who the key players are, we should not simply focus on individuals who are in the upper echelons of the organization chart. The important issue is not where people stand in the hierarchy but whether they have the capacity to affect the project outcome either positively or negatively. If this serves as the guideline for identifying key players, then we see that on a data base development project, humble data entry clerks might be key players; on a market survey project, telephone interviewers might be key players.

Consider what a list of key players in a hypothetical office relocation project might look like:

- *Players within the organization:* upper management, project staff, office director, purchasing department, budget office, people being relocated, managers of the operations being relocated, data processing department, maintenance department, facilities management group.
- *Players outside the organization:* customers, architectural consultant, interior design consultant, real estate agents, moving company, insurance company, electric power company; if the move entails building a new facility, the list of outside players might grow explosively, including key players such as the general contractor, subcontractors, the zoning board, and the county permits office.

Each of these players has the power to affect the project. That is, each of them through their actions or inactions can affect the project schedule, budget, and specifications.

What Are the Goals of the Players? The creation of a list of key players alerts us to the people to whom we must devote some attention because they can affect the outcome of our project. Once we have identified them, we need to find out what motivates them. Knowledge of their goals provides us with insights into how we should deal with them.

Discovering the goals of key players requires us to develop the skills of a psychologist. Not only are we concerned with the players' stated goals, but we are interested in their hidden goals as well. Identifying hidden goals is not easy since they not only are hidden from us but—to the extent that they operate at a subliminal level—may be hidden from the players themselves.

In the office relocation example, the office director may have presented the following goals to upper management in order to gain their support for the move:

- To move to larger facilities in order to accommodate a growing work force
- To move to facilities with modern amenities
- To be located nearer to customers

However, she may have harbored an additional goal that she did not articulate: to move away from headquarters so as to gain a degree of independence of action. Furthermore, she may have unconscious goals of which she is only dimly aware. For example, she may be an inherently restless person who needs periodic infusions of major change in order to charge her batteries. Conscious awareness of all these goals gives the project manager special insights into the character and desires of a key player. With this knowledge, the project manager will have some guidance on what to do and what to avoid.

Many project professionals have difficulty identifying the goals of key players. Some are simply insensitive to the needs and wants of other people and totally lack empathic skills. Others are uncomfortable playing the role of psychologist. This is especially true of introverted technical individuals who are more comfortable with things than with people. Given the difficulty that many people have in identifying goals of key players, it may be wise to conduct this exercise in a small group where two or more heads may indeed be better than one.

Who Am I? This is the "know thyself" step. To be politically effective, project managers must know their own strengths and limitations, particularly as they bear on the project at hand. For example, how does the project match with their values? Do they see it as a Mickey Mouse effort that misuses their talents? Do they resent the fact that the enormous work load interferes with their weekend plans? If the match between the project requirements and their goals is a poor one, this will negatively affect their attitude and commitment to the project, which in turn will color their political effectiveness.

Other important knowledge project managers should gain about themselves can be gained by addressing the following questions:

- In the eyes of my colleagues, am I physically and socially attractive?
- Do I have good written and oral communications skills?
- Do I have a good grasp of the technical and administrative issues involved in this project?

For detailed guidance on understanding oneself better, the reader should read Richard Boles's *What Color Is Your Parachute?* (1994), one of the most successful business books of all time. The central premise of this book is that individuals cannot be successful in planning their careers if they do not understand their wants, needs, and capabilities thoroughly.

Step 4: Define the Problem, Then Identify and Implement a Course of Action

Steps 1 through 3 have prepared the political groundwork that enables project managers to factor important political considerations into their decisions. Only now are they ready to offer solutions to problems. Unfortunately, most project managers skip Steps 1 through 3 and begin the decision-making process at Step 4. That is, they define the problem and begin offering solutions before they have an appreciation of the political issues that underlie the matters they are addressing.

Having done their political spadework, project managers will have a different perspective on the situation facing them than they otherwise would have had. The real nature of the problems facing them will look different when viewed through political spectacles than when political issues are ignored. What originally may have seemed to be a straightforward technical matter is now seen as something more complex, something fraught with traps and hidden obstacles. Armed with their knowledge of the political landscape, managers are in a good position to blaze a trail through the thicket.

Of course, mere awareness of key issues is not enough. Effective political action requires that project managers use their awareness effectively. They must *behave* in a politically appropriate manner. For example, they must know when to employ finesse in their dealings with others and when to use a club. They must avoid gaffes such as saying the wrong things to the wrong people at the wrong time. They must develop a good sense of timing, knowing when to introduce new initiatives and when to pull back. They must identify how much pressure they can apply to pursue an objective, being sure not to be too aggressive or too timid.

Building Authority

Over the years I have been maintaining a list of different kinds of authority project staff employ. Each time I come across a new form, I add it to the list. The full list has some thirty distinct kinds of authority that I have identified. Many of these border on the trivial or are counterproductive, so I offer here an abridged list.

Formal Authority

People who are new to project management and technical people who see the world as governed by clearly defined rules tend to depend heavily upon formal authority. They believe that the very status of project manager confers upon them a substantial degree of authority. They see themselves as bosses. They expect others to recognize their authority and to respond to it appropriately.

Unfortunately, this is not how organizations work in the real world. Formal authority often is not very helpful to project managers unless it is accompanied by what is called *borrowed authority*. That is, for formal authority to be effective, it must be closely associated with the will of someone who is an obviously powerful player—typically someone in a high position in the organizational hierarchy. When this condition exists, the requests of the project manager can be interpreted as requests of the powerful player. Going against the project manager is in effect going against the will of someone with clout.

Technical Authority

Technical people tend to view the world through a prism of technical competence. The value of their bosses, colleagues, and subordinates is often measured in terms of their perceived intelligence and technical abilities. A great source of frustration for technical staff is to work for someone who they feel is a technical lightweight. They may be distressed that this individual's lack of know-how is hampering their efforts. They may also resent that they are subordinate to someone whom they perceive to be inferior to them intellectually.

The implications of the technical ethos are clear: project managers working directly with technical staff must possess some degree of technical authority if they are to earn the respect of the staff. It should be noted that this reality extends beyond the purely technical environment of scientists and engineers. Accountants, marketers, attorneys—any staff members with finely developed skills—require a fairly high level of technical competence in their supervisors. When such technical authority is absent, it is easy for staff to dismiss the efforts and desires of their bosses and colleagues with "Don't take him seriously because he isn't all that sharp technically."

Technical authority is not achieved easily. The expertise that underlies it is gained through education and experience over an extended period of time. If we do not have it when we assume our project responsibilities, we face a disadvantage that cannot be remedied easily.

Charismatic Authority

People who possess charismatic authority are able to get others to do their bidding through the force of their personality. The benefits of possessing some measure of charismatic authority are obvious. A major benefit is that charisma can serve as an important component of leadership. Through the sheer force of personality, the charismatic leader may be able to get project staff to commit themselves more fully to the project—that is, to work long hours, to take risks they normally would avoid, and to be creative in problem solving.

There are two common problems with charismatic authority. First, when things go wrong—as they often do on projects—project staff may come to question the basis of this authority and may perceive the charismatic leader as a master of form who lacks substance. The same charisma that serves as the basis of managerial strength may become an object of derision.

Second, it is not clear how project managers can develop charisma. Some argue that it is an inherent component of personality—that you either have it or you don't. Others maintain that the fundamental elements of charisma can be learned. Most likely, it is not an either/or situation. That is, some people can acquire certain charismatic traits through study and practice, whereas others are going to be hopelessly uncharismatic no matter how many hours they spend trying to learn how to win friends and influence people.

Purse-String Authority

Those who control resources can parlay this into a significant source of authority. With purse-string authority we face a classic carrot-and-stick reward situation: those who cooperate with us are rewarded by gaining access to needed resources. Those who do not are denied these resources. Clearly, there is strong incentive here for our staff and colleagues to see things our way.

The big problem with purse-string authority is that most project managers have little control over resources. The people assigned to their projects are borrowed resources who report to other managers. In addition, they often have only marginal control of their budgets.

Having said this, I would like to add that the picture is not as bleak as it may seem. With a little imagination, project managers and staff can see that they control more resources than they might think. For example, they have a measure of control over one of the most precious of all resources: *time.* They can reward the hardest workers with time off. (As one of my colleagues at a Fortune 50 company quipped, "To reward their good behavior, I occasionally give my finest workers a Saturday off from work.") They may also be able to adjust staff schedules for the convenience of individual workers.

Project managers also control work assignments. As a reward for effective work, the best workers can be given the most challenging assignments. To the extent that project managers regulate the allocation of equipment (for example, computers, photocopy machines, and fax machines), this can be seen as a resource to be employed. The rewards and punishments that can be employed by project managers to build authority are discussed in more detail in Chapter Seven, which looks at team building in a matrix environment.

Bureaucratic Authority

The essence of bureaucratic authority is captured in the words of Lyndon Johnson, who was one of the most effective politicians in the U.S. Congress. He advised, "Learn how the system works so that you can work the system." The great appeal of this form of authority is that with a little effort, anyone can develop it. The basis of bureaucratic authority is knowing the rules by which the organization runs and using this knowledge to achieve desired objectives. It is common knowledge that in a parliamentary debate, the individuals who have mastered Robert's Rules of Order have an edge over those who have not. Similarly, those who have mastered the rules of the organization have an edge over those who are only marginally aware of these rules.

What are the rules that should be mastered? They come in a great many varieties. There are rules for the hiring and firing of personnel, rules governing the types of equipment that can be acquired, procurement rules, contract rules, budget-cycle rules, ethics rules, leave-time rules, rules impinging upon our personal conduct outside the office . . . rules, rules, rules. Most of us view these rules as impediments to doing a good job. We have minimal tolerance for them and follow them with little or no enthusiasm—we may even ignore them outright. We do not appreciate how with a little study, we can turn these rules to our advantage. To see this, consider the following example.

Emily Ando was overwhelmed with the administrative chores associated with the project she was managing. She was spending more time filling out time sheets, budget reports, requests for tuition remission, performance appraisals, and so on than she was doing active project work. She went to her boss, Maureen Reilly, and told her of her problem. She asked Ms. Reilly for administrative help. Ms. Reilly said she would see what she could do.

One month later, Emily still had no help. She went to Ms. Reilly and reminded her of her plight. It was clear that Ms. Reilly had forgotten about Emily's request. Emily pleaded once again for administrative help, and once again she received assurances from Ms. Reilly that she would look into the matter. Two weeks later, Emily stopped Ms. Reilly in the hallway to inquire about progress in obtaining administrative assistance. Ms. Reilly was vague in her response. Emily was getting nowhere.

By chance, the same day that Emily had her last encounter with Ms. Reilly, she ate lunch with a budget officer who complained to her about the increase in his work load now that the end of the fiscal year was approaching. "Suddenly everyone is worried about the money they haven't spent this year. They know that if they don't spend it they lose it." Emily knew practically nothing about the budgeting process in her organization, so she had her companion explain it to her briefly. She learned that a department's unspent money was returned to the general fund at the end of the fiscal year.

When she returned to her office, she immediately telephoned Jack Marx, who maintained Ms. Reilly's department budget and who was on good terms with Emily. She asked him about the department's budget status, explained her need to him, and learned that there was a $15,000 line item in the budget for college interns that had not been spent in three years.

The next day, she met with Ms. Reilly and told her about the intern position, and how the department would once again lose the money obligated for the position. Ms. Reilly was shocked to learn that this money was not being used by her department and immediately authorized the creation of a job slot titled "Project Administrative Intern." Three weeks later, Emily had a young graduate student taking over the administrative duties that had plagued her so.

By gaining knowledge of how the budget system worked in her organization, Emily Ando was able to have her will prevail. Whether she recognized it or not, she was behaving in a politically effective manner.

Other Sources of Authority

The five sources of authority discussed so far do not exhaust the list of the kinds of authority project managers can try to develop. However, they do encompass the most common types of authority that project staff are likely to encounter. Other sources of authority include the following.

Authority Based on Competence. I put this at the top of the list because it promotes my view that one of the most powerful weapons individuals have is their competence. My experience suggests that people who are very good at what they do achieve a level of respect that translates into power. Highly competent individuals add value to their organizations. They make their managers and colleagues look good. People ignore them or mistreat them at their peril. They epitomize the maxim "Nothing succeeds like success."

Follow-Through Authority. One element of competence is the capacity to actually do what you promise. Follow-through is a scarce commodity. I have asked several hundred managers, "Of the promises made to you over the past year, what percent were actually kept?" Answers typically range from 5 to 20 percent. One company I worked with in the 1970s was populated with highly talented scientists, most of whom had earned Ph.D.s from world-class universities. The president of this company told me that the single greatest frustration he faced was the fact that "despite their considerable talent, our people can't seem to bring things to closure."

Imagine the power of being perceived as a person who keeps his or her promises!

Authority Based on Trust. Managers who can keep a confidence, who avoid the sordid aspects of politics, and who function consistently according to well-defined standards can develop a strong measure of authority based on the trust others put in them. Too often, people operate according to what is expedient. Those who resist expedient solutions, even when this may lead to short-term discomfort, are a minority of the general population. If their general trustworthiness is recognized, they are powerful.

Management by Intimidation. Sad to say, there is a place for occasional cage rattling in project management. Workers who consistently come to the office late and leave early might respond positively to managers who are not afraid to raise the decibel level of their voices. Vendors who have been promising for three months that a crucial part is in the mail might actually deliver the part in response to explicit threats of negative action. However, as a dominant approach, management by intimidation seldom is effective. In the long run, it is a demotivator. Furthermore, it breeds resentment, so those who live by the sword should be prepared to die by the sword.

Authority Based on Physical Appearance. Many studies have demonstrated that how you look helps define the perception other people have of you. Each year thousands of bright young executives spend a substantial portion of their incomes in an attempt to "dress for success." Actually, the issue is not whether the Rolex watch you recently bought will lead to a promotion. Rather, it is that you should be sensitive to what is considered an appropriate appearance in a given circumstance. The owner of a health spa is not going to inspire confidence in the efficacy of her weight reduction program if she herself is grossly overweight. A biker wearing a three-piece Brooks Brothers suit will be viewed with suspicion by his Hell's Angels colleagues. In many software shops, a plaid flannel shirt, blue jeans, biker boots, a beard and a ponytail are standard fare for programmers. This same ensemble would raise eyebrows in the boardroom. The point is, project staff should recognize that their physical demeanor has an impact upon their authority. They have the power to increase or diminish their authority through their personal grooming habits and their sartorial choices.

Authority of the Initiative. Back when I was chairman of the Management Science Department at George Washington University, I found myself in a position closely akin to what project managers face. I had ultimate responsibility for the actions of a large number of tenured professors, adjunct faculty, doctoral teaching fellows, and office administrative staff (sixty people in all), yet I had no direct control over any of them. In my department, the department chair is not a boss but rather a servant of the department, an enabler who allows things to run smoothly. I found quickly that the best way for me to establish authority over my flock was to initiate things. I alerted faculty to the availability of grants and contracts and helped them write proposals; I offered clerical assistance to faculty and graduate students who were serious about publishing their research results; I raised money to purchase desktop computers for all the faculty and some of the doctoral students. Through these initiatives, I operated in a proactive fashion. The targets of my actions were put into a reactive mode. I initiated, they responded. This served me well as the basis of my authority. It also served my department well in that faculty, staff, and graduate students got the support they needed to operate more effectively.

Similarly, project managers can undertake initiatives to strengthen their authority. For example, they may request staff to suggest better ways to carry out tasks, present new project ideas to their bosses, or provide functional managers with suggestions on how to do their jobs better. In taking the initiative, they operate proactively, placing others in a reactive posture. With initiative comes a certain measure of control.

For this approach to work, the initiatives that are undertaken must be sound and achievable. They must capture the imaginations of the individuals to whom they are directed. If they are introduced properly and are well received, they will confer upon the individual introducing them an aura of leadership.

Crisis Authority. In Chapter Three, I mentioned that some of my Japanese students had commented that a common way to establish authority in Japanese organizations is to announce crises. For example, it may be a Friday afternoon, and the project team members are ready to return home for a weekend with the family. Just before they are scheduled to leave, the project manager rushes breathlessly into the room and describes a major crisis that has just arisen. In order to meet this crisis, the team members will have to stay late for work this evening and are expected to work on Saturday and Sunday as well.

Crisis authority is commonly employed in the East. Even in the West, the occasional raising of a crisis can be an effective way to build authority. A well-motivated team will rise to the challenge and will be willing to sacrifice some of their personal lives for the good of the project. However, as a long-term strategy, the continual raising of crises is bound to fail. Westerners are willing to go only so far to meet the needs of the team. Their individualism requires that their personal needs take priority over the team's needs. A manager who is constantly dealing with crises is perceived to be out of control.

Old Boy Network. Many of my students tell me that an important source of authority in their organizations is not what they know, but whom they know. They are, of course, describing what has come to be known as the "old boy network." In this era of sensitivity to gender-specific language, some of my female colleagues talk about "the Sisterhood." Actually, what is being described here transcends sexual stereotyping. The key point is that decisions are made to a great degree on the basis of personal connections.

I don't see anything inherently wrong with these personal networks as long as their influence is moderate. They are one of the many communications channels existing in a typical organization. They may enable the organization to get things done when formal communications channels become clogged. We all belong to some personal networks. We should use our connections when doing so helps us to achieve our objectives. These personal networks become a problem when they are the dominant mechanism by which actions are carried out. When this occurs, they no longer are simply another communication channel. In fact, they lead to the repression of the free flow of information since they become the only meaningful communication channel.

Other forms of authority that have come to my attention include name-dropping, weaseling, mothering, blackmailing, mentoring, and tendering. I'll leave it to the reader's imagination to deduce what these forms of authority entail.

Using Authority Effectively

It should be recalled that the whole purpose of developing authority is to have our will prevail over others in an environment where we have little clout. For this to happen, we must develop several bases of authority. Being strong in only one area is not enough. For example, if all we possess is technical authority, we run the risk of being branded as narrow-focused techno-nerds. Or if all we have is charismatic authority, we may develop a reputation for possessing a great deal of fluff and little substance.

In respect to authority, the old adage about "more is better" holds true. Effective project managers should develop as many bases of authority as possible. This should be done consciously. Project managers should periodically—say, once a month—ask themselves, "What can I do to strengthen my base of authority?" Then they should go through the list of the various sources of authority to identify those areas where they can strengthen themselves. They should ask questions such as: How can I build up my formal authority? My technical authority? My bureaucratic authority?

Managing Our Managers

To be effective, project managers must know how to manage their own managers. A complaint frequently issued by project managers is that the powers above them in the organizational hierarchy are not supportive. Lack of support can take a number of different forms. For example, higher-level managers may not provide the resources they promised, may be unclear in defining their goals, may not use their power to open doors for team members, or simply may not listen to what the team members have to say.

I suspect that responsibility for the problems of managing our managers rests equally on the unsupported managers and on their bosses. Oftentimes when I investigate the accusation that a manager's boss has not been supportive, I find that the complainants have not operated in a manner deserving support or have not clearly articulated their need for support. Their bosses do not support them because they are not pleased with their work efforts or because they are unaware that a need for support exists.

However, truly nonsupportive managers do exist, and it is unfortunate when we are assigned to work with them. I have encountered many individuals for whom it would be horrible to work. I feel great sympathy for the individuals they "supervise."

The discussion on "managing our managers" is broken into two parts. In the first part, attention focuses on steps project managers can take to better articulate their need for support. In the second part, I look at how to deal with the truly nonsupportive boss.

Articulating the Need for Support

If project managers want the support of their bosses, they must do whatever they can to be continually in the bosses' field of vision. Project managers who disappear for three months in order to work in isolation should not be surprised if their bosses do not support them. They have fallen into the classic trap of "out of sight, out of mind."

Project managers can maintain their visibility in a variety of ways. One is regular status briefings. Once a week, managers can brief their bosses on project progress. In doing this, they keep communications channels open. When problems arise, they can be addressed as part of a regular programmed process so that bosses don't get the impression that the only time the project achieves visibility is when it is in trouble. Furthermore, if bosses are made part of the regular decision-making process, they develop a stronger stake in the project's success. Their support of project efforts is likely to increase.

Regular written reports are another way to maintain project visibility. Monthly status reports keep upper management apprised of project developments. Exception reports can be generated when problems arise that need their attention. Periodic milestone reviews alert them to the accomplishment of major components of the project plan. In addition to offering upper management information on project developments, these written reports also allow project managers to maintain an audit trail of their actions. If they are accused of keeping their bosses in the dark about some matter, they need merely pull out the pertinent documentation to show that this is not true. The point here is that project managers should not view reports as an administrative pain; rather, they should recognize that reports, when used effectively, enable them to operate more effectively.

Dealing with the Truly Nonsupportive Boss

I have been fortunate in my personal work experience. I have never worked for a nonsupportive boss. But I know they exist. I encounter them occasionally in my consulting assignments and hear about them from students both at my university classes and training classes.

Working for nonsupportive bosses can be exceedingly unpleasant. If their lack of support stems from incompetence, their employees may find themselves trapped in a situation where bad decisions—or perhaps no decisions—are made, where goals are ill defined, or where managerial ineptness leads to insufficient resources and overcommitments. If lack of support is rooted in simple meanness, then employees must struggle to survive the machinations of a bully boss.

There is no simple solution for dealing with the truly nonsupportive boss. The most obvious step the unfortunate employee can take is to move to a better job environment. Even the world's greatest managers will fail if they must operate in an inordinately hostile environment. Of course, this may not be possible since there are limits to job mobility in most organizations.

A more proactive step is to overwhelm the nonsupportive manager with competence. *All* managers cherish employees who can solve their problems for them. Effective employees make their managers look good. In general, all managers, including nonsupportive managers, will support willingly those employees who make their lives easier and who offer them the opportunity for glory. The obvious problem of logic here is that it may not be possible for competent employees to demonstrate their competence if they do not have the support needed to allow them to shine. Still, they are better off striving for excellence than retreating into a protective shell.

Another approach project managers can use to deal with the truly nonsupportive manager is developing powerful allies who can protect them from the consequences of their manager's bad management practices. Examples of powerful allies might be their boss's boss, managers who control resources, and their boss's peers. A danger inherent in this approach is that it can backfire. The boss may view the project manager as insubordinate. Others may perceive him or her as a political operator and not a team player.

Conclusions

The theme of this chapter has been that politics is inevitable on projects. Therefore wise project professionals will strive to develop good political skills. With such skills, they will improve the likelihood that they can affect the outcome of events in a way that is favorable to them. Without political skills, they will have little control over events.

Unfortunately, all project professionals are not equally successful in developing political skills. Political action is closely tied to personality, and it is evident that some project managers have personalities that allow them to be politically effective, while others do not. But for most project professionals, there is some hope. This chapter has made no attempt to change personalities. What it proposes is essentially a method project personnel can use to increase their political *sensitivity*—their awareness of the political currents on their projects and recognition of the outcomes of political action and inaction.

At the heart of the method is the project manager's effort to be conscious of political issues—through periodic reviews of the list of sources of authority provided earlier or through periodic enumeration of those individuals who will be affected by the project and who can have an impact on its outcome. At a minimum, increased political sensitivity will help project professionals reduce the number of political blunders they make. Beyond this, it may suggest courses of action that can strengthen their ability to have their will prevail in an environment where they have substantial amounts of responsibility without corresponding levels of authority.

Chapter Seven

Building Teams

with Borrowed Resources

When we think of teams, the image of a sports team immediately springs to mind. Standard team-related concepts, such as team spirit, are usually pictured in the context of athletes striving together to develop the ability to defeat their opponents. Coaches and athletes are popular dinner speakers, and the topic of their speeches often centers on team building.

Unfortunately, the similarity of sports teams and project teams is remote. Sports are characterized by clarity: the rules of the game are known and can be found in the rule book; the goal of the game is clear—to win; the core group of players is fairly constant; they have clearly defined roles; they learn to function as a unit through constant practice; in the heat of the game, team members can identify each other readily by the color of their uniform; and the team is offered strong guidance on how to perform through the directives of the coach (who, incidentally, wields carrots and sticks and therefore is a boss).

Projects, in contrast, are characterized by fuzziness: often there are few clearly established rules governing the project effort; the project goal is often obscure, partially because most projects have multiple goals that may contradict each other; the team is composed of a constantly changing set of players who are used as needed and then returned to their functional homes; team member roles are unclear; team members do not have an opportunity to practice their skills as a unit—sadly, the project is the practice session; and project managers are not bosses.

The reason that project teams do not look like sports teams is that they entail the employment of borrowed resources. If you wanted to design a management approach that would make team building truly difficult, you would invent the matrix management concept! Matrix management provides the underlying principles that govern most project activity. Imagine sports events being carried out like projects: each week the composition of the team would change, players would get their weekly playing assignments through a lottery system, team size could fluctuate, the rules of the game would be dynamic, and coaches would have no power over their players. When applied to a sports example, the standard practices employed in project management appear laughable.

How can team spirit be built in such an environment? I recall a class I held several years ago in which, after a discussion of difficulties in team building on projects, one student asked plaintively, "Is it hopeless then? Is it basically impossible to build a sense of team identity on projects?"

This question caught me off guard. The tenor of our discussion certainly suggested a feeling of hopelessness, but experience counsels that there are highly motivated project teams out there in the real world. I have been a part of such teams and have seen many other examples in my career. Still, I was not sure how to answer the student's question, so I took a Socratic approach.

"What do you think?" I asked the whole class. "Is it hopeless?" The class response was exciting. The gist of their answer was that no, it is not hopeless. A large number of students talked about approaches on their projects that had contributed to team building. The exercise was so successful and elicited so much student participation that I have used it in every project management class I've taught since that time. Nearly four thousand people have participated in the exercise.

I soon noticed that the "tricks" for team building employed by my students fitted a pattern. From class to class, they were saying the same thing. Basically, their advice fell into three categories. One set of tricks involved making the team as tangible as possible. Most project teams are so dynamic as to be only marginally tangible. Team membership is constantly changing. To build commitment to the team, the team itself should be made as concrete as possible since most people are reluctant to charge into the fray on behalf of an abstraction.

Another set of tricks focused on identifying rewards for good behavior. Clearly, because most project managers have little or no control over resources, they are not able to effect elaborate rewards. However, with a little creative thinking, they will see that a good reward system can be built even when control over resources is limited.

My students called the third category of tricks "the personal touch." The point is that through their personal actions and attitudes, project managers can motivate their borrowed staff to walk the extra mile. Certainly, if they possess a bad attitude, they will demotivate their staff quite easily.

Each of these three areas of team-building "tricks" will now be discussed in more detail.

Make the Team as Tangible as Possible

Project teams are highly dynamic. Team members are constantly changing. For example, on a project to provide external customers with a product, the team may be weighted heavily with members from the marketing department at the outset. As the project evolves along its life cycle, needs analysts and requirements specialists may join the team and play a central role. Most of the marketing staff may drift away and attempt to generate new business elsewhere. Once needs and requirements have been established, designers may begin playing an important role as the needs analysts and requirements specialists in their turn drift away. When a solid design has been developed, builders take over. As they build whatever it is they are making, they are periodically assisted by testers. Documenters also enter the picture periodically, generating systems documentation, user documentation, training manuals, and the like.

The example offered here is quite typical. It is not evident that the various individuals who play a role on the project really see themselves as part of a larger entity, a cohesive team. Why should they? Like the blind men, all they encounter are pieces of the elephant. The lack of a cohesive team identity can lead to an absence of a feeling of belonging. Team building will not occur under such conditions.

Very often, project teams are an abstraction. Only the project manager and possibly some members of senior management may see the team in its entirety. The team members themselves see only snippets. If project managers want a motivated team, they must work to make their teams as concrete as possible. How can this be done? Following are frequently employed approaches to make the team more palpable.

Hold Productive Meetings

The most obvious purpose of meetings is to convey information to the participants. A less obvious purpose is to reinforce the identity of the group. At meetings, the players get to see each other in the flesh. There is nothing abstract about sitting in a room with a dozen of your teammates, some of whom you may not have seen before. Obviously, meetings are an instrument to make the team more tangible.

A particularly important meeting in project management is the *kickoff meeting*. As the name implies, this meeting is held at the outset of the project and is designed to get the project rolling. Features of a typical kickoff meeting include presenting the project charter (a tangible) that defines project goals and authority; identifying team players and issuing a team roster (a tangible), which includes addresses and phone numbers of the team players; identifying key milestone dates, which can be presented via a milestone chart (a tangible); and establishing rapport among the team players.

Another important meeting category is the *status review*.

This is a periodic meeting (weekly, monthly) that focuses on defining project progress. Attention is directed to such things as budget and schedule variances and problems in the execution of the project. On smaller projects, it may be desirable to have all team members present during the status updates. On larger projects, this may be impossible, owing to limitations of time and space. In this case, it is advisable to establish rotating attendance at these meetings in such a way that every month or so each team member has an opportunity to meet with all other team members. The value of status meetings to team building is that they remind the players that they are not Lone Rangers but are a part of a larger group.

Meetings need not be formal. Beer and pretzel parties, milestone parties, and social functions, like the team softball game, are informal meetings that help reinforce a sense of belonging to something concrete among the team players. Meetings need not even have attendees present in one place: some of my AT&T students tell me that the most common meetings they attend are telephone conference calls.

Create a Team Space

The single best way to give project staff a sense of belonging to a real team is to locate them all at one site. In this way they see each other every day. Through their constant interaction, they learn something about each other. Co-location does not assure good relationships—remember the adage that states that familiarity breeds contempt—but it does affirm a sense of team identity.

The key problem with co-location is mundane: few organizations have the resources or space to put a large number of people into a consolidated area. Even when resources are bountiful, it may not make sense to relocate people to the project area if the project will be complete in a matter of a few months.

If co-location is not practical, a good substitute is the creation of a "war room." I have seen war rooms used to good effect on many projects. They can be quite humble—no more than glorified closets, in fact. Or they can be elaborate "situation rooms." In any event, they are a tangible embodiment of the project effort. The full array of project-related documentation should be kept here. The walls are often filled with PERT charts, Gantt charts, budget curves, and resource-loading charts. Information on the project history can be stored in loose-leaf binders on the bookshelf. A conference table enables project staff to gather in one place to mull over project ideas. An added advantage of a well-configured war room is that it impresses outsiders. I recently came upon a project that had a major budget increase because top management was highly impressed with the demeanor of the war room.

Create Team "Signs"

Semiotics is the science of signs. A readable introduction to this field can be found in Jack Solomon's *The Signs of Our Time* (1988). Semioticians tell us that the signs we employ advertise our aspirations and motivations. They are symbols reflecting deeper realities. Important signs that can help create team identity are a team name and logo. The power of these symbols should not be underestimated. At a meeting, I once encountered a well-dressed man wearing a tattered navy blue tie. The tie caught my attention because it did not go with his elegant suit. Upon looking at the tie, I saw it had a pattern on it.

"Isn't that the Hubble space telescope on your tie?" I asked him.

"It certainly is," he said with pride. He explained to me that he was with Ford Aerospace and that these ties were distributed to all the men who worked on the multibillion dollar Hubble space telescope project. "I wear it nearly every day," he added. Its heavy use was evident. "It's a badge that identifies me to other Hubble team members. Occasionally I'll have people from another contractor organization come up to me and tell me they are also on the Hubble team."

To this man, the tie had taken on great significance as an insignia identifying his connection with a prestigious project.

A common practice on project teams is to affix the team name and logo to an assortment of items. I have seen team T-shirts, coffee mugs, pens, stationery, caps, and pins. Purveyors of these goods jokingly refer to them as "trinkets and trash."

Publicize Team Efforts

A project public relations effort can solidify a project's image, thereby making the team more tangible. To the extent that a project team is recognized externally, a sense of identity will be forged among its members. One way to publicize project efforts is to make sure that the project is mentioned regularly in the organization's newsletter. In this day of easy desktop publishing, the project may establish its own newsletter for circulation throughout the organization. To further heighten the project profile, team members should offer public presentations on project work whenever possible. The key point of this public relations effort is to increase public awareness of the team's work, setting it apart from the rest of the organization.

Develop Rewards for Good Behavior

A second broad approach to team building on projects is to institute a reward system to motivate team members to do their best and to reaffirm good behavior. The obvious problem here is that project managers seldom have control over resources that would serve as the basis of the rewards. They cannot provide raises, offer bonuses, or extend vacations. In most cases, they do not even have responsibility for filling out performance appraisal reviews for their team members. So how can they use carrots and sticks to motivate their teams?

They must use their imaginations. A little thought will show them that they control more "resources" than they might think:

- They can write letters of commendation for good performance.
- They have a measure of control over job assignments and can make sure that good workers get choice assignments.
- They have a measure of control over scheduling assignments and may be able to adjust schedules to accommodate the needs of exemplary workers.
- They may be able to provide "comp time" for workers who have been working sixty-hour weeks.
- They can recommend employees for corporate bonuses.

- When new equipment arrives, they can offer it to the best workers.
- They can take workers (and possibly their spouses as well) to dinner.
- They may have some input into deciding who gets what perquisites (for example, parking spaces, corner offices, offices with windows—in one company I know, an important status symbol is the quality of trash basket one has).
- They can offer team members increased visibility by allowing them to give briefings to upper management.

The central point here is that despite the lack of direct control over budgets and personnel, project managers can establish rewards to motivate their team members. To do this effectively, they must take stock of those things they *do* control and consciously employ them as rewards.

Develop an Effective Personal Touch

The third category of project management team building tricks focuses on the one-on-one relationship between project managers and their team members. The basic question here is: Does the project manager's personal behavior inspire team members to work as hard and effectively as is necessary to get the job done? Most of the suggestions in this category employ common sense. Like the Golden Rule, they are good precepts that should guide all of our dealings with people.

Suggestions for developing good personal touch capabilities include:

- Provide positive feedback on performance. Say thanks now and then. (I have worked with project teams where project managers issue gold stars to employees as an indicator of their pleasure with good performance. It works!)
- Publicly acknowledge good performance. For example, at the

status review meeting, point out that a given employee has completed her work ahead of schedule.

- Show interest in the team members. Learn something about
their background and interests. *Know their names!* (To support
their memories, many project managers keep records of team
member facts on 3x5 cards.)
- Be a "shirt sleeve" manager. Demonstrate a willingness to do the
dirty work alongside the other team players. (One project manager told me of an incident where his team was working well
into the morning hours on an important project. Outside a
blizzard was raging and all the team members would rather have
been at home in bed. The project manager showed his concern
for the team by calling them regularly *from his hotel in the
Virgin Islands.* After the third phone call, the team members
were so irritated with their boss that they packed up and went
home.)
- Be accessible. Practice open door policies and management by
walking around.
- Be clear in defining your expectations and in describing work
requirements. Staff are justifiably angered by managers who
give them vague guidance on what they should do ("Do what
you think is appropriate") and then later criticize them for doing the wrong thing.
- Be consistent and stick to the rules.
- Empower team members to make decisions.
- Acknowledge special occasions—birthdays, anniversaries, and
the like.
- When critical milestones have been achieved, celebrate this with
milestone parties.
- At least two important Don'ts should be observed: don't publicly criticize team members, and when problems arise, don't put
the blame on the team.

A word of caution: project team workers are not stupid. If
they perceive project managers employing motivation tricks in a
cynical way as a tool of manipulation, they will be turned off. The
team-building effort must come from the heart. Otherwise, it will
backfire on the project manager and lead to team disintegration.

Self-Managed Teams: Prospects and Pitfalls

In this section, I will digress a moment to examine one of the management "hot buttons" of the 1990s: self-managed teams. At the present time, organizations are actively experimenting with different team structures to help them operate more effectively in a viciously competitive global business environment. These experiments are exciting and demonstrate the vitality of management thought in many leading organizations.

By the mid 1990s, the concept of self-managed teams achieved prominence. Business magazines such as *Fortune* and *Business Week* extolled the virtues of this approach. Books and seminars proliferated on how to employ self-managed teams in organizations. Tom Peters praised them in his influential *Liberation Management* (1992). Most of the material on self-managed teams focuses on how they have produced miracle results in organizations. Few words of criticism are directed at this approach.

With self-managed teams, team members define the approach they will take to getting a job done. Collectively, they make key personnel decisions—work assignments, performance appraisals, hiring decisions, and, occasionally, firing decisions. The team members call the shots, and upper-management intrusions are minimized.

The press praises self-managed teams as a mechanism to empower workers to do the best job they can. The theory is that when people make their own decisions, they have a greater commitment to executing them effectively. Furthermore, people who are close to the work have a better sense of what is needed to do a good job than managers far removed from the day-to-day action.

When they function properly, self-managed teams can be awesome. Back when I was actively involved in research and software projects, the teams I belonged to were largely self-managed. Our projects were carried out under contract, so the specifications we were to achieve were externally defined. Beyond that, we wrote our own rules. For the most part, our projects were well done and our customers were highly satisfied with our efforts. Top management was delighted with this approach since the team assumed total responsibility for the work effort. When problems arose, the team would figure out how to deal with them. If the solution to a problem required that we work seventy hours for a week, we would work the seventy hours without complaint.

The problem is that self-managed teams often do not work as advertised. To see this, one need merely recall that Yugoslav enterprises were pioneers in the area of self-management. While in Dubrovnik in 1980, I observed self-management firsthand. The self-management I saw there confirmed the old adage that when everybody is in charge, no one is in charge. Yugoslavia never developed the reputation as a world-class producer despite its self-management practices. By the 1990s, the focus on self-management quickly disappeared as the country disintegrated into fratricidal chaos.

Gerald M. Weinberg's concept of *egoless teams* was a variant of self-management that emerged on software projects in the early 1970s (see his book *The Psychology of Computer Programming*, 1971). The basic idea underlying egoless teams is that team members have collective responsibility for their products and should behave as if they are interchangeable parts. Hierarchies and selfishness are out, group focus and joint decision making are in.

I have interviewed people associated with more than thirty projects who were members of egoless teams. They highlighted a number of pitfalls they encountered in their group-focused efforts. These included the following:

- There is a danger that leadership will be lacking if the group focus requires everyone to buy into team solutions.
- Decision making may be slow if team consensus must be carefully nurtured.
- In order to avoid group conflict and to achieve group consensus, solutions occasionally appeal to the lowest common denominator.
- People have egos.

Whether a self-managed team approach is appropriate must be determined on a case-by-case basis. The idea of empowering a team is certainly appealing. Through such empowerment, vital team energies might be tapped that otherwise would be suppressed. Workers would take a greater interest in their efforts. They would work harder and smarter to achieve the team's goals. Beyond this, there is the democratic appeal of self-management. In the West, we like to think that people should be given as much control over their destinies as possible.

However, self-managyement is not a panacea. Success is certainly not built into it. It will not succeed unless

- Upper management truly empowers team members to make independent decisions.
- Team members demonstrate leadership qualities and are not frightened of responsibility.
- Team members are highly motivated and are willing to do what it takes to get the job done.
- Team members form a cohesive body of players—they are not borrowed resources temporarily assigned to work on the project.

The last point represents a major obstacle in applying self-managed team concepts on project teams. Today, the dominant mode of structuring teams is to employ borrowed resources: when we need particular resources, we draw them from the resource pool; when we are done with them, we send them back home. This approach is too dynamic to lend itself to self-management.

Structuring the Team

To a large extent, the potential problems of self-managed teams are hard-wired due to the self-managed team structure. The principal components of this structure are:

- Group decision making
- Lack of clearly defined leader
- Diffuse accountability

Slow decision making, the need for compromise, and potential aimlessness are all potential consequences of this structure.

In this section we examine structural issues in some detail. In particular, we focus on the management consequences of structure. The discussion is an extension of the ideas I presented in

Managing Projects in Organizations (1987). Interest in the management implications of structure gained a measure of popularity in the early 1990s under the rubric of *organizational architecture* as a consequence of work done by David Nadler and the Delta Consulting Group (see Nadler and others, 1992).

The principle examined here is the converse of one of the most famous dictums in architecture. Louis Sullivan, the great American nineteenth-century architect, promoted the concept that "form follows function." Basically, what this means is: "If you tell me what will happen in a given space (function), then this will suggest the appropriate architectural design to me (form)."

We will examine the converse proposition: "Function follows form." In other words: "You show me the structure of a project team (form), and I will predict accurately the managerial consequences (function) of that structure."

The power of this approach can be seen through a simple example. Let's say we are examining the following rudimentary structural proposition: "A team is getting larger." What are the managerial consequences of this growth? One is that communication channels between team members grow explosively. This matter was discussed in Chapter Two ("Managing Complexity"). For example, with two people, there is one pairwise channel (for the purposes of this discussion, we will ignore the two-way flow of information). With three, there are three channels; with four, six channels; with five, ten channels. In general, if there are n people, the potential number of pairwise channels is $n(n-1)/2$.

This explosive growth in communication channels has enormous managerial implications. For example, project managers on large projects spend disproportionately more time on administrative chores than project managers on smaller teams. Consider that the project manager of a five-person team has only 10 pairwise communication channels to oversee, whereas the project manager of a twenty-person team (hardly a large team) has 190. Overseeing communications channels translates into all sorts of administrative and tracking chores.

As the number of channels grows, the need for formal structured procedures increases. It reaches the point where on very large projects (in the billion dollar range), sixty-five cents out of every dollar goes to maintaining the administrative infrastructure that keeps the project functioning. Only thirty-five cents goes to directly productive activities.

Other implications of growing team size are a greater chance of communication breakdown; a need for more office space, desks, and equipment; less attention spent on the needs of individual team members; and so on.

The point is that the managerial consequences of structure can be anticipated in advance. The manager who has just been promoted from head of a five-person team to head of a twenty-person team had better be prepared for the fact that she will no longer have time to do hands-on technical work along with the other team members. She will spend much of her time on the phone, in meetings, and pushing paper.

Following are two case studies focusing on the structural aspects of two projects. These case studies are not hypothetical. They represent real situations that arose in two real companies.

Euro-Lan

Euro-Lan is a European-based systems integrator that specializes in installing local area networks (LANs) in businesses. It recently won a competitive bid to install LANs in the local offices of a large insurance company that had major operations in the United Kingdom, France, Germany, and Spain.

Responsibility for managing the project was given to Euro-Lan's Development Group in Paris because this group was charged with advancing Euro-Lan's LAN implementation capabilities. Euro-Lan operations in France, Germany, the UK, and Spain each had responsibility for installing the LANs in the insurance offices in their own countries.

Unfortunately, the national operations of Euro-Lan functioned as semiautonomous fiefdoms, each with its own profit and loss responsibilities. Consequently, communications between the project coordinator in Paris and his counterparts in Germany, the UK, and Spain were indirect, going up and down national chains of command as pictured in Figure 7.1.

Figure 7.1. Euro-Lan: Insurance Company Project.

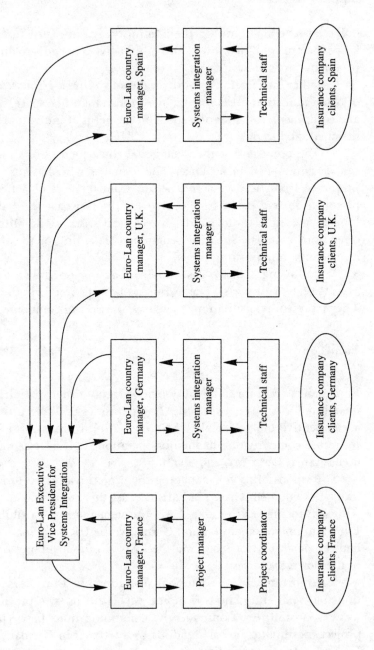

The functional implications of this structure are obvious and led to serious problems on this project. They are as follows:

- Communications between the project coordinator and his counterparts in Germany, the UK, and Spain were painfully slow. Consequently, Euro-Lan was unable to respond quickly to customer requests, which led to unhappiness on the part of the client.
- Because any given communication had to pass through so many hands, the likelihood that messages would become distorted was great. By the time a request from Paris reached technical staff in Germany, the UK, and Spain, it had undergone so much filtering that the actual instructions received varied measurably from country to country.
- The project coordinator lacked even the most rudimentary degree of authority over technical staff in the other countries. A substantial proportion of his requests to these countries were ignored.
- Conflicts between the different national groups had to be elevated to Euro-Lan's vice president of systems integration in order to be resolved since the communications structure used in this project made her the key arbiter to deal with cross-divisional problems. The VP became exasperated by the continual bickering on this project as even trivial issues were brought to her for resolution.
- Problems induced by the communications architecture on this project were aggravated by financial structural issues. For example, in managing the project budget, Euro-Lan's Paris office allocated the lion's share of profit to Euro-Lan/France. Operations in Germany, the UK, and Spain basically were reimbursed for their costs and were allocated a minuscule profit. This led to a great deal of resentment in the non-Paris operations and chilled any spirit of cooperation that might have existed.

Scan Systems Inc.

Scan Systems Inc. was awarded a contract to replace the bar code scanning equipment for all of Wonder Toy Company's ninety-five retail outlets. Key players in the project are pictured in Figure 7.2. On the Wonder Toy side, a project manager was assigned from the Information Technology Department. Her responsibilities were principally to generate requirements and to monitor the performance of Scan Systems Inc. The Information Technology Department was given a central role in the project. In fact, they were the ones who generated the request for proposal to which Scan Systems Inc. responded. They were also instrumental in selecting Scan Systems Inc. from among five bidders. The vice president of finance was an important player since this project was undertaken in response to his request. Similarly, the vice president for operations was involved since bar code scanning enabled Wonder Toy to track inventories.

On the Scan System side, a project manager was assigned. He had total responsibility for overseeing the installation of scanning hardware and software in the ninety-five Wonder Toy retail outlets. He had access to about twenty technically capable staff members who would carry out day-to-day activities on the project. Because Wonder Toy required that the software run on the unique B-Zar Operating System, Scan System hired a B-Zar specialist as a consultant. The account manager who shepherded the project during the preaward phase and was instrumental in developing the winning proposal continued to work on the project as a customer liaison. Finally, since this project entailed the delivery of some six hundred scanning units, Scan Systems' manufacturing group was actively involved in the project effort.

The Scan Systems project manager was highly experienced with this type of project. He did a "structural analysis" of the situation and saw immediately some structurally based challenges that he had to be prepared to deal with. The following were some of the key challenges:

- Decision-making authority was diffuse on the customer side. Although the Wonder Toy project manager might appear to be a key decision maker, in fact she was a minor player because three powerful players—the Finance VP, Information Technology VP, and Operations VP—could make independent decisions

Figure 7.2. Scan Systems Inc.

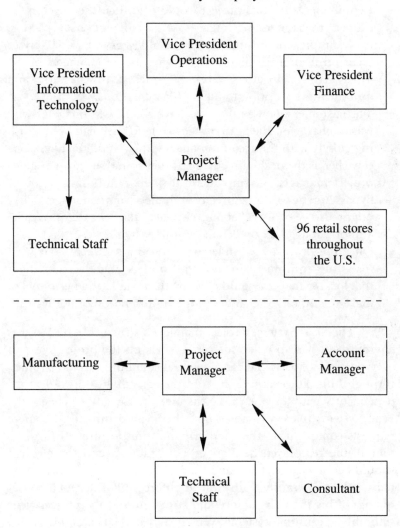

Wonder Toy Company

Scan Systems, Inc.

by virtue of their power. In fact, if there is a major divergence of interest between the information technology and finance groups, all decision making can become bogged down.

- Requirements for this project would be difficult to develop because of the contending interests of the different sets of players. For example, the information technology group was likely to focus on technical functionality, whereas the managers of the ninety-five retail outlets were more interested in usability and minimizing disruption to their daily operations.

- The customer side was likely to have a confused image of who was in charge on the Scan Systems side. If they had been working closely with the account manager, they would be likely perceive her as the person in charge. If they found the Scan Systems project manager unsympathetic to their requests, they might bypass him by working directly with the account manager. They might also be confused about the role of the consultant. Was he authorized to speak on behalf of Scan Systems?

- Once the project was under way and the technical staff were installing equipment in the retail outlets, there was a danger that local managers would pressure the installation personnel to make unauthorized changes to the configuration of the system.

The Scan Systems project manager's structural "fix" to this environment was to make his central role on the project clear to everyone and to insist that consequential communications be routed through him. For example, he told the consultant not to deal independently with anyone in the customer organization. He got the Scan Systems players to agree that they would funnel all change requests coming from the client organization to him. In turn, he told all the key players at Wonder Toy that any requests they had should be directed to him—and that the other players at Scan Systems were cooperating with him to enforce this rule. As a consequence of his proactive stance and structural fix, the project went smoothly. Scanning systems were installed on time and within budget, and generated high levels of customer satisfaction.

Conclusions

The basic unit of project work is the project team. Unfortunately, project environments are so dynamic that teams operating in this environment do not look like regular teams. On projects, team members are borrowed resources. They come to the project, do their work, and then return to their functional homes.

A key concern of project professionals is how to engage in team building in such an environment. Normal conditions that promote team building—for example, co-location of team members, stable membership of players, the availability of carrots and sticks to motivate people—do not exist on most projects.

An additional complication is that project teams today increasingly involve partnering arrangements, in which members from the customer organization are part of the team. Some of the issues involved in partnering were discussed earlier in Chapter Three ("Managing Change"), which examined a popular partnering arrangement called rapid prototyping.

This chapter has shown that although team building is difficult under standard project conditions, it is not impossible. Caring project managers who employ a little ingenuity can devise ways to build team spirit in an environment that seems rather hostile to it. But they must recognize that team building will not occur by accident. It requires conscious and conscientious effort.

Chapter Eight

Selecting Projects

That Will Lead to Success

Not so long ago, the common wisdom maintained that the manager's principal jobs were to organize and direct. Such an outlook was appropriate in the hierarchical organizations that dominated Western business life until recently. Today, however, we live in an age of flattened organizations and inverted pyramids. Much of the organization's work is carried on by outsiders through outsourcing arrangements and strategic alliances. Managers are now charged to empower and support their work force rather than to direct them. So much of what was standard managerial fare a decade ago looks positively archaic today.

One thing has still not changed, however. Whatever else they do, managers still have major decision-making responsibilities. This is not to say that they make decisions unilaterally. Now more than ever, in fact, decision making is a cooperative effort between managers, the work force, and customers. In such an environment, the job of managers is not to call the shots independently but to assure that effective decisions are made. They can do this in a

174

number of ways. For example, they can create an environment where they, their work force, and customers can interact productively to arrive at decisions.

Effective decision making does not occur by accident. In this chapter we examine some of its core elements, particularly as they relate to the selection of projects. The discussion can be generalized to cover other selection decisions as well—choosing staff, vendors, designs, and so on.

The Essence of Choice

Rational decision making is fundamentally a process of prioritizing options. The best options go to the top of the list, the worst to the bottom. Consider the choice to buy a car. In this case, buyers consider a number of different selection criteria, including price, performance, styling, safety, and prestige. In the absence of an explicit decision-making methodology such as the analytical hierarchy process, they intuitively assess the performance of the target cars on each of these criteria and then sum up the results. Car A may get top billing on price, performance, and safety but be rated as average on styling and prestige. In contrast, Car B may receive the highest ratings on styling and prestige but middling ratings on price, performance, and safety.

Which car ranks higher? The answer depends on how the buyer grades practical considerations (price, performance, and safety) versus considerations of status (styling and prestige). If practical considerations are paramount, then Car A is chosen. If status considerations dominate, then Car B is chosen.

In view of the fact that decision making entails prioritization, whatever decision-making tools we use should have a built-in capacity to rank order the options. This is precisely what lies at the heart of the specific project selection techniques that we examine in this chapter. What they all have in common is the goal of rank ordering the options.

Benefit-Cost Ratios

The term *benefit-cost analysis* refers to the attempt to systematically weigh the benefits associated with an option against the costs. This can be done in a highly informal manner, as when we divide a page into two columns, labeling one "pros" and the other "cons." It can be done more formally through the creation of sophisticated mathematical models of benefits and costs.

In this section, we discuss one of the more commonly employed approaches to weighing benefits against costs: the benefit-cost ratio. The ratio is created by developing a quantitative estimate of benefits (usually measured in monetary terms), developing an estimate of costs, and dividing the latter into the former. Consider the following primitive example of how a benefit-cost ratio might be created to provide us guidance on what project to select:

$$\text{B/C} = \frac{[\text{Estimated Sales}] \times [\text{Estimated Profit Rate}] \times [\text{Probability of Success}]}{\text{Estimated Costs}}$$

Let us assume that the estimated sales volume is \$100,000, the estimated profit rate is 10 percent, and the probability of success is 80 percent. These three values multiplied together yield the expected value of profit. That is, \$100,000 × 10 percent yields a profit of \$10,000. It is 80 percent certain that this will be achieved, so by calculating 80 percent of \$10,000, we determine that the expected value of profit is \$8,000.

Let us further assume that the estimated project costs are \$4,000. Our benefit-cost ratio is determined by dividing the expected value of profit by estimated cost, or \$8,000 by \$4,000. The resulting ratio is 2.0.

It should be noted that this ratio is not an abstract number. A ratio of 2.0 tells us that for every dollar invested in the project, we can anticipate \$2.00 in benefits. In other words, the ratio is a measure of "bang for the buck." If this ratio accurately portrays the per-dollar impact of an investment, it can be a valuable tool in our project management toolbox. The relative merits of two or more projects can be established by comparing their benefit-cost ratios.

In finance, the benefit-cost ratio is called the *profitability index* because it tells us whether an option is profitable. When the ratio is greater than 1.0, it is profitable because benefits exceed costs. When it is less than 1.0, it is not profitable because costs are greater than benefits. A ratio of 1.0 indicates that benefits perfectly offset costs—we neither make nor lose money.

Estimating Benefits and Costs

The benefit-cost ratio is a quantitative tool, and as such it requires that the variables being analyzed be quantified. Most typically, benefits are measured in monetary terms. The example offered above shows how this can be done. In this particular formulation, benefits are measured by estimating profits in the simplest way possible.

Computations of benefits can grow more complex than this. An elaborate modeling of benefits can become quite formidable, filled with exotic integral signs and Greek characters. For example, anticipated benefits might be captured by a mathematical growth function using integral calculus. The effects of depreciation, salvage value, and taxes might be factored out, further complicating the formulation. When all is said and done, the mathematical formula describing benefits might look like something copied from a book on rocket science.

Obtaining data to calculate ratios can be troublesome. Where do the data come from? Ideally, the organization conducting the analysis has been collecting data over a period of time and has developed a historical data base that can be employed. If it is an important project, many departments might contribute to the estimating process: the marketing department might contribute possible sales and price estimates; the manufacturing department, information on projected production runs and costs; and the finance department, data on costs.

It is certain that even the best data will be a bit soft. We are talking, after all, about gazing into a crystal ball to predict the future, and the future is always vague. It is therefore a good idea to establish a range of possible outcomes: a best case, worst case, and most likely scenario. By uncovering the full range of options, decision makers have a better sense of the consequences of their actions.

Unfortunately, the reliability of much of the data being generated through this process may be low because of problems inherent in making estimates. For example, many of the people involved in generating the data may be amateurs in the realm of cost estimating, pulling numbers out of thin air. Or perhaps the optimism of key players makes it impossible to see the downside of certain projects. Difficulties of estimation are described in detail in Chapter Nine.

Measuring Benefits as Cost Avoidance

Clearly, when one is selling a product or service to an external customer, it is easy to construe benefits as income streams. But what of situations where we do not have income streams? Governments always encounter this situation because they do not operate to generate profits. In the private sector this also occurs, commonly on internal projects designed to improve an organization's operations, as when equipment or information systems are upgraded. For example, it is difficult, if not impossible, to calculate increases in profitability associated with the purchase of a new financial accounting system.

So how can benefits be calculated when there are no income streams associated with an activity? One can measure benefits as *cost avoidance*. That is, one uses benefit-cost ratios to identify options that will save the organization money.

To see how this works, consider the following example. A government scientific laboratory is looking for a way to analyze blood samples more effectively. Currently, their procedures are labor intensive. They seek out modern blood analysis machinery that can automate the process extensively. Three products emerge that can help them carry out their work more effectively. Each of these products meets the lab's technical requirements for blood analysis. The laboratory decides to conduct a benefit-cost analysis to assist it in selecting the proper piece of equipment.

In calculating benefits, the lab first computes the cost of analyzing blood under current procedures. Then, using data supplied to it by the vendor combined with estimates made by its own personnel, the laboratory estimates the cost of analyzing blood for each of the three candidate products (net of the costs of purchasing the equipment in the first place, as well as the cost of a maintenance contract). It determines the annual cost savings associated with each of the products to be $120,000 for Product A, $80,000 for Product B, and $160,000 for Product C. Clearly, Product C will provide the laboratory with the greatest level of cost savings.

These cost savings must be assessed against the purchase price of the equipment plus additional costs, such as the price of a maintenance agreement. Assuming that the equipment has a useful life of five years, the lab divides the total purchase price by five and adds on the annual maintenance fee to derive an estimate of annualized costs for the equipment. The estimated annualized costs are $80,000 for Product A, $60,000 for Product B, and $160,000 for Product C.

In calculating benefit-cost ratios, the laboratory finds that they are 1.5 for Product A, 1.33 for Product B, and 1.0 for Product C. This analysis tells us that from a purely financial point of view, Product A gives the most bang for the buck.

Common Problems with Benefit-Cost Ratios

In using benefit-cost ratios, project staff should be aware of a number of common pitfalls.

Focus on the Measurable. Obviously, this approach has a bias toward what is readily measurable. It tends to ignore things that are hard to quantify. However, sometimes the immeasurable can be very important. For example, in calculating benefits, have we taken into account the downstream secondary and tertiary consequences of our project? Possibly a seemingly unimpressive project might be laying the groundwork for major breakthroughs in the future. Have the potential downstream benefits been factored into the benefit-cost ratio for this project?

Other hard-to-quantify factors include the amount of good will generated by the project, its "fit" with corporate goals and the corporate culture, and its contribution to building core competencies in the organization (for example, increasing technological capabilities). If factors such as these are not included in the benefit-cost analysis, the resulting ratio will offer a skewed view of the value of benefits in relation to cost.

Inadequate Specification of the Benefit-Cost Model. When computing a benefit-cost ratio, an obvious question that arises is: Does the benefit-cost model we have created accurately reflect reality? In statistics, this is called the *specification problem*. There is bound to be some divergence between reality and the model since models are an approximation of reality. The key issue is whether the specified model deviates *dramatically* from reality, providing us with seriously misleading information.

We have just seen that the exclusion of nonmeasurable factors from the model might lead to distortions. But there may be problems even with the measurable factors. For example, our model of benefits may assume that they grow exponentially over the next five years when in fact their growth is linear. Or our model may neglect to take into account the salvage value of a product when this may measurably affect how benefits are calculated.

To minimize the negative effects of model misspecification, the model should be continually tested against reality and subjected to criticism. Alternative forms of the model should also be explored to determine how sensitive it is to variations of its specifications.

Size-Independent Nature of the Ratios. Given two project options, one whose benefit-cost ratio is 3.22 and the other whose ratio is 2.80, the "obvious" choice is to support the first option. However, consider the data that might have gone into the construction of these two ratio values:

Option A: B/C = ($3,220/$1,000) = 3.22

Option B: B/C = ($2,800,000/$1,000,000) = 2.80

A review of the data underlying the ratios changes our perspective on the relative merits of the two projects. A large company would find Option B more desirable than Option A because it involves larger amounts of payback. The payback of Option A is "chicken feed." Consider that from an investment point of view, Option B is one thousand times larger than Option A (that is, it would take one thousand Option A projects to equal one Option

B project because a million dollar investment is a thousand times larger than a thousand dollar investment).

The point here is that benefit-cost ratios are size-independent. They tell us nothing of the dimensions of the underlying investment and payback. There are an infinite number of ways that a ratio of 3.22 can be generated: 0.322/0.100, 3.22/1.00, 32.22/10.00, 322/100, etc. In comparing two benefit-cost ratios, we want to be sure that we are not comparing an elephant with a mouse.

Unknown Payback Periods. If Project Option C has a benefit-cost ratio of 3.22 and Project Option D has a ratio of 2.80, Option C would appear to be more attractive than Option D. However, if the payback period associated with Option C's benefits is longer than that of Option D, Option D may be the more desirable choice. In interpreting benefit-cost ratios, it is generally important to examine the cash inflow and outflow structures associated with benefits and costs respectively. The overall ratio may blur important information contained in the cash flow data.

The Telescope Effect. In Chapter Ten, which covers procedures for estimating project costs and schedules, the telescope effect is described in some detail. Small errors of estimation can telescope into major errors if these errors occur consistently. For example, if an estimator consistently overstates benefits by 10 percent (and understates costs by 10 percent) in the benefit-cost equation shown at the beginning of this chapter, the resulting benefit-cost ratio will overstate benefits by 48 percent. When such an effect takes place, undeserving projects obtain support based on faulty estimates.

Buss's Technique for Rank Ordering Projects

In 1983, an interesting article written by Martin Buss appeared in the *Harvard Business Review*. Entitled "How to Rank Computer Projects," it described a benefit-cost project selection methodology that does not depend on employing quantitative data but that still shares some of the key features of benefit-cost ratios. The following discussion expostulates on Buss's ideas but modifies them slightly in light of my own experience in employing them.

Buss's approach requires that a small project selection team be put together—say, during a quarterly review session—to review at one time a number of project proposals. Ideally, the team members represent different perspectives. For example, a hypothetical team might have the following composition: one member from the marketing department, one from finance, one from production, and one from engineering.

The team members are charged to go through the pile of proposals and to evaluate each of them according to key project selection criteria. Although each organization can create its own specialized criteria, experience shows that four criteria serve the project selection process effectively: financial, technical, developmental, and organizational. Each of these criteria is viewed from the perspective of benefits and is matched against project costs. The matching of costs against benefit for the four selection criteria is pictured in Figure 8.1. The matching takes the physical form of a three-by-three grid.

Grid A matches costs of the candidate projects against anticipated financial benefits. As the grid illustrates, nine possible scenarios emerge. Project costs can be high while financial benefits are also high; costs can be moderate while benefits are high; costs can be low while benefits are high; and so on.

The team begins the process by evaluating the first proposal according to its relative costs and financial benefits. After some discussion, a team consensus should emerge as to which of the nine cells best captures the essence of the project. In our example, the team determines that Project 1's costs are "medium," as are its financial benefits. This process is repeated with the other proposals. One by one, they are assigned to their appropriate cells in the grid.

Most proposed projects are likely to fall into the cells along the diagonal of the grid. I call the diagonal the "you get what you pay for" cells. Along the diagonal, the relative benefits of a low-cost project are low, the relative benefits of a medium-cost project are medium, and the relative benefits of a high-cost project are high. Projects assigned to these cells are analogous to projects with a benefit-cost ratio of 1.0. They neither make nor lose money. Benefits and costs basically offset each other.

The most desirable cell is found in the top left-hand corner:

Figure 8.1. Buss's Grid Approach to Project Selection.

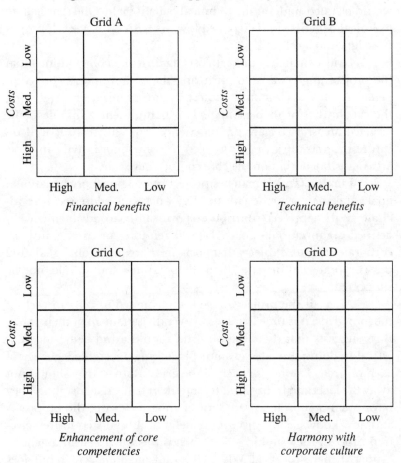

Grid A

Costs: Low, Med., High

High, Med., Low

Financial benefits

Grid B

Costs: Low, Med., High

High, Med., Low

Technical benefits

Grid C

Costs: Low, Med., High

High, Med., Low

*Enhancement of core
competencies*

Grid D

Costs: Low, Med., High

High, Med., Low

*Harmony with
corporate culture*

here projects have high benefits but low costs. The least desirable cell is the one in the bottom right-hand corner: here projects have high costs and low benefits. In general, any projects assigned to the diagonal or to the cells above the diagonal are supportable: they do not lose money. Projects assigned to cells below the diagonal are money losers.

Once all projects have been assigned to their cells in Grid A, attention turns to Grid B. Here project costs are matched against technical benefits arising from the project. A project that leads to a technical breakthrough that can lead to further technical advances would be rated high on the technical benefit scale. One that had no technical benefits would be rated low. As with Grid A, each project is assigned to a cell.

Grid C matches project costs against the contributions that the project might make to nurturing the organization's core competencies. By carrying out a project, is the organization developing the capabilities of its personnel? Is it gaining entry into desirable targeted areas? Is it gaining experience that will serve it well on future projects? If a project is seen to contribute heavily in these areas, it is rated high on the core competency scale.

Finally, Grid D matches project costs against organizational goals and the corporate culture. Key questions addressed here include: Will a project contribute significantly to advancing well-defined organizational goals? Does it reinforce or run against the corporate culture? Projects that go against organizational goals and the corporate culture are doomed to failure and should not be supported.

After all the projects have been assigned to cells in each of the four grids, it is time to make an overall assessment of their value. Buss suggests that the selection team should avoid being too analytical in doing this—for example, by taking a weighted average of each project's "score" for each of the grids. Rather, they should put away the facts and figures and trust in their collective insights. They have spent a substantial amount of time reviewing the proposals and now know each project intimately. As a final step in the selection process, they should assign each project to a cell in a generic "super" benefit-cost grid. When all is said and done, which cell does Project 1 belong in? Project 2? Project 3? And so on.

Buss's approach to rank ordering projects is appealing for at least two reasons. First, it offers a method for conducting a benefit-cost analysis that does not require the organization to develop a quantitative model that might be misspecified. Yet it still shares key features of benefit-cost ratio analysis. For example, the cell to which a project is assigned roughly corresponds to benefit-cost ratios greater than, equal to, or less than zero. In addition, the process is rigorous in that the selection team must be explicit about selection criteria.

Second, the approach depends on the informed collective judgment of the members of the selection team. Because the team members reflect a broad range of perspectives, their decisions are less likely to reflect a narrow outlook. They arrive at their conclusions after measured debate on the merits and shortcomings of different projects in respect to different criteria. Through the process of give-and-take discussion, all features of the project—drawbacks as well as strengths—will have been exposed and reviewed. Because any position can be challenged, project optimists will be forced to justify their rosy projections. The Buss approach is very much a Japanese-style management tool.

Poor Man's Hierarchy

An exciting development in management science in the 1980s was the rapid growth in the popularity of a decision-making tool called the Analytical Hierarchy Process (AHP). This technique was developed in the 1970s by Thomas Saaty. Its applications to management decision making are described in Saaty's book *Decision Making for Leaders* (1982). AHP has caught people's fancy because it generates quantitative values based on subjective judgments.

A detailed description of this technique lies outside the realm of this book, partly because the mathematics are a bit arcane (they involve the computation of such things as eigenvalues and eigenvectors). However, a pared-down treatment can be offered here. Because it is only a shadow of the full AHP, I call it the "poor man's hierarchy." I developed it as an introduction to AHP concepts for managers lacking a solid mathematical background. After teaching it to many managers and employing it on consulting assignments, I found that it is a good decision-making tool in its own right.

The central objective of the poor man's hierarchy is to enable decision makers to rank order options in a relatively painless fashion. It does this by having managers compare each of the options pairwise. The point is best illustrated by means of an example. Let's say that a small group of managers and technical staff are brought together to select a new site to establish manufacturing operations. In using the poor man's hierarchy, their first task is to identify what criteria should go into the decision-making process. They choose these criteria after give-and-take discussion. They might ultimately decide that the key selection criteria are availability of cheap labor, proximity of the site to a good highway and a major airport, proximity of the site to key suppliers, cost of land, availability of investment incentives from the local government, and tax policies in the region.

After the criteria have been selected, they are rank ordered according to priority by making pairwise comparisons between the criteria. The comparisons are made by addressing the following types of questions: Which is the more desirable criterion, availability of cheap labor or regional tax policies? Proximity to key suppliers or regional tax policies? Availability of cheap labor or proximity to key suppliers? These questions are raised for all possible pairs of questions.

The process of asking questions and tracking the answers is facilitated by the creation of a square grid, as pictured in Figure 8.2. The selection criteria are listed along the side of the grid as well as across the top. This enables the decision makers to make sure that they address all possible pairwise combinations of criteria.

Cells in the grid are filled in according to the following rule: if the criterion along the side of the grid is preferable to the criterion listed across the top, then a "1" is placed in the cell. If the criterion on top is preferable, then a "0" is placed in the cell. Note that the diagonal cells are blanked out since it does not make sense to compare a criterion to itself. Note additionally that comparisons need only be made for cells above the diagonal. Whatever value is put in a cell above the diagonal, the opposite value will be put into the corresponding cell below the diagonal. For example, the "1" appearing in the cell linking "suppliers" to "land cost" appears as a "0" in the corresponding cell linking "land cost" to "suppliers."

Consider the criterion "suppliers" in Figure 8.2. The "0" in the cell under "cheap labor" tells us that cheap labor is rated higher than access to suppliers. The "1" in the cell under "transportation" indicates that access to suppliers is deemed more important than access to good roads and an airport. Similarly, the "1" under "land cost" indicates that access to suppliers is more important than the cost of land. And so on.

By adding up the numbers across a row, we obtain a total

Figure 8.2. Illustrative Example of the Poor Man's Hierarchy.

	Cheap labor	Transportation	Suppliers	Land cost	Government incentives	Tax policies	Score
Cheap labor	***	1	1	1	1	1	5
Transportation	0	***	0	1	1	0	2
Suppliers	0	1	***	1	1	0	3
Land cost	0	0	0	***	1	0	1
Government incentives	0	0	0	0	***	0	0
Tax policies	0	1	1	1	1	***	4

score. This score signifies the number of times a criterion won in its comparisons with other criteria. The higher the score, the higher the number of wins. By implication, the higher the score, the higher the ranking of the criterion. In Figure 8.2, it is evident that the ranking of criteria is, from highest to lowest, cheap labor (5 points), tax policies (4 points), access to suppliers (3 points), access to good transportation facilities (2 points), land cost (1 point), and government investment incentives (0 points).

In making pairwise comparisons, we may produce logical inconsistencies. For example, we may say that A is preferable to B and B is preferable to C, but in comparing A and C we may say C is preferable to A—a logical inconsistency. In the poor man's hierarchy, inconsistencies will show up as tie scores. For example, "transportation," "suppliers," and "land cost" may all achieve a score of 2. (This will happen if we state that "transportation" is more important than "suppliers" and "transportation" is less important than "land cost.") As Saaty points out in his work, inconsistencies are not inherently bad. They may simply reflect the fact that our model has not taken into account all pertinent decisional dimensions.

The poor man's hierarchy is useful in many contexts. It was noted at the outset of this chapter that the essence of rational decision making is the rank ordering of options. The whole point of this technique is to assist in the rank-ordering process. It is done very simply, by comparing options two at a time. Thus this technique is a generic decision-making tool. It can be employed to rank order projects, vendors, employees, promise dates, and so on. When my daughter Katy was eight years old, she used it to select whom she would invite to her birthday party (she wanted to invite twenty friends, but there was enough room for only twelve).

I used it once in a faculty committee meeting established to identify a suitable commencement speaker. The committee members easily generated a list of about fifteen possible prospects. However, we found it impossible to achieve a consensus on how they should be rank ordered. Finally, I convinced my fellow committee members to rank order the candidates through pairwise comparisons. We had no problem at all choosing one candidate over another in a pairwise mode. The whole process took about ten minutes. At the end of that time, we had our overall rank ordering. Everyone agreed it reflected the consensus of the group. What seemed to be an impossible task when tackled as a whole was easily carried out when reduced to small, workable pieces.

The Murder Board

For project selection to be effective, no proposition should be allowed to go unchallenged. If the project champion states that her project will generate a 20 percent return on investment if supported, she should be prepared to defend that statement rigorously. If the team engineers say that a particular component in their proposed system will outperform existing components by a factor of five, they should be able to back up their projection.

A highly effective project selection methodology has arisen based on the proposition that no idea should go unchallenged. It is given the rather macabre name of *murder board*. It is a simple method, both in concept and execution.

With the murder board approach, a panel of reviewers is put together to review project proposals. The panel is made up of people from different parts of the organization. For example, one member might come from marketing, another from finance, another from engineering, and another from production. The panel is charged to scrutinize the project proposal carefully. In fact, they should tear it apart and try to show how it is not workable.

The project champion is charged to go before the panel and make the best arguments possible in support of the proposal. He should be prepared to field tough questions and to deal with a skeptical audience. Of course, to be effective he should have back-up documentation and employ it when necessary.

Effective use of a murder board allows organizations to catch problems during the talking stage, before large sums have been committed and designs have been cast in concrete. This process tempers the unchecked optimism of project champions and makes it less likely that their infectious fervor will lead the organization to support unsound ideas. For this approach to work, all parties in the process must recognize that its objective is not to punish and humiliate the project champion but rather to distinguish between solid and shaky propositions.

An example of a murder board in action has been captured in the *In Search of Excellence* video. It shows a project champion going before a high-level murder board at 3M (which includes the company's CEO) in an attempt to get the organization to support the development of optical disk production capabilities. The project champion is subjected to intense questioning and is clearly rattled. His defense is good, however, and in the end he receives support to go ahead with his project.

The murder board approach likely will be used in conjunction with other approaches. For example, the project champion may be required to develop a benefit-cost ratio to support her arguments. In the final analysis, the murder board serves the function of "reality check," an attempt to make sure that arguments in support of project ideas do not have built into them the seeds of their own destruction.

Peer Review

The dominant form of project selection in scientific areas is called *peer review*. This approach is employed to select billions of dollars of research projects each year under the auspices of government agencies such as the National Science Foundation, the National Institutes of Health, and the National Institute of Standards and Technology. In addition, it is employed to select projects in industrial labs such as Bell Labs and IBM's assorted laboratories.

With peer review, projects are evaluated by "peers," individuals who are technically competent to assess the technical merits of a proposal. Typically, three or more peers receive a copy of a proposal. They are asked to review the proposal independently. After examining it, they are asked to assess its merits according to a number of criteria. The National Science Foundation criteria, for example, ask for an assessment of such things as the project's technical merits, the competence of key players (in particular, the principal investigator), and the value of the management plan. The assessment is usually noted on a scoring sheet, where each criterion is given a score ranging from 1 (low score) to 5 (high score).

After the reviewers have all had a chance to score the proposed project, their assessments are collected and examined jointly. If all three reviewers give the project a low score, it will certainly be rejected. If it receives mixed reviews, it is not likely to be funded in this era of tight budgets. Even the enthusiastic support of all the reviewers is no guarantee of funding.

Peer review has long been criticized as a highly subjective approach that is susceptible to distortions, such as bias in favor of an old boy network. One study by Jonathan and Stephen Cole found that peer review is only marginally better than coin flipping in identifying winning projects. So why is it employed?

The answer to this question is more closely tied to the politics of science than to rational decision making. The scientific community is reluctant to be reviewed by nonscientists and to be accountable to nonscientific selection criteria. It will be interesting to see whether this outlook will be able to survive the tight budgets and societal demands for accountability that we will encounter in the upcoming decades.

General Rules for Selecting Projects

This chapter has focused on a handful of rational techniques that can be helpful for decision making. Clearly, there is more to project selection than technique. Before concluding the chapter, I would like to put these techniques into a broader decision-making context. Following are some general rules for project selection that, if followed, will lead to better choices.

Rule 1: Be Explicit About What Is Important in Choosing Projects. Project selection should occur in accordance with clearly defined selection criteria. These criteria should be written in large, boldface type. They should be taped onto the walls in the room where selection decisions are being made. They should be ritualistically recited at the outset of each selection meeting. During the selection process, people should not be distracted by the wealth of interesting possibilities that the organization *can* pursue—rather, they should focus on what the organization *needs* to pursue, as captured in the selection criteria.

Rule 2: Identify Explicit Procedures for Choosing Projects, then Stick to Them. Project selection should not occur by accident. An approach to choosing projects should be developed and rigorously adhered to. Even powerful players in the organization should be required to stick to the procedures. In this way, decisions become less arbitrary. Also, a check can be placed on those powerful players who irresponsibly push for a particular project "because it seemed like a good idea at the time."

Rule 3: Be Prepared to Rigorously Challenge All Assertions. No statement about possible benefits or costs associated with a project should be immune from challenge. Project champions tend to lose sight of possible problems. The picture they paint of project benefits is typically rosy. By the same token, project critics often picture a proposed project in the worst possible light, adducing all manner of facts to back up their position. The most effective way to temper excessive optimism or pessimism is to question the veracity of key assertions made by project champions and critics.

Rule 4: Constitute a Project Selection Team Whose Members Represent a Broad Array of Stakeholders. All projects serve multiple purposes and have multiple impacts. Clearly, the project selection team should be made up of individuals who represent a broad array of perspectives. A typical selection team for a private sector project should have members who reflect the varying perspectives of engineering, marketing, finance, and production.

Rule 5: Involve Key Project Personnel in the Selection Process. In a survey I conducted of a sizable number of project managers, I found that only 20 percent reported being involved in the selection of the projects they work on. For most project managers, the selection decision is made without their input. They are given project management responsibilities after the decision has been made. There are at least two good reasons for including key project personnel in the project selection decision. First, if these people have a role in choosing a project, they will automatically have a stake in it. They will be more energetic in pursuing project goals because they had a role in establishing them. Second, if they are part of the project selection process, they will understand the rationale for conducting a project. In this way, continuity can be maintained between the project selection and project execution phases in the project life cycle. Too often, when key personnel do not understand the original rationale of a project, they redefine this rationale to suit their outlook, and this leads to problems of continuity.

Conclusions

The selection of projects is serious business. It should not be carried out in an offhand manner. Too often, insufficient attention is given to whether a particular project idea has real merit. Thus projects may be selected to satisfy the hunches of powerful players. Or they may be selected simply to keep staff busy or to spend end-of-the-year money.

A big problem with offhand project selection is that it leads to the ineffective use of resources. Support of a project to satisfy short-term exigencies may lead to long-term fiascoes. Those making the decisions often forget that by committing resources to a poorly conceived project idea, they are tying up those resources. They have not taken into account the opportunity costs of their decision. If a truly good project prospect arises in the future, they may no longer have the resources to pursue it because their resources are tied up in marginal undertakings.

Chapter Nine

Estimating

Realistic Costs, Schedules,

and Specifications

to Ensure Project Success

I spent the late spring of 1989 in Beijing on a World Bank consultancy assignment. This was during the time of the Tiananmen Square turmoil. I worked with two groups of project managers: one in the chemical engineering industry, the other in shipbuilding. The environment in which we carried out our sessions was a bit distracting. As we talked about managing projects, we could hear the cheers and chants of student and worker demonstrators outside.

"What do you find to be the single greatest problem of project management in your jobs?" I asked my students.

They answered with amazing consistency. "If we are to get support for our projects," they said, "we must state that we can do the project for nearly nothing. Once the project is authorized, we spend all of our time scrambling for resources."

This problem is certainly not unique to China. In organization after organization, I hear the same refrain: "We are committed to doing the job with insufficient resources." Having worked with many project managers in a large number of organizations, I have

194

reached the conclusion that the great majority of projects being carried out today are underresourced by 20 to 30 percent. What is particularly bothersome about this situation is that cost and schedule overruns are hardwired into these projects. If we are committed to doing 1,000 person-hours of work with only 750 person-hours of labor, something's got to give.

The conscious "lowballing" of cost and schedule estimates is not the only source of poor estimation on projects. Consider the following list of problems. We continually underestimate technical glitches that can arise. The people doing the estimating generally are amateurs. Events arise in the environment that invalidate our informed guesses. Project champions are so blinded by the opportunities their projects present that they don't see the pitfalls. Our clients begin changing project requirements, with measurable budget and schedule impacts. And so on.

To a certain extent, every cost and schedule overrun can be traced back to a failure of estimation. Even when the root cause of an overrun is sloppy project execution, we can complain that the estimation did not take into account the likelihood of such sloppiness.

Causes of Poor Estimation

Problems in estimating costs and schedules have been with us a long, long time. No doubt Imhotep was disappointed more than once by the poor estimates his architects provided him in the building of the pyramids. When we explore the causes of bad estimation, we see why the problem is so intractable: on a typical project, there are *several* causes of difficulties, all functioning at the same time and all conspiring to prove our best guesses to be inadequate. In this section, we look at key problems.

Inexperienced Guessers

One major cause of poor estimation is that the people making the estimates don't know what they are doing. Most cost and schedule estimates are conducted in the following way: individuals with certain technical expertise and others with responsibility for carrying out tasks are asked to provide estimates of what it will take to carry out their pieces of the project. These individuals generally scratch their heads, think back to past experiences, make a few phone calls, and then come up with their estimates. Usually, there is no consistency of outlook among these individuals. The assortment of scattered predictions they make is then brought together in a haphazard way and offered as the official estimate.

The problem, then, is that most estimates are being made by amateurs. Amateur estimators typically fall into the following traps:

- They tend to be optimistic about what is needed to do the job and consequently understate potential problems.
- They tend to leave things out of their estimates. For example, in estimating the cost to install a computer system, they forget to include the cost of the cable that will link the computer to the printer (this is called the "missing components" problem).
- They follow no consistent methodology in deriving their estimates, so that it is difficult to recreate the rationale for their estimating procedures. It is likely that the estimate they make on a Monday will differ measurably from the same estimate made on a Thursday.

There are two good ways to deal with inexperienced estimators. First, they should be given training on estimating processes. This training will teach them that there is an art and science to estimating. Over the years, methodologies have emerged (for example, parametric cost estimating) that enable individuals to make quite precise time and cost estimates. There are even societies that focus on estimating procedures, such as The American Association of Cost Engineers. The students should be required to learn and employ these solid estimating methodologies.

Second, the organization should develop tight methods and procedures for cost and schedule estimates. The procedures can be form driven so that estimators need merely fill out a form to get the estimates they need. As part of this process, estimators should be supplied with checklists of items that should be included in the estimates. Explicit methods and procedures for estimating will increase the consistency of estimates in the organization and will counter the amateur's propensity to contribute to the "missing components" problem.

Lack of Continuity Between the Preaward and Postaward Phases

Organizations that employ a sales force to sell their products and services encounter a common problem: during preaward negotiations, the salespeople promise clients features and services that the project and production staff cannot provide. The explanation of their behavior is simple. In most organizations, salespeople derive a substantial portion of their incomes from commissions. The more sales they make, the greater their commissions. If they see a sales opportunity slipping, they may be tempted to cut prices excessively or to make product or service commitments that will be difficult or impossible to meet.

Once project staff take over a project in the postaward phase, they may find themselves in a no-win situation. The price of a service provided to the client may be lower than its cost to the company. Technological enhancements may be promised that lie outside of the organization's capabilities. Or commitments may be made to achieving impossible deadline dates. What project staff face here is programmed failure. This may manifest itself in outright financial losses or customer disappointment when expectations have not been met. In any event, project staff may find themselves blamed for problems they did not create.

There is no easy solution to this problem. Organizations are often reluctant to take their sales staff off commission for fear that this will dull their killer instincts. What some organizations do is put together an account team that includes sales, project, production, and maintenance people. If the salespeople begin to make unachievable commitments, the other members of the account team can rein them in.

Bad Technical Guesses

As Chapter Four on risk management makes clear, the future is always uncertain. The financial impact of this uncertainty can be devastating when it results in bad technical guesses as to what needs to be done on a project. Newspapers are full of stories about technical problems that hold up progress on projects like the B-2 bomber and the Hubble space telescope, leading to massive cost and schedule overruns.

We encounter technical glitches on most of our projects. The simple project to cut a doorway between two offices turns into a nightmare when we discover that the wall separating the offices is not sheetrock but brick. Our attempt to change the oil filter on our car becomes a four-hour ordeal when we discover that the oil filter is just centimeters out of the reach of our hand. A crucial component on our telecommunications equipment fails on Friday afternoon, right before the beginning of a three-day weekend.

Thorough planning and the employment of good quality management practices can avert many of these surprises. But others are truly bolts out of the blue that cannot be anticipated. Therefore estimators should assume the worst in making their estimates. They should establish contingency allowances to deal with the "unknown unknowns" that are bound to arise. They should be skeptical of any technical guesses that assume that everything will work fine the first time through.

Changes to the Project

Projects face constant pressure for change. This pressure arises from several sources. Some of it comes from the environment. For example, a competitor's introduction of a new product may lead to changing market conditions that the project team must adjust to. Or government's changes to environmental regulation may force the team to alter the way it does its business. Or macroeconomic fluctuations, such as a sudden surge of inflation, may invalidate key assumptions built into the cost- and schedule-estimating procedures.

Pressure for change also arises from within the organization. For example, technical glitches may require stopping the project until the problems are fixed. Or technical staff may want to redesign something in their search for perfect solutions.

Finally, clients can be a major source of change. As the deliverable becomes more concrete and clients see what they will be getting, they may not like what they see and demand alterations. Or they may be stimulated by what they see and suggest enhancements. Another common source of client-induced change derives from shifts of key personnel in the client organization. For example, the new division director may put the project on hold until he or she has a chance to review it.

The problem with change is that it typically causes some measure of cost and schedule overruns. Consequently it can lead to failures of estimation. Cost and schedule estimators must factor the effects of change into their estimates. Unfortunately, specific changes are difficult to predict. The best way to anticipate change is to carry out a risk assessment that identifies the overall stability of the project environment (see Chapter Four). If the project is dealing with untried technology, if it is being supported by a cost-reimbursable contract, or if the client organization is in turmoil, it is likely that the project will experience substantial change. In this case, estimators should build large "fudge factors" into their estimates of individual activities, thus providing for substantial contingency allowances.

Beyond this, the project organization should have strong change management procedures in place. Without change management, "scope creep" will ensue. What started out as a modest undertaking will grow into a costly behemoth. Cost and schedule overruns will occur, and the estimating process will be undermined. (More is said about change management in Chapter Three.)

Psychological Factors

As people mull over new project ideas, they often grow excited about the possibilities. The new project may offer interesting technical and marketing challenges. It may also hold the promise of increasing profitability dramatically. Soon there is a psychological commitment to carrying out this project. This can translate into a blinding optimism about the project's prospects.

The impact of unchecked optimism on cost and schedule estimating can be enormous. What is especially disturbing is that optimism can distort the estimates in subtle ways that are not easy to spot. Consider how this occurs in the following story.

The 10 Percent Optimist

Marvin and his development team are very excited about the prospects of building a new Whambangatron. They have roughly scoped out their ideas and now must present a proposal for project support before the project review board. An important component of the presentation will be the business case for the Whambangatron. Marvin must present a benefit-cost analysis describing the business consequences of carrying out the proposed project.

Unfortunately, Marvin is so enamored of the project idea that he becomes a "10 percent optimist." That is, in making his estimates he unconsciously overstates benefits by a small amount—10 percent. He also tends to underestimate costs by 10 percent. It would seem that the consequences of Marvin's modest optimism would be marginal. Actually, the consequences are dramatic.

In order to estimate benefits, Marvin predicts that total sales resulting from the Whambangatron will be $1,100,000. In reality, they will be $1,000,000. He further estimates that profits will be 11 percent of sales, resulting in profits of $121,000 (that is, 11 percent of $1,100,000). In reality they will be 10 percent, or $100,000 (that is, 10 percent of $1,000,000). After carrying out a risk analysis, he determines that the probability of success for this project is 88 percent, meaning that the expected value of profits is $106,480 (that is, 88 percent of $121,000). In reality, it is 80 percent, giving an expected value of profits of $80,000 (that is, 80 percent of $100,000).

In estimating costs, Marvin unconsciously shaves 10 percent off of true costs. He states that project costs will be $81,000, whereas in reality they will be $90,000.

In computing a benefit-cost ratio, Marvin divides his estimated benefits of $106,480 by his estimated costs of $81,000. The resulting ratio is 1.31, meaning that for every dollar invested in the project, $1.31 will be generated. In reality, the true benefit-cost ratio is $80,000 divided by $90,000, or 0.89. Because the true ratio is less than 1.00, the project is actually going to lose money.

Note that Marvin's modest 10 percent optimism has telescoped into a projection that overstates the benefit-cost ratio by 47.2%! The project review board will be making a decision on the basis of a flawed estimate, and the project, if supported, will find itself in serious trouble.

The problem here is not that Marvin made imperfect estimates. Most people would be delighted if they could predict the future with 90 percent accuracy. The problem is that his optimistic estimates were *applied consistently* for each variable that went into his benefit-cost equation. This led to a compounding of the estimation error. Imagine what his benefit-cost ratio would be if he decided to boost his estimates by another 10 percent in order to strengthen his case before the project review board!

The best way to deal with the problem of the 10 percent optimist is to place skeptics on the cost-estimating team. No individual estimate should be permitted to go unchallenged.

Lowballing

Lowballing occurs when the project organization says it will do a job for less money than it will actually cost. Obviously, if organizations spend more than they make, they will not stay in business very long. So why do they lowball?

The great hope is that the low bid will get them the job. Once they have it, then they count on making their money through change orders or follow-on business. The lowball bid is the project management equivalent of a "loss leader."

For many years, skilled contractors could play the lowball game and make money on it. This was particularly true in the government arena, where contracts would be awarded primarily on the basis of cost. Project management on these contracts concentrated chiefly on tracking change orders. Each time government wanted a change, it would be billed generously. The nickels and dimes added up, and by the end of the contract, the contractor was in a profitable situation.

The lowballing strategy has lost its appeal in recent years. In part, contractors find that as a consequence of budget shortages, government is not pressing for expensive change orders any more. So they may offer to do a job at a low cost but may not make up their losses through change orders.

The idea of bidding low in hopes of getting follow-on business has probably never been a good one. In government work, the logic of such an approach simply does not make sense because follow-on work is competed for openly, and once again, work will go to the low bidder. Even in private sector work, the lowballing strategy frequently backfires. The initial strategy is to get a foot in the door for follow-on business. Unfortunately, because the project is underfunded, it may get into trouble, leading to missed deadlines and quality problems. Given such poor performance, the client is not inclined to conduct repeat business with the project performer.

Customers increasingly realize that policies where work goes to the low bidder do not always serve their interests. At first glance, it appears that competitive bids resulting in awards to low bidders lead to cost savings and good bargains. What often happens, however, is that this process creates situations where contractors get in trouble. As a Defense Department colleague once asked me, "Would you want to leap out of an airplane wearing a parachute built by a low bidder?"

The new emphasis is on value. In the early nineties, the federal government successfully awarded a number of significant contracts based on value rather than cost. Losing low-bid contractors have protested this new policy, but it has successfully been defended by procurement authorities.

Politics

Occasionally, an organization's best cost and schedule estimates are overridden because of political concerns. Professional cost estimators spend countless hours gathering cost information and feeding it into their sophisticated cost models. After some serious number crunching, a solid cost estimate emerges. This estimate is then forwarded to upper management, who, after glancing at it briefly, cross it out and put in a value that is more acceptable politically. Patrick Tyler, in his book *Running Critical* (1986), describes how precisely this kind of scenario at General Dynamics led to one of the greatest cost overruns in history. It also resulted in the tarnishing of the careers of some prominent people, including Admiral Hyman

Rickover—father of the U.S. nuclear navy—and General Dynamics' CEO.

Political meddling in cost and schedule estimating is an everyday occurrence in some organizations. In order to get support for their projects, project staff doctor their estimates to make them more palatable to powerful players. The best antidote against such political meddling is the establishment of objective, clearly defined procedures for project selection. The procedures should be set up so that no players, no matter how powerful, can unilaterally impose their will on the selection process.

Traditional Approaches to Cost Estimating

Traditional approaches to cost estimating generally fall into one of two categories: bottom-up or top-down. The bottom-up approach is concerned with gathering vast amounts of detailed cost data on each component of the project. Once the data are gathered, they are rolled up for an overall estimate of costs for the whole project. The top-down approach, also called *parametric cost estimating*, eschews the detail and derives estimates on the basis of historical experience. It is a statistical approach.

Bottom-Up Cost Estimating

The bottom-up approach focuses on tracking all cost elements associated with a project. Total project cost is simply the sum of the costs of all the individual elements. The question is how to identify these cost elements in a systematic fashion. The most common approach to doing this is to employ a work breakdown structure (WBS) as a guide to identifying cost elements.

This means that before cost estimates can be made, a detailed WBS must be constructed. Cost data are then gathered at the bottom-most level of the WBS, which is called the *work package* level. These data are then aggregated to the next WBS level, which provides budget insights into activities reported at this level. They are further aggregated until we reach the highest level of the WBS, at which point we have an overall cost estimate for the project.

This bottom-up roll-up process is illustrated in Table 9.1.

Table 9.1. Bottom-up Cost Estimating with the WBS.

WBS #	Task	Cost
10.0.0	Project: Pour concrete foundation	*14,900*
10.1.0	Conduct survey	*1,200*
10.1.1	Measure foundation dimensions	900
10.1.2	Mark foundation dimensions	300
10.2.0	Clear debris	*1,300*
10.2.1	Remove shrubs	700
10.2.1	Remove rocks	600
10.3.0	Excavate	*4,700*
10.3.1	Obtain equipment	1,200
10.3.2	Dig hole	3,500
10.4.0	Pour foundation	*7,700*
10.4.1	Insert concrete forms	1,100
10.4.2	Pour concrete	6,000

Note: Work package data appear as normal type. Rolled-up data appear in italics.

Work package data appear as normal type. Rolled-up data appear in italics. In this example, work package data include both labor and material costs. A more refined WBS can distinguish between different costing categories.

Parametric Cost Estimating

Parametric cost estimating is also called *top-down estimating*. It focuses on formulating cost estimates by examining fundamental parametric relationships. In mathematics, *parameter* is a fancy word for what our elementary algebra teachers call *constants*. For example, in the equation of a straight line—$Y = mX + b$—m and b are parameters, whereas Y and X are variables. There is an additional hidden parameter in the straight line equation: the exponent of X is understood to be 1.0.

Parameters define the fundamental structure of the relationships of variables. For example, in the straight line formula, m represents the slope of the line (how steeply it rises) and b the point at which the line intersects the y-axis. If the parameter associated with X changes from 1.0 to 2.0, giving us $Y = mX^2 + b$, we no longer have a straight line but rather a parabola.

In everyday life, we encounter many parameters that offer us guidance on how to conduct our affairs. For example, gasoline may sell for \$1.25 per gallon. Here, the \$1.25 is a parameter. If I buy two gallons of gas, I pay \$2.50; three gallons, \$3.75; and so on. Or consider another example: the speed limit on the Interstate is 55 miles per hour. If I travel four hours, I will cover 220 miles.

Similarly, there are many parameters governing the relationship between variables in business. For example: experience tells us that a yard of concrete will cure in so many hours. The learning curve suggests that if we increase the production run of our widgets by 80 percent, their unit costs will decrease by 20 percent. In doubling the height, width, and depth of a structure, we generally increase our material requirements eightfold.

With parametric cost estimating, we identify fundamental parameters that offer us insights into the cost of our project. This is illustrated in a simple example in Table 9.2. The table shows a cost estimating approach I used for several years to price small-scale research and software projects. In conducting my project business, I often found myself in a position where I would be meeting with a client and the client would raise a point similar to what follows:

"David, since I've got you here, let me ask you something that has nothing to do with our current project. We are thinking about upgrading the management information system that tracks our inventory. . . ." The client would then proceed to describe briefly his requirements for the upgrade.

Table 9.2. Example of Parametric Cost Estimate.

Professionals (500 person-hours @ \$20/hr)	\$10,000
Technical support (4 × professional hours, that is, 2,000 hours, @ \$15/hr)	\$30,000
TOTAL DIRECT WAGES	\$40,000
Fringe benefits + overhead (determined by accountants to be 1.06 × Total Direct Wages)	\$42,400
Total Labor-Related Costs (Fringe benefits + overhead + Total Direct Wages)	\$82,400

"So, David, what would an upgrade like this cost? Roughly, of course." At this point, the client would typically give me an earnest look. "Don't worry about being precise in your estimate. We won't hold you to it." After he stated this last sentence, I perceived the client's nose to grow a little bit, like Pinocchio's.

I thus found myself in a situation where I had to respond to a client's inquiry quickly if I was going to exploit a new business opportunity. The client wanted an answer *now*. He didn't want me to tell him I'd get back with an estimate one week from now.

Generally, I was able to give an estimate that I could live with by using a simple top-down estimating procedure. Let's say that I knew from experience that the work required to do the job would occupy a professional programmer for one-fourth of a person-year. This translates into five hundred person-hours of effort (note the useful parameter: two thousand person-hours a year roughly constitutes one person-year of work). Given my initial estimate of the amount of professional work needed, everything else falls into place due to fundamental parametric relationships.

One person-hour of professional effort costs $20, so five hundred person-hours of effort cost $10,000. In my company, experience shows that for every hour of professional effort, four hours of technical support effort are consumed (a parameter), so the proposed project will require two thousand person-hours of technical effort at $15 per hour ($30,000). Thus labor costs will be an anticipated $40,000. Corporate auditors, who review the financial books carefully each year, have determined that fringe benefits and overhead can be computed by taking direct wages and multiplying them by 1.06 (a parameter). Thus the fringe benefits plus overhead related to this project will amount to $42,400. Total salary-related costs will be $82,400. Note that I had to estimate only one thing: person-hours of professional effort needed to do the job. Once that estimate was made, everything else fell into place.

In addition to the $82,400, we will want to add nonsalary costs to our estimate. Some of these nonsalary costs can be determined parametrically. For example, experience may show us that on a typical project, for each $15,000 of salary-related costs, we spend $1,000 in report reproduction and $800 in travel. Other nonsalary costs may have to be computed according to the specific context of the project. For example, we may have to rent special hardware to create a good platform to develop software that will run on the client's computer system.

The parametric cost-estimating example provided here is very simple. Highly sophisticated parametric cost-estimating models can be developed. One famous model was developed by RCA and is called PRICE. Clients can rent this model to help them perform cost estimates on highly complex projects, such as building a nuclear power plant, installing a telecommunications system, or designing a commercial aircraft. Complex parametric cost-estimating models are made up of hundreds of equations that specify parametric relationships derived from historical data. They have proven to be useful cost-estimating tools.

Bottom-Up Versus Top-Down Estimates

Which is a better procedure: bottom-up or top-down estimating? The answer, of course, depends on context. Bottom-up estimates require you to develop a detailed WBS. At the earliest stages of a project, this may not be possible since the future is still highly uncertain. It may also be difficult to do this on high-flux development projects. In these cases, estimates may have to be based on a top-down estimating procedure.

On the other hand, the building of a detailed WBS is desirable on projects that have been carried out repeatedly. In this case, ample historical data exist, providing project staff with the information they need to construct a good WBS. Large, complex projects also demand WBS-based bottom-up cost estimates. On such projects, there is too much complexity and too much at stake to leave things to chance. Building a detailed WBS on a large project is costly and time consuming, but the costs of the effort more than offset losses that would be incurred through sloppy planning.

When possible and practical, it might be a good idea to do *both* bottom-up and top-down estimating. These two approaches can serve as a check on each other. If the resulting estimates are wildly disparate, then the estimators had better review their estimates to see the sources of disparity.

Life Cycle Cost Estimating

When I was a boy, my father would occasionally astonish me with some revelation that caught my fancy. Once when we had gone to a drugstore together to purchase a package of razor blades, he took me to the display shelf for razors and showed me the price of different brands. They were all quite cheap—somewhere in the range of two dollars.

"See how cheap these are?" he asked. "The manufacturers sell their razors cheap to get you to buy their product. Where they really make money is in selling you razor blades. So you may pay two dollars to buy the razor initially, but over a year you will spend much more than that buying razor blades."

Recently, it has been noted that this same principle is being applied on a grander scale in the selling of automobiles. Automobile dealers today sell new cars close to a break-even price. Where they fatten their profit margins is in postsales servicing.

We have the same principle at play in the project management arena. Project costs are often small in comparison to postproject operations and maintenance costs. In the software industry, Barry Boehm has shown that about 70 percent of the cost spent on software systems today is directed at maintenance (Boehm, 1987).

Clearly, in pricing something—whether a razor blade or a sophisticated weapons system—cost estimators should take into account the cost over its life. What initially appears to be a low-cost project may turn out to be quite expensive when viewed from a life cycle perspective.

By creating detailed WBSs, project staff can obtain a good sense of what work needs to be done on the project. They can use this information to estimate costs through a bottom-up cost estimating procedure. Most project staff, however, are unfamiliar with what will happen to the deliverable in the postproject phase. What *are* the key cost elements of operations and maintenance?

Broadly speaking, operations and maintenance costs typically fall into the following categories.

Installation

After a deliverable is developed, it frequently must be installed on the customer's premises or some other appropriate place. For example, a newly developed software system may need to be installed on the customer's mainframe computer, or a telecommunications switching system may need to be installed in the office. Installation can be a project in its own right—it has its tasks, milestones, costs, and specifications. With highly sophisticated systems, the costs of installation can be substantial.

Training

Training costs should not be ignored. To appreciate the costs of training, consider the following example. A client of mine once gleefully recounted to me how he negotiated the price of a scheduling software package (Package A) down from $600 per package to $500 per package. The vendor for a competing package (Package B) would not come down from their $600 price, so my client decided to purchase ten units of Package A.

"I saved a thousand dollars by going with Package A," he chortled.

I smiled at this news. As I smiled, I carried out a quick mental computation of the costs of Package A versus Package B. From personal experience, I knew that it takes three days of training to get project staff proficient on Package A, whereas the training time for Package B is two days. At that time, the cost associated with three days of training was about $200 per day per student. The training cost for thirty students being trained on Package A would thus be $18,000. The comparable cost for Package B would be $12,000, a $6,000 difference. Instead of saving one thousand dollars, my client actually lost $5,000 because of the additional training costs associated with Package A. The source of his problem was that he only looked at the shelf price of the product and ignored its life cycle costs.

Repairs

The systems we develop ultimately break down. Sometimes the breakdowns occur because parts wear out. This is a characteristic of mechanical systems. Anyone who has bought or leased a photocopy machine—which has many moving parts—has become well acquainted with photocopy repair service personnel.

Occasionally, the source of breakdowns is embedded in the deliverable—for example, poor design or bug-ridden software. Software that erases a portion of memory each time the F2 key is hit will need to be rewritten.

Preventive Maintenance

When we submit our systems to routine scheduled maintenance, we are undertaking preventive maintenance. We do this, for example, when we take our car to Jiffy Lube every six thousand miles for a change of oil. The purpose of preventive maintenance is to avoid breakdowns by keeping the system functioning effectively throughout.

The impact of preventive maintenance on our life cycle cost estimates will vary dramatically according to the nature of the system we are dealing with. Mechanical systems with many moving parts have a higher need for preventive maintenance than purely electrical systems.

Back-Up Systems/Disaster and Recovery

In many aspects of our lives, we are heavily dependent upon the functioning of automated systems to serve us. When the Boeing 767 first came out, pilots quipped that they were now obsolete since the aircraft is almost fully automated. On Wall Street, trading volumes of 200 million shares per day are made possible through computerized programmed trading. Each day billions of dollars of transactions are executed between banks through electronic funds transfers. The antilock braking systems of automobiles are computer controlled.

This dependence on automation has a dark side to it. What if the computers break down, we lose electric power, or our software is flawed? Will our personal lives or the affairs of our company, community, or country go into a tailspin?

The growing dependence on automated systems has led to a growth industry called *disaster and recovery*. D&R is a risk management approach that is concerned with anticipating problems and developing strategies to cope with them. Consider, for example, a bank's concerns about its dependence on computer systems to maintain all of its financial transactions. If an earthquake, fire, flood, software error, or power surge knocks out its main computer system, can the bank continue to operate effectively? What will happen to the billions of dollars of deposits and loans whose records are maintained electronically?

The bank's range of D&R actions varies substantially. At the low-cost end (the "cool site" option), the bank can make an arrangement with other banks to use their facilities in case a disaster strikes. This requires that the bank constantly back up crucial data and store the backups in a safe place.

At the mid-cost range (the "warm site" option), the bank can establish the shell of a parallel operation at a separate site. For example, it can rent office space to use in the event of a disaster. Salvaged equipment can be moved to this site, additional equipment can be rented, and operations resumed.

At the high-cost end (the "hot site"), the bank can continually run a parallel operation at another site. This is the safest option: if disaster hits one site, little is lost since the second site continues to function normally. It is also enormously expensive.

From the perspective of life cycle cost estimating, it is apparent that one cost element that cannot be ignored is the cost of D&R. Even low-cost contingency plans will have a measurable impact on overall costs.

Salaries and Materials Associated with Running the System

Obviously, a major contributor to the life cycle cost of a system is the salaries and material costs associated with running the system. These must be included in the life cycle cost estimate. The material costs include costs of spare parts. With a high maintenance deliverable (such as a fighter aircraft), these can be considerable—greater, eventually, than the initial cost of the system.

Overhead

Overhead costs include all those nondirect costs necessary to keep an operation running, such as electricity, rent, and insurance.

Clearly, substantial overhead costs will be incurred in the postproject phase.

Strategies for Dealing with Poor Estimates

People working on projects often confront situations where they must grapple with the consequences of poor estimates. That is, they find themselves with insufficient resources to do their jobs. The only groups I have encountered that do not routinely struggle with limited resources are those dealing with research and development projects. R&D projects are sufficiently ill defined that staff can work around resource constraints.

In view of the near-inevitability of underbudgeted projects, project staff should develop strategies for dealing with them. The strategies break down into two categories: those designed to avoid bad estimates and those designed to deal with their consequences once the project is under way.

The focus of this chapter up until now has been on *avoiding* bad estimates. This can be done by professionalizing the organization's estimating procedures. For example, procedures should be established for developing WBSs and using them to conduct bottom-up estimates. Historical data should be gathered to identify parameters that can be employed in parametric cost estimates. Common estimating pitfalls, such as excessive optimism, political pressures, and poor estimating models, should be recognized and avoided.

Attention now turns to *reacting* to the consequences of poor estimates. That is: What should be done if it is determined that there are insufficient resources to carry out the job? The course of action to be taken depends upon *why* there are problems, the nature of the project team's relationship with customers, and whether the project is being executed under contract.

First, why are there problems? Is it fundamentally a question of poor execution or of unrealistic estimates at the outset? If the problems reflect poor execution—inexperienced workers, sloppy planning, poor change control—the solution must focus on tightening execution. If they reflect built-in overruns caused by bad estimates, the estimates must be revisited through rebaselining. In either case, if the project is hopelessly bogged down in a cost and schedule quagmire, serious thought must be given to *rescoping*—project management jargon for changing the plan to match reality. It may entail adding additional budget to the project or cutting back on planned tasks or both.

In trying to understand why problems exist, project staff should determine whether the problems are occurring in a politically charged environment. This is important to know. Political environments are notoriously messy. In such environments, rational solutions are less important than "politically correct" ones. For example, do we find ourselves slipping into a cost overrun situation because our boss has made unrealistic and unachievable promises to customers or upper management? If so, how do we raise the point that the underlying problems have been caused by the actions of a powerful player within our organization? How do we resolve such problems? Questions such as these must be answered in the context of the specific situation facing the project team. They are always difficult to deal with.

Second, what is the nature of the relationship of the project team to customers? Are the customers kept at arm's length or are they partners on the project? Is the relationship primarily conflictual or harmonious? Clearly, problems can be worked out best in an environment where the project team and customers pursue common goals and have a good relationship based on mutual trust and understanding. In this case, the developer and the customers will agree to adjustments of schedule, budget, and specifications in order to allow the project to succeed. If the relationship is confrontational, chances are that problems will compound problems. In the worst case, disputes end up in court.

Finally, is the project being carried out under contract? If so, is it a fixed-price or cost-reimbursable contract? With fixed-price contracts, project staff will not receive much sympathy for their problems. A major exception to this rule is when the problems are caused by customers changing project requirements. When this occurs, they should be charged for their changes and schedules should be updated to reflect the new circumstances.

The whole point of the fixed-price contract is to nail down the requirements for cost, schedule, and specifications at the outset so that they are not subject to continual adjustment. By signing the contract, both buyer and performer agree that a given deliverable will be produced for a specific price, by a specific time, according to specific requirements. With such a contract, developers assume the risk of overruns. By the same token, they can capture the benefits of any cost savings that may occur and can translate them into profits.

With a cost-reimbursable contract, project staff find themselves in a more flexible situation. In theory, increased costs in project work can be passed on to the customer. (In practice, spending limitations can be identified, but these do not carry the same weight as the built-in constraints developers feel when they are spending their own money.) There is often a lesser sense of urgency when project staff face cost and schedule problems under a cost-reimbursable contract.

Following are some specific strategies that can be pursued when a project team finds that, owing to estimation problems, it lacks sufficient resources to perform effectively.

Use Data to Illustrate the Problem of Lack of Resources

I call this the intellectual approach. Data and logic can be employed to demonstrate to the powers who control resources that there simply are not enough resources to do the job—that project staff cannot create a silk purse out of a sow's ear. If a convincing argument is made, then the resource powers may free up additional resources for the project or may agree to pare back on project requirements.

An excellent tool for illustrating resource limitations graphically is the resource-loading chart, also called the resource histogram. I once worked with a company that was misestimating budgets and schedules by factors of five. I worked with their staff to identify how people's time was committed over the next three-month period. I then plotted the data on a resource-loading chart. The results are found in Figure 9.1.

This chart clearly shows one explanation for this organization's horrendously poor time and cost estimates: their resource

Figure 9.1. Using the Resource-Loading Chart to Highlight Insufficient Resources to Do the Job.

commitments on projects far exceeded their resource capacity. In the case of the illustrated resource—a statistician—his time was being allocated to projects as if he could do the work of three people. Of course he could not. Failure was programmed into his projects.

An interesting aside in this case is that the statistician was largely to blame for the overcommitment of his time. He was unable to say no to requests from various project managers who needed his skills because he did not want to disappoint his colleagues. Of course this short-term desire to please colleagues led to long-term disenchantment with his performance when colleague after colleague found their projects stymied by bottlenecks created by the statistician.

The director of projects in this organization was astonished by the data pictured in the loading charts for all the company's resources. She used the charts in a briefing to upper management. They were equally amazed and immediately increased the budgets for project activities.

Unfortunately, in a politically charged atmosphere, the intellectual approach can fall on deaf ears. In this situation, appeals to rationality may not be effective.

Strengthen Change Management Procedures

Anyone who works in the construction industry knows that a major source of profits comes from change orders. Even fixed price contracts won through a low-bid process can be quite profitable if change orders are tracked carefully. For example, if the customer wants an electrical outlet moved eighteen inches to the left of where it appears in the engineering drawings, the contractor can make the change but will charge handsomely for it. Ultimately, the nickels and dimes add up to fat margins.

The experience of the construction industry suggests that tightened change control procedures may be a significant means to get an underresourced project on track. One problem with this approach is that it may alienate customers, who begin to see the developer as a skinflint who is intent on extracting every penny possible from them.

Prioritize Goals

Project staff members who find themselves overcommitted by 30, 60, 100 percent or more must face a cold reality: they are not going to get all their work done! In the long run, they are put in an untenable situation and something's got to give. This requires long-term solutions such as increasing staff or reducing work load. In the short run, however, project workers and their immediate managers have got to determine how to handle their efforts over the next month or two. Probably the worst thing they can do is to run helter-skelter from assignment to assignment, plugging leaks. Such an approach will assure that nothing is brought to a satisfactory conclusion.

What they should do is make some hard decisions revolving around the question: Which goals are worth achieving now and which should be abandoned, either temporarily or permanently? That is, they should establish priorities.

Chapter Eight ("Making Choices") offers a broad array of approaches to establishing priorities. The approach suggested here is quite simple: employ Pareto's eighty-twenty rule, which states that most of the problems or opportunities we face (say, 80 percent) are attributable to a small number of causes (say, 20 percent). The rule is employed frequently in quality control. Quality managers are instructed not to expend their energies trying to locate all quality problems but rather to focus their efforts on identifying the core problems that contribute to the majority of problems.

By the same token, project staff who find themselves under-resourced should direct their efforts to high-impact activities. They should systematically identify the 20 percent of actions that can contribute to 80 percent of progress on the project. Having identified them, they should work on them and momentarily cast aside low-impact actions. Obviously, what constitutes high-impact and low-impact actions must be determined in the specific context facing project staff.

Conclusions

A substantial portion of schedule slippages and cost overruns are rooted in poor estimates of what it will take to do a job. Some of these bad estimates are a result of ineptitude in estimating budgets and schedules. The people making the estimates don't know what they are doing. Others are a consequence of project players—particularly upper management and sales staff—making promises that are unrealistic. Still others are the results of conscious attempts to lowball: offer to do a job for less than cost in order to get the business.

Bad estimates ultimately create problems for the organization. Consistently bad estimates can even lead to bankruptcy as the organization struggles with a string of damaging cost overruns. One unfair consequence of poor estimation is that as project teams incur schedule slippages and cost overruns, the problems are attributed to poor execution, and team members are blamed for their incompetence, when in fact these problems are a product of poor estimation.

For organizations to carry out projects effectively, they must estimate as accurately as possible what it takes to get the job done. Through careful estimation, they will spot projects that are likely to be profitable as well as those that will lead to trouble.

Chapter Ten

Outsourcing

to Control Costs,
Focus on Core Work,
and Expand Resources

An important trend in recent times has been the growing use of outsiders to carry out an organization's business. This employment of outsiders is called *outsourcing*. Consider the following evidence of the growing impact of outsourcing on business affairs: in 1990, General Electric employed half the work force it did in 1980, yet it was generating twice the business volume! Some of this is attributable to productivity growth. But a large share is attributable to an increased dependence on outsiders to carry out GE's work.

The underlying rationale for outsourcing is clearly economic. Companies have determined that they can do business more cheaply by working with outsiders than by relying on their internal work force. This happens in various ways.

With offshore production, companies take advantage of the low cost of overseas labor. For example, in Asia or Mexico they can find workers whose wages are a small fraction of what American workers demand (in the mid 1990s, American wages were eight times greater than Mexican wages). Initially, in the 1960s and 1970s, the job shift to offshore producers occurred in low-skills areas, such as assembling. Increasingly, as the education level of the populations in poor and middle-income countries has increased—and as the education level of Americans has declined—work is shifting to higher–value-added areas, including engineering and software development.

Outsourcing also occurs domestically. In the United States, domestic outsourcing is a response to cost-cutting pressures facing American companies. By cutting back on employment and shifting the work to contractors, American companies experience enormous savings because they do not pay for such worker benefits as insurance and pension plans. Furthermore, in some environments, such as manufacturing, outsourcing shifts the burden of maintaining inventory and storage onto suppliers, thereby incurring substantial cost savings for the outsourcer.

An interesting phenomenon that is a spin-off of present-day outsourcing is that frequently the people doing the work on the outside are former employees of the outsourcing company. During a downsizing exercise, they may have been released from the company, only to be rehired later as contractors. Not everyone is unhappy with this arrangement. The outsourcing company saves large sums by not paying fringe benefits to the employees, and the employees have a greater degree of independence than they did while working for the company. The price of this independence is, of course, lessened security.

Outsourcing is driven by more than the desire to economize. It is also a tacit recognition that the old adage of "big is better" no longer holds true for a whole range of activities. The "big is better" philosophy emerged from more than a century of industrial experience. In traditional manufacturing, large-size efforts lead to economies of scale. The low-cost producer is the one who can produce large runs of widgets. In its extreme form, the drive to become large led companies to attempt to control the whole production process in order to achieve total self-sufficiency. A car company might get into the iron and coal business in order to obtain the steel needed to make cars. It might own rubber plantations in South Asia and tire-making plants. Of course, it would also develop capabilities in forging, machine tooling, metal cutting, and assembling. To sell cars, it would need advertising, distribution, and servicing capabilities. The achievement of total self-sufficiency is called *vertical integration.*

Today, the "big is better" outlook is on the wane in most areas. For one thing, the financial and intellectual capital necessary to run a vertically integrated enterprise in today's complex and competitive environment is daunting. It is hard enough for a company to excel in its core business; to be a first-rate performer across a range of business borders on the impossible. Second, there is a feeling that the advantages of economies of scale may be offset by the cumbersomeness of running something so big and complex. Experience shows that large organizations are inordinately bureaucratic and incapable of responding quickly to market challenges. Third, when a company commits itself to operating self-sufficiently on a large scale, it is increasing business risk. It invests capital and time to achieve a particular solution. If that solution fails in the marketplace, the company is a big-time loser because it has placed all its eggs in one basket.

The "big is better" outlook has been replaced by a "lean and mean" perspective. Large companies are consciously shrinking the size of their operations. In doing so they are increasing their profitability. They focus on maintaining a core of activities and depend on outside sources to provide them with the auxiliary goods and services needed to carry out their business. In doing so, they are also shifting business risk to the outsiders. If an outsider's particular solution does not work, outsourcers need only turn to other solutions offered by other outsiders.

In this chapter, we examine different forms of outsourcing, explore its implications for project management, and investigate the principal mechanism for effecting it: the contract.

Forms of Outsourcing

Outsourcing can take different forms. At one end of the spectrum, it may involve nothing more than hiring someone temporarily to execute a task. At the other, it may entail having outside contractors carry out the lion's share of the company's work. Some of the more common outsourcing arrangements include the following.

Consultants

Perhaps the simplest form of outsourcing is employment of a consultant to undertake needed work. This is done frequently in the broad areas of accounting, training, design, and software development, as well as in specialized technical and business areas.

Operating with consultants offers the outsourcing company a great deal of flexibility. In most areas of work, there is a fairly clearly defined market of consultants, so the company can pick and choose among a broad array of candidates. If this month we need an expert trainer conversant with the Oracle data base language, we can hire one for a week of work. If next month we need training on project-scheduling software, we can hire someone else. Because of the ready availability of these capabilities on the outside, there is no need to develop them in-house.

Another advantage of hiring consultants is that they do not add to the burden of fringe benefit costs. The company's commitment to them is limited to paying their wages. When they have done their job, the company's commitment ends.

Yet another advantage of consultants is that if the company is unhappy with their performance, it simply ceases to employ them—no hassles with unions and labor sensitivities here.

The chief difficulties with consultants are problems that are common to all forms of outsourcing. For example, how well do the outsiders know the business? If it is important that they know the business well, a large fraction of the consultants' time may be dedicated to learning the business. Not only is the company paying them to educate them (thereby increasing their value in consulting with others), but it may find that the education effort disrupts ongoing activities as the consultants consume the valuable time of core personnel in their attempts to get up to speed.

A second problem focuses on the issue of commitment. Are the consultants fully committed to achieving the company's most deeply held goals? In fact, do they even know what these goals are? Since consultants are often paid on a time-reimbursable basis, there is always the danger that their greatest commitment is to racking up the number of hours they put into the project. The more time they spend on the project, the more they get paid.

Finally, there is a problem of access to company secrets. Most companies have a range of secrets that they do not want to fall into the hands of their competitors. Common examples of these include information on production costs, technical processes, market targets, operating procedures, technical data, growth strategies, and sources of internal problems. For outsiders to do their jobs effectively, they may need access to these secrets. Is the company really willing to provide them with such access? Generally, the secrecy issue is handled by having consultants sign nondisclosure agreements, but will they really abide by them? How will the company know if they do not?

Personal Services Contracts

Recently I spent a week on site at a facility of a Fortune 50 company. Because I had been working steadily with this group, they issued me a contractor's badge, complete with unflattering photo. As I walked through the corridors of this facility, ate lunch in the cafeteria, and visited clients in their offices, I became powerfully aware that about 20 percent of the people I encountered were—like me—wearing contractor badges. I asked my hosts who these people were. I was told that they represented a cross section of activities being conducted at the facility: some were secretaries, others were facilities maintenance personnel, still others were systems developers, and so on.

Contract labor is a growing phenomenon in organizations. It is no longer uncommon to see a contracted secretary sitting at a desk adjacent to one occupied by a full-time corporate secretary. The motivations for hiring contract labor are the same as for other forms of outsourcing: to save money and maintain flexibility. In addition, I have encountered cases where professionals are hired initially as contract workers in order to test them out. If they are perceived to provide value to the organization, they may ultimately be offered a full-time job, complete with all the benefits. If not, they continue to work as contract workers or are released.

Two obvious problems stand out here. First, there is confusion as to where the contract workers fit into the existing organization. Are they second-class citizens? How seriously do full-time employees take them? Will full-time employees see them as a long-term threat to their jobs?

Second, individuals working on personal services contracts do not have much security. They often do not know whether they will still be employed by the company two or three months from now. They may have to cover the costs of essential services—such as insurance and retirement—out of their own pockets. (If their incomes are inadequate, they may decide that they cannot afford such services.) From society's point of view, a big question is: Are we willing to accept that an increasingly large portion of our fellow citizens are living lives of desperate uncertainty? From the company's point of view, there is a question of how effective workers can be when they feel insecure.

Organized Suppliers of Specialized Services

Contract labor does not require that the contracted work force be bereft of any benefits. We see this in companies that have been set up to provide specialized services to other companies. A common example of this is security services: most businesses hire specialized companies to provide them with security services, including security guards, electronic monitoring capabilities, and alarm systems. Other examples include food service, printing services, and maintenance service. In recent times, higher–value-added services are emerging as well. Included here are training, design, marketing, and data processing services. The employees of these specialized companies may be fully employed by them (although not always—consider the Kelly Services model) and may thereby be beneficiaries of a full range of fringe benefits.

Suppliers of Parts and Materials

Some of the most dramatic outsourcing that is occurring involves having outsiders supply a company with the parts and materials it needs to produce its goods and services. Even previous champions of self-sufficiency, such as IBM, are increasingly turning to outsiders in this area.

Because it is vital that the parts and materials provided be of the highest quality, outsourcing arrangements are handled very carefully. In some cases, they are carried out through the formation of strategic alliances. For example, a large producer of computers may establish a joint venture with a chip manufacturer to supply the computer maker with needed semiconductor chips. Through the joint venture, the computer maker can exercise some measure of control over its supplier.

When dealing with an arm's-length supplier, producer and supplier must establish close relations to minimize misunderstandings and to build a joint commitment toward a successful venture. The producer must be assured of open and reliable access to quality parts and materials. The supplier must be confident that its customer is dependable in both the short and long run. Today we call this kind of arrangement *partnering*.

Outsourcing in Project Management

Outsourcing is not new to project management. In two lines of business, in fact, it has been the basic way project work has been carried out for decades. In construction, projects are often run by a general contractor, whose job is to select and manage a battery of contractors and subcontractors. To a large extent, the essence of the general contractor's job is simply contracting per se. This is the way large and small buildings, airports, dams, and other civil engineering products have been constructed for decades.

The second line of business that depends heavily on outsourcing is government business. The great share of government work is conducted through contracts. Government seldom builds weapons systems, highways, or computer systems by using its own employees. The work is typically done by private, outside contractors. Government has been conducting its business this way for centuries.

What is new is that outsourcing is now being promoted in nontraditional areas. It is not unusual these days to have software developed by outsiders; training conducted by contractors; reports edited, printed, and distributed by a modern, computer-based print shop; designs developed by outside engineering companies; and so forth.

Actually, most project personnel do not feel particularly awkward with this situation since it is a natural extension of the matrix. In a classic matrix organization, data processing, training, printing, and design resided in functional departments within the organization. The acquisition of needed resources entailed a form of internal contracting whereby the number of resources to be committed, their charges, and their time of commitment would be specified. What has happened in the era of outsourcing is that the internal contracting inherent in matrix organizations has been replaced by external contracting with outside performers. However, for the outsourcing approach to work, project staff must develop contracting skills. A violation of the terms and conditions of an internal contract may result in a slap of the hand; such a violation on an external contract could possibly lead to a lawsuit.

Contracting

The principal mechanism for outsourcing is the contract. Simply put, a contract is an agreement between buyer and seller stipulating the rights and responsibilities of each in respect to a specific transaction. The transaction may be something as simple as procuring ten thousand pencils. Here the contract document may be less than a page long. It may be highly sophisticated, involving the construction of a space vehicle to be used on a mission to Mars. In this case, the contract document may be the size of a telephone book for a large city.

The contract process is broken into two phases: preaward and postaward. In the preaward phase, the buyer sets out to identify prospective sellers. Once a likely candidate has been found (perhaps through a competitive bidding process), the detailed terms and conditions of the contract are negotiated. Finally, the contract is signed and an award is issued.

The postaward phase focuses on oversight of contract performance. The key question here is: Is the contractor performing its duties on time, within budget, and according to specifications? Close monitoring of the contract is particularly important for buyers on *cost-plus* (also called *cost-reimbursable*) contracts.

This last point highlights an important consideration in

contracting: How has the contract been structured? There are many ways to structure contracts. We will focus on the two broad forms most commonly employed in project management here: fixed-price contracts and cost-plus contracts. The differences in these approaches is of more than academic interest to project managers. The type of contract employed has a major bearing on the management challenges they face.

Fixed-Price Contracts

With a fixed-price contract, both buyer and seller agree that the project deliverables will be produced for an agreed-upon price. For example, a contractor may be contracted to write a seventy-five-page user's guide that will describe how to utilize a new management information system. The contract stipulates that the contractor will be paid $10,000 for the document upon delivery on or before March 15. If the contractor's expenses are $6,000, she can experience a profit of $4,000 on the project. On the other hand, if her expenses mount to $11,000, she experiences a $1,000 loss. The key point here is that it makes no difference what the contractor's expenses are: the price of the product is "fixed" at $10,000.

The management implications of this form of contract are strong. The burden of project risk lies on the performer. The great risk is that expenses will outstrip the contract price. In such a situation, the contractor will experience a loss. In theory, the buyer does not need to oversee the execution of the project with care. Given the fixed-price nature of the project, the issue of overruns is irrelevant to the buyer.

It should be noted that performers face good opportunities for gain with this type of contract. If they operate efficiently and realize cost savings, they can broaden their profit margins dramatically. Every dollar saved translates to a dollar increase in profit.

Fixed-price contracts are most appropriate for routine implementation projects (for example, building the thirtieth house in a subdivision, installing telephone switching equipment in an office, conducting a credit check on a loan applicant). If a particular project has been carried out many times before, cost estimators have a good sense of what project costs will be, so they can estimate these costs with a high degree of precision. These cost estimates provide important insights into how to price the project. When bidders place their bids, they can be reasonably confident that their costs will be lower than the bid price, thus assuring them a profit on the project.

Fixed-price contracts are generally not appropriate for high-risk development projects (for example, conducting research, designing new software, building a space station). With such projects, estimates of project costs are very speculative, owing to the unique nature of the work being carried out. If actual costs are much higher than the cost estimators anticipated, these costs may exceed the project price, putting contractors into a situation where they lose money. If the losses are great enough, the contractor may go bankrupt. Not surprisingly, competent contractors are reluctant to bid on high-risk projects if they are funded through a fixed-price contract.

It was implied earlier that with fixed-price contracts, buyers typically need not monitor the project effort closely since the risk of overruns lies with the contractor. There are occasions, however, when close scrutiny of the project effort is appropriate. In particular, if contractors begin having problems on their projects, their difficulties may translate into difficulties for the buyer. In extreme cases, cost overruns may force contractors to close down operations. Now buyers find that they have nothing to show for the money they have spent. A close monitoring of the project effort can give buyers advance warning of impending problems and allow them to prepare for unfortunate contingencies.

Cost-Plus Contracts

The dominant contract form employed on development projects is the cost-plus contract (also called a cost-reimbursable contract). With this type of contract, contractors are reimbursed for their expenses. They are also awarded a profit above and beyond their expenses.

Obviously, the risk of cost overrun with this type of contract rests squarely on the buyer. If contractors' costs are covered, then they have no worries about losing money. Without such worries, cost discipline may grow lax.

This high level of risk for buyers requires them to establish administrative mechanisms to monitor project progress closely. As a consequence, the administrative costs of the project are driven up because contractors now must spend a sizable portion of their time reporting on their progress.

Why do buyers award cost-plus contracts when these contracts pose such a great risk of cost overruns to them? The answer is simple: high-quality contractors will not bid on risky development projects that might drive them into bankruptcy. The only way to get them to bid on such projects is to underwrite the risk by covering project costs.

Cost-plus contracts can be structured in different ways to reduce incentives for contractors to engage in excessive spending. Three dominant types of cost-plus contracts have emerged: cost-plus-fixed-fee (CPFF), cost-plus-incentive-fee (CPIF), and cost-plus-award-fee (CPAF). Each of these will be discussed in turn.

Cost-Plus-Fixed-Fee (CPFF) Contracts. The CPFF contract removes incentives for excessive spending by limiting the contractor's profits to a fixed amount, regardless of project costs. The CPFF approach can be best understood through a simple numerical example.

Contractor A wins a contract award of $1,000,000 to design a new product. During the contract negotiation process, the buyer agrees to pay Contractor A a 10 percent fee of $100,000 for the work performed. Thus the contract price is $1,100,000. Because the fee is fixed at $100,000, Contractor A will be paid that amount if it does the work for $900,000. Similarly, it will receive $100,000 even if project costs go beyond the $1,000,000 target. The point is, there is no incentive here for the contractor to overspend.

The CPFF contract is very attractive to contractors engaged in high-risk development work. With this form of contract, the buyer effectively becomes a risk capitalist, underwriting the risks associated with a new, speculative venture. Developers undertake work that would otherwise be too risky to engage in. Through this process they acquire new skills that help them grow.

To a large extent, California's Silicon Valley and Route 128 outside Boston were built with Defense Department CPFF contracts. Consider how this worked: after World War II, many scien-

tists and engineers involved in the war effort returned to their jobs
in academia. Having worked with the military for a number of
years, they were now wise to the ways of defense procurement. Back
home many of them set up small independent business operations
in order to continue their relationships with the military.

Let's say one particular group of engineers invests $5,000 to
establish a storefront operation on Route 128 (prices were low in
1947). Then they discuss an idea for a new radar component with
their former colleagues in the army. They submit a proposal for a
$1,000,000 CPFF contract to support them in their development
work. During the negotiation phase it is agreed that they will be
paid a fixed fee of $50,000.

Consider what the contracting engineers have gained here.
They have received what amounts to $1,000,000 in risk-free capital
to develop new capabilities. Later, they can use these new capabilities to increase their business opportunities. Furthermore, they
have a locked-in profit of $50,000. They will receive this profit even
if the product does not pan out. In view of the fact that their initial
investment was $5,000, this translates into a 1,000 percent rate of
return on their investment!

Cost-Plus-Incentive-Fee (CPIF) Contracts. Although the CPFF does
nothing to encourage cost overruns, neither does it actively attempt
to save money. The CPIF contract, in contrast, provides carrots and
sticks to encourage cost-effective project performance. It has rewards
built into it for saving money, and punishments for profligacy.

Here is how the CPIF contract works: before the contract is
issued, buyer and contractor negotiate target cost, target price, and
target profit for the project. If contractors do the work for less than
the target cost, they will share the cost savings with the buyer. Thus
the actual price of the contract decreases—saving the buyer money—
while the contractors' profit increases.

If the contractors exceed target costs, this decreases profits.
For the contractors, this is less risky than the situation they face
with a fixed-price contract since project costs will be covered by the
buyer. However, like the fixed-price contract, poor performance is
punished—in this case, profit margins are reduced.

Cost-Plus-Award-Fee (CPAF) Contracts. An increasingly popular form of contracting among buyers is the CPAF contract. It offers them more flexibility in dealing with contractors than a CPIF contract. Under the CPIF contract, rewards and punishments are effectively determined by formulas. With CPAF contracts, subjective judgments can be included in determining rewards.

At the outset of a CPAF contract, an award pool is created. The funds that are set aside can be used to reward contractors for good performance. The level of award is determined by an award committee, which reviews contractor performance. Awards are not made only according to objective criteria (as they are with CPIF contracts); they can also take into account subjective factors (such as the attitude of the contractor).

Contracting: Preaward

As the name implies, the preaward phase is concerned with events leading up to the issuance of a contract award. Two key issues must be resolved here: one is source selection and the other contract negotiation. Each of these issues will be discussed in turn.

Source Selection

The principal objective of source selection is to identify who will carry out the contracted work. Obviously, many factors must be taken into consideration before this issue can be resolved. The size of the project, the complexity of the work to be done, risk, and procurement rules help determine what sources we select. For example, on most government projects the rules require that contractors be selected through a competitive bid process. However, in special cases competitive bid procedures can be waived. An example of this is the sole source contract, which is issued to a contractor who has unique capabilities in conducting the needed work.

In general, with small, simple efforts, informal source selection procedures are followed. A list of possible performers can be quickly generated through some exploratory phone calls to people who know the business. Typically, when the list contains from three to five prospects, the search procedure ends. One by one, the prospects may be contacted to find out what they charge and whether they would be interested in doing the work. Follow-up discussions may occur to define the buyer's requirements more carefully and to identify what the potential contractors propose to do. Finally, the prospects are asked to submit short proposals that outline their work plans, describe their capabilities, and provide cost and schedule estimates. The final selection decision is made by reviewing the proposals. In addition, impressions of the competency of the bidders gained through discussions with them may play an important role in the final decision.

Requests for Proposals (RFPs)

With large awards and complex work efforts, highly formal source selection procedures are carried out. Too much is at stake to depend on an informal approach. The process may begin with the buyer developing and issuing a *request for proposal* (RFP). The RFP provides bidders with the guidelines they need to prepare a proposal. Some of these are procedural, describing the format the bidders' proposals should take (for example, how many pages long it should be or how it should be structured), identifying points of contact in the buyer's organization, and describing the buyer's policies regarding such things as equal employment opportunity.

Others are substantive. A work statement is provided, telling bidders what the nature of the proposed work is. The bidders are expected to build the substance of their proposals around this work statement. In addition, guidelines are offered regarding the amount of work the project should entail (for example, "It is anticipated that the project will consume 22 person-years of effort"). Bidders scrutinize this section carefully since it gives them insights into how much the buyer is willing to spend on the project (for example, "A person-year of effort typically costs $120,000, so the labor costs associated with a 22 person-year project lies in the neighborhood of $2.64 million"). Finally, a deadline date for proposal submissions is given, and criteria for evaluating the proposals are provided (for example, "In evaluating bids, cost will be given a weight of 50 percent, personnel qualifications a weight of 20 percent, technical solution a weight of 15 percent, management plan a weight of 10 percent, and facilities a weight of 5 percent").

A well-formulated RFP is a vital first step in managing a successful contracted project. Its work statement provides bidders with the cues necessary for them to put together detailed proposals. A poorly fashioned work statement will lead bidders astray and will result in unsatisfactory solutions to the buyer's problems. Later on, in the event of contract disputes, the contractor may point to the original poorly formulated work statement as a leading cause of project problems.

If the proposed effort is truly large and complex, development of the RFP may become a major undertaking in its own right. It may, in fact, become a stand-alone project. Consider how much precise and detailed information must be contained in an RFP associated with a project to build the next generation fighter aircraft or a nuclear power plant. Development of such an RFP can take years to carry out.

Advertising the Tender

It is generally in the buyer's best interest to have as many qualified bidders as possible become aware of the proposed project. Generally, the more bidders the better. (This is not always true: if too many responses are received, who will have the time to evaluate all of them?)

For potential bidders to become aware of the proposed project, the project must be advertised as a tender. The specific mechanism for doing this depends on the particular circumstances of the project. All openly bid U.S. government contracts, for example, must be advertised in a document called *Commerce Business Daily*. Typically, the advertisement describes the proposed contract in a few sentences and then gives possible bidders a phone number or postal address that they can employ to get more detailed information. Municipalities often advertise their upcoming contracts in a special section of the local newspaper. Data processing contracts to be issued by companies might be advertised in data processing trade journals. Small Third World countries often advertise capital construction projects in the international magazine called *The Econ-*

omist. Basically, buyers advertise where they think they will get results.

Evaluating the Bids

Once the bids have been submitted, they are opened and reviewed. On large, complex projects, this process can be time consuming because there is so much material to look over. Evaluations of proposals proceed according to evaluation criteria that have been established. For each bid, the qualifications of the proposer's personnel must be assessed and noted. Similarly, evaluations must be made of work plans, management capabilities, proposed solutions, proposed costs, and so on.

Through the evaluation effort, a winnowing process takes place. Some bids may be completely off target from a cost point of view and can be rejected out of hand. Others may display marginal capabilities and receive a low score. Still others may be viewed as competent and fairly priced and may be put on a "short list" of possible candidates.

At this point, when several possible contenders have been identified, the buyer may contact each contender to clarify various points. Some preoffer negotiation may occur here. Occasionally, the buyer may have the short-listed bidders submit a *best and final offer* (BAFO); this allows bidders to make a final pitch to sell their projects.

Ultimately, of course, a decision is made to accept the offer made by one bidder. When this has been done, the process is still not complete. At this point, a detailed contract, based on the offer contained in the proposal, must be negotiated and signed.

Contract Negotiations

Note the iterative nature of the process described so far: first, buyers specify their needs for goods and services in an RFP. The substance of the need is described in the work statement. Then bidders react to the RFP by creating proposals, which they submit to the buyers for review. During the review process, the buyers have an opportunity to adjust the bidders' approaches through discussions and requests for clarification. Finally, a decision is made to accept one bidder's proposal, and this serves as the basis of a contract.

The process does not stop here, however. Many important details must be worked out and included in the contract. Common items for negotiation include:

- *Data rights.* In the information age, information is often an organization's most valuable asset. Who has rights to the data generated through the project, the buyer or the contractor?
- *Penalties.* The contract will surely have clauses that cover actions to be taken in the event that things do not go according to plan. These are usually described as penalties. For example, what penalties will contractors pay if they do not deliver their products on time? What penalties will be instituted if they walk away from the contract? How much extra will buyers be charged if they make late payments?
- *Payment schedules.* The contract needs to specify how payments will be made. Common approaches include progress payments, made in conjunction with the achievement of prespecified milestones; monthly cost reimbursement for time expended on the project and materials purchased; pro rata payments issued evenly over the life of the project (for example, four payments of $25,000 every two months on an eight-month, $100,000 project); start-up payments; closeout payments.
- *Fee structure.* On cost-plus contracts, as discussed earlier, buyer and performer negotiate the details of fee structure. *Fee* refers to the profit that is built into the project. On cost-plus-fixed-fee contracts, the negotiations focus on a specific fee amount that will be paid, regardless of the cost of actually executing the project. On cost-plus-incentive-fee contracts, a fee schedule is laid out, showing how the fee will increase if the performer does a better job than planned and how it will decrease if they begin slipping schedules and overrunning budgets.
- *Schedule of deliveries.* Buyers invariably are impatient to receive the goods and services covered in the project as soon as possible. During contract negotiations, they may press to accelerate the proposed schedule of deliverables offered by the performer. Performers often resist this pressure out of fear that they will be

committing themselves to unachievable targets. Ultimately, a compromise is reached and hard-nosed delivery dates are included in the contract.

When the negotiations end, both parties sign the contract. It now becomes the basis of most project activities.

Proposal Development Teams

Bidders must organize themselves to respond to RFPs. First, they must review the RFP to see whether it is worth bidding on. If the proposed work lies outside their domain, if they sense that the contract is "wired" to a predetermined contractor, or if they believe that many companies will submit a bid, they may decide not to write a proposal.

If they choose to bid on the RFP, then they must organize a proposal writing team. In many companies, the proposal development effort is guided by people from the marketing/sales department. They create a team that can work together to write a responsive proposal. Typically, key team members are technical people who can provide credible technical insights into how the proposed project might be carried out. In addition, pricing specialists may work on the team in order to price the effort. Functional experts from areas such as manufacturing, quality assurance, and data processing are consulted when needed. Physical production of the proposal is put into the hands of professional editors, who may also write large segments of it.

A major problem in writing proposals is the tendency of the proposal writing team to stray from a focused view of what will satisfy the customer. In their brainstorming sessions, they may grow excited about exercising new capabilities and "pushing the envelope." Gradually, what they propose to do may no longer have a bearing on what the customer needs and wants.

In order to keep the proposal properly focused, many companies subject the evolving document to "sanity checks." For example, at the time that a tight outline of the proposal is first created, it may be required to pass through a *pink team* review. The pink team is a group of people outside the proposal team who are asked to review the proposal outline from the perspective of the buyer. They identify flaws in the presentation in the early stages of the proposal development. Hopefully, their comments will keep the proposal on track. Their suggestions can be adopted at a time when it is still easy to make adjustments to the presentation.

Later on, after a draft of a fully developed proposal has been created, the document might be subjected to a *red team* review. Like pink team members, red team members view the proposal from the perspective of the buyer. Their function is to see whether the proposal is still responsive to customer needs and wants. If it has weaknesses, they suggest changes that can be made to it before it is finally issued.

Contracting: Postaward

Once a contract has been issued, energy is concentrated on executing the project. The big question now is: Is the work being carried out on time, within budget, and according to specifications? Postaward contract management efforts are primarily directed at addressing this question. They do this through contract monitoring.

There are two principal components to the monitoring effort. One entails regular reviews of progress—say, monthly reviews of status reports. On cost-plus contracts, these monthly reports enable buyers to track cost and schedule performance in detail. It is important that they do this since they are paying for the work directly. In the reviews, attention focuses on examining cost and schedule variances, where *variance* is defined as planned performance minus actual performance. It is important to examine cost and schedule variances concurrently. By itself, a cost underrun for a given month may be interpreted to represent cost savings. However, when viewed in conjunction with schedule data, it may become evident that costs were underrun because work was not being done and that the project is in fact behind schedule.

A second component of the monitoring effort entails looking at whether the contractor is achieving predetermined milestones effectively. Over the years, various standard checkpoints have emerged over the project life cycle. For example, on development projects, preliminary design reviews (PDRs) and critical design reviews (CDRs) are often built into the monitoring process. However, most of the milestones to be reviewed are project-specific. Was Phase I completed on June 4, as planned? Was a particular component tested by August 10, as planned? Has the first draft of user documentation been edited by March 31, as planned?

As the project is carried out, there is a high probability that there will be pressure to change the project's original scope. Perhaps an unanticipated technical glitch requires a different approach to solving problems. Perhaps a new player decides to change the specifications in order to satisfy his or her whims. Perhaps delays demand that more people be put on the project to get it back on track.

The problem with change is that it typically leads to cost overruns. Obviously, when additional work is being done, costs will rise. But even when there is not additional work, change can have negative cost consequences—there is often a cost associated with abandoning old commitments and making new plans.

In order to deal with change, change control procedures must be implemented during the postaward phase. These procedures have important contractual implications. With well-established procedures, distinctions can be made between authorized and unauthorized changes. Clearly, customers do not want to pay for unauthorized changes made by contractors. By the same token, contractors do not want to implement unauthorized changes for which they will not be paid. A common dispute on contracts revolves around whether specific changes were authorized and who pays for them. Change control is discussed in more detail in Chapter Three.

Customer Acceptance and the Handover

If one point of the typical contract can be called "the moment of truth," it would be customer acceptance. *Customer acceptance* is a term employed in project management to indicate that point in the life cycle when the customer determines whether the deliverable meets the terms and conditions of the contract. This determination frequently occurs in conjunction with tests of the deliverable (for example, a first article test) to see whether it meets specifications, as well as a customer walk-through in which the contractor reviews different features of the deliverable with the customer, step by step. If the customer accepts the deliverable, it is determined that the contractor's obligations have been met. The project is over and the contractor can move on to other fertile fields.

Problems often arise at the customer acceptance stage. Disputes typically stem from different interpretations of the contract's terms and conditions. Customers may complain that the deliverable does not satisfy all their needs and wants, as captured in the statement of work. Contractors may counter this argument by showing test results that prove that the work statement has been satisfied. When the situation is viewed objectively, it frequently becomes apparent that both parties are correct—the differences in opinion are rooted in interpretation, not in willful misconduct on the part of one or the other player.

The consequences of a dispute at this point can be dramatic for both buyers and contractors. Buyers do not get the deliverable they need. As the dispute lingers on, the lack of the deliverable may have adverse effects upon their operations. Contractors do not receive final payments for their work. Furthermore, as long as the contract is still on the books, they must expend energy and resources to deal with it. If a final contract sign-off is delayed indefinitely, this can become costly and tiresome.

There are a number of common causes of problems at the customer acceptance phase. Some of them are tied to the fact that earlier in the project, buyers and contractors did not come to grips with their different perspectives. For example, as the deliverable becomes more tangible, it may be clear to buyers that what is emerging is not what they reckoned on. However, both parties want to avoid conflict, so they put off making hard decisions, hoping that somehow the problems will take care of themselves. Of course, they seldom do. It is generally a good idea to deal with problems early on when they are small and can be handled with relatively low-cost solutions.

Other problems are rooted in the dynamic nature of projects. Throughout their lives, they may be subjected to a barrage of change: players, budgets, technology, and the environment are in constant flux. A technical requirement written into the work statement at the outset of the project may take on a different meaning six months later owing to a change of context. This type of situation is typical of all but the shortest and most trivial projects. Both buyers and contractors must recognize this fact and prepare to deal with it. They should build in periodic reviews of project requirements to make certain that perspectives on them do not begin to diverge. They also should implement tight change management procedures to avoid "scope creep."

Still other problems arise because of mismanagement on the part of contractors. For example, in order to get an award, they may "lowball" their bids (that is, submit a bid whose price is unrealistically low). As the money runs out and it becomes clear that there are not enough funds to finish the project, they may grow churlish and cut corners. Another example: because of poor management, project documentation may be treated as an afterthought. As the project approaches its end, it is difficult to bring things together coherently, owing to a lack of good documentation. Chaos ensues. The customer loses confidence in the contractor and questions the quality of the deliverable.

Conclusions

Outsourcing has grown into a dominant business practice. Today we find many companies trying to cut back on their operations even as they attempt to grow their businesses. They do this by farming out large portions of their operations to outsiders. A key slogan of the opening years of the twenty-first century is that companies are destined to be "lean and mean." This stands in marked contrast to the traditional view of "big is better."

Outsourcing has a long tradition in project management, particularly in the construction industry and on government contracts, where it has been the principal mode of operation for decades. But even in project management, the degree of outsourcing has hit new highs as more activities are being outsourced across a broader range of organizations. It has reached the point where outsourcing should reside in the toolboxes of all effective project managers. In particular, contracting skills have become a sine qua non of project management.

The focus on outsourcing leads to an interesting management dilemma. How do you motivate people when they do not work directly for you? Management practitioners and theorists have long recognized that organizational success is closely tied to motivation. Among the best known management theories are those dealing with the motivation of employees, including Maslow's hierarchy of needs, McGregor's Theory X and Theory Y, and Herzberg's hygiene factors versus motivators.

Interest in motivation theory is based on the following proposition: a properly motivated employee will move mountains to get the job done. Business history is replete with stories of companies that made it to the top because their work forces were populated with workers who had a passion to be the best. A recent example of this is the spectacular success of Walmart.

The gist of most motivation theories is that the strongest motivator is opportunity for self-growth. (The preferred term among many management theorists is *self-actualization*.) But the presumption is that workers operate in a stable environment. Maslow (1954) stipulated this when he stated that a set of key needs—physiological, safety, group belonging, self-respect—must be satisfied before self-actualization can take place. Similarly, Herzberg (1959) suggested that an environment of stability and consistency (his hygiene factors) must exist before self-actualization can be realized.

The outsourcing environment is not particularly conducive to stability and loyalty. Outsourcing is driven primarily by unvarnished financial concerns. In the 1980s and 1990s, we have seen massive layoffs of blue-collar and white-collar workers alike in the name of downsizing. The traditional moral contract between large corporations and their employees appears to have been broken. A key management challenge in the future will be to determine how to spur people to move mountains in this environment.

Chapter Eleven

Integrating Cost and Schedule Control

to Measure

Work Performance

A well-known joke in project management circles states that the last 10 percent of a project typically takes 50 percent of the effort. We often encounter projects that are stuck at the 90 percent mark for months. It happens so frequently that I have given it a special name: the 90 percent hang-up. The problem is not that project staff are suddenly encountering insurmountable obstacles; rather, it is that the reporting on the amount of work achieved has been incorrect. On most projects, staff do not know how to measure work performance effectively.

Perhaps the most important control information project managers have is data on the amount of work that has been done. If they do not know how much work they have accomplished, they cannot really know whether they are overspending or underspending, or whether they are near to meeting their schedule objectives. Effective project control requires that project organizations generate accurate measures of work performance.

Traditionally, work performance data are collected by having project staff report on "percent of task complete" month by month. Staff are usually left to interpret what this means on their own. Most report percent complete based on gut feeling. I call this the "dartboard school" of work performance measurement since one has the sense that the data are chosen by throwing darts at a board. Their reliability is low. It is likely that five people reporting on percent of work complete will offer five different assessments.

Occasionally, staff may review their budget expenditures and report the percent of budget spent as their estimate of work complete. Unfortunately, in the real world of project management, the correlation between money spent and work done is weak, so this is not a good measure. Furthermore, with this approach project staff are not providing new insights to the organization since the accounting department already knows how much of the budget has been spent.

So how does one measure work performance? This question is the key concern of this chapter. As we shall see, the answer centers on the concepts of earned value and integrated cost/schedule control.

A Graphical Approach to Integrated
Cost/Schedule Control

The interpretation of cost and schedule variance data must be undertaken cautiously. If the project accounts show that we have a positive cost variance of 10 percent in March, we should not jump to the conclusion that we have saved money. Perhaps the positive variance reflects the fact that we have not done much work. If we have not done the job, it may be that we have not spent our money. Similarly, a negative variance of 10 percent does not necessarily mean that we have overspent. It may reflect the fact that we did more work than planned in March.

Common sense suggests that to have an accurate perception of project status, we should look at cost and schedule variances concurrently. A 10 percent positive cost variance actually reflects a true savings if we are on or ahead of schedule. A negative 10 percent cost variance indicates overspending if we are slipping our schedule, or even if we are on schedule.

An effective way to examine cost and schedule variance is to use cumulative cost curves (also called S-curves) and Gantt charts. Employment of these control tools allows staff and managers to assess overall project status at a glance. This is seen in Figure 11.1, which employs Gantt charts and cumulative cost curves to illustrate three different scenarios. The Gantt chart in Figure 11.1a shows that the project is fundamentally on schedule, and the cumulative cost curve shows that money is being spent in conformance with the budget. This reflects a situation where progress appears to be going according to the plan.

Figure 11.1b shows that tasks are being accomplished earlier than planned. At the same time, more money is being spent than budgeted in the time period under review. This reflects a situation of "crashing," in which extra resources are thrown into a project to either maintain or accelerate schedule.

Figure 11.1c shows the worst possible situation. The project is experiencing both schedule slippage and a cost overrun.

The beauty of the simultaneous use of Gantt charts and cumulative cost curves is that managers can determine at a glance what their project status is. Furthermore, integrated cost/schedule control portrayed through graphical means is an effective communication tool. As such, it can be employed to report project status both to upper management and project staff in a way that is easy to understand. Another advantage of the graphical approach is that today's project scheduling packages typically generate good-looking cost and schedule charts so that producing the graphics is no problem.

The principal deficiency of the graphical approach is that it is cumbersome from an analytical perspective. The graphs provide a visual impression of project status. By themselves, they do not offer other important information, such as the rate at which the budget is being spent vis-a-vis the amount of work being accomplished, the contribution of individual tasks to budget and schedule performance, or the percent of the work that has been carried out. In addition, on projects of moderate or substantial size, the number of Gantt and cost curves that must be generated can be overwhelming.

Figure 11.1. Integrated Cost/Schedule Reporting.

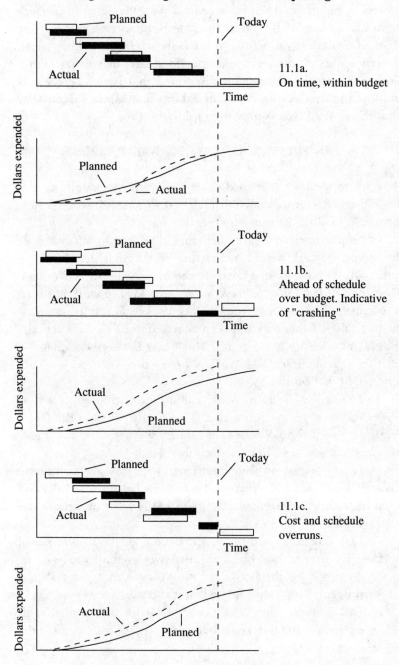

11.1a.
On time, within budget

11.1b.
Ahead of schedule
over budget. Indicative
of "crashing"

11.1c.
Cost and schedule
overruns.

In the next section, we examine an analytical approach to reviewing budget and schedule status called the *earned-value approach*. It is one of the more clever techniques developed in the arena of management. Although it has its origins in the late 1960s, its early use lay exclusively in the domain of large defense programs. Today, project managers have discovered that it can be usefully employed in small projects as well as large ones, and its popularity on projects of all sizes is growing rapidly.

The Fifty-Fifty Rule for Measuring Work Performance

Here we introduce the earned-value approach by examining one method cost accountants have developed to measure work performance. It is called the *fifty-fifty rule*.

Employment of the fifty-fifty rule is quite straightforward. At the moment a task begins, we assume we have achieved half its value, where value is measured by the budgeted cost of the task. Thus for a $1,000 budgeted task, we assume $500 in work has been accomplished the moment the task begins. We do not assume that the full value of the work has been achieved until the task actually ends. Thus once our hypothetical $1,000 task has been completed—whether it is completed early, late, or on time—we say we have achieved $1,000 worth of work.

The utility of the fifty-fifty rule in measuring work performance can be seen in Figure 11.2. This figure portrays the Gantt chart for a very simple, four-task project. To keep the arithmetic simple, each task has a budgeted value of $100.

Task 1 begins on time, and when it begins, we assume we have accomplished $50 in work. Task 1 finishes on schedule, and upon its completion we note that the full $100 value of the task has been achieved.

Task 2 begins on time, so we assume we have done $50 of work. At the time of its scheduled finish, work remains to be done, so we do not close the books on it. We note that the task has achieved its full $100 value only when it is complete.

Task 3 begins late. We do not indicate the accomplishment of any work until the task actually begins. At that time we note the

Figure 11.2. The Fifty-Fifty Rule.

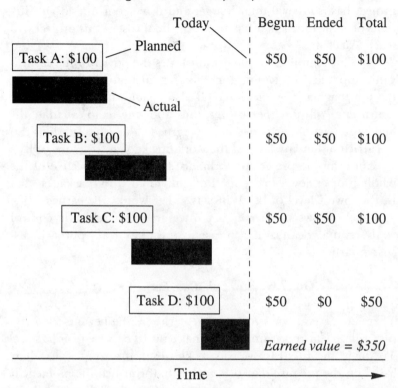

	Begun	Ended	Total
Task A: $100	$50	$50	$100
Task B: $100	$50	$50	$100
Task C: $100	$50	$50	$100
Task D: $100	$50	$0	$50

Earned value = $350

Time ⟶

achievement of $50 in work. The task slips its deadline. Not until it actually finishes do we state that it has achieved its full $100 value.

Finally, we see that Task 4 begins late and that as of today it is still incomplete. Consequently, we report that it has only achieved half its value, that is, $50.

In making a status report, we compute that as of today we have achieved $350 worth of work out of a planned $400 of effort. The measure of the $350 of work performed is called *earned value*. The fact that $350 of work out of a planned $400 of work has been achieved suggests that we have reached 87.5 percent of our target.

Notice that we have said nothing about how much it cost us to accomplish our work. Let's assume that a tally of time sheets and invoices tells us that we spent $700 to achieve $350 of work. Thus for each dollar actually spent, we attained fifty cents of value. If this project has a $10,000 total budget and if we continue to get fifty cents of value for each dollar spent, the final cost of this project will reach $20,000!

This simple example demonstrates the power of the earned-value approach. It gives us a method for calculating the percent of the job that has been achieved. It also enables us to measure the "burn rate" of our expenditures, thus allowing us to calculate the budget impact of our performance. Earned value computations can be carried out at any level of the work breakdown structure (WBS): we can examine project performance from the perspective of the whole project down to the level of individual work packages (that is, the lowest level of the WBS). In other words, the earned-value approach allows us to conduct integrated cost/schedule control analyses analytically, in contrast to the graphical approach discussed earlier.

Other Ways to Calculate Earned Value

There are several ways to calculate earned value beyond the fifty-fifty rule. Data processing personnel tend to be very conservative. To them, the fifty-fifty rule is recklessly optimistic because it is based on the premise that the work is half-finished the moment it is begun. Anyone who has written software code realizes that half-finished software has no value. Consequently, they employ the zero-one hundred rule in calculating earned value. That is, when a task begins, it is not assumed that anything has been accomplished. Only when the task is complete is it given its full value. In the example provided in Figure 11.2, the total earned value as of today is $300 with the zero-one hundred rule. This means that the project has achieved only 75 percent of its target.

The favored way to calculate earned value is to make computations based on historical experience. I will illustrate this with a simplified example of a company that assembles computers. The assembly process involves five steps. First, auxiliary memory chips are installed on the motherboard. Experience suggests that when this step is complete, the assembly process has achieved the 25 percent mark. Then the motherboard is installed in the chassis (the 30 percent mark). After this, a hard drive is installed in the hard drive slot (the 70 percent mark). All cables are linked to their appropriate connectors (the 85 percent mark), and then the chassis is slipped into the computer housing (the 100 percent mark).

To calculate earned value status each month, a tabulation is made of the number of computers found at each stage of the assembly process, and a weighted average is computed estimating the total value of work achieved during the month. For example, suppose the work value of a complete assembly operation is $100. If during the review of work in progress it is found that five computers have had auxiliary memory installed, then the value of work achieved for these computers is $100 × 5 × 0.25 = $125.

Calculating earned value based on "gut feeling" is permitted but is the least preferred approach. In this case, a task leader might guess that she has achieved 85 percent of her $1,000 assigned effort, indicating that she has accomplished an earned value of $850 worth of work.

A New Look at Cost and Schedule Variance

The traditional approach to measuring cost variance has been to subtract actual costs from planned costs. A negative variance suggests that more has been spent than planned; a positive variance indicates that less has been spent than planned. For example, suppose that for the month of March we planned to spend $1,000 but actually spent $900. This would yield a positive cost variance of $100. As we saw earlier, this cost variance cannot be interpreted meaningfully by itself. It must be examined in conjunction with information on schedule status.

With the earned value approach, we take a different tack to calculating cost variance. It is computed by subtracting actual costs from earned value. Staying with the example offered in the paragraph above, if earned value is computed to be $850, then cost variance will be $850 – $900 = –$50. This means that we paid $900 to do $850 in work. For the work we have done, we have overspent by $50. *Note that cost variance here is being assessed against the value of the work that has been performed.* In this case, it is not necessary to look at the Gantt chart to determine that we have overspent our money. By itself, the cost variance data indicate that we have spent too much. Any negative cost variance figure suggests overspending, and positive cost variance indicates cost saving.

Schedule variance is defined as earned value minus planned cost. In our example, this is $850 - $1,000 = -$150. In words, this says that although we were supposed to have achieved $1,000 in work, we only accomplished $850, giving us a work shortfall valued at $150.

Note that schedule variance is being measured in monetary units, not time units. At first this appears peculiar because people normally think of schedules in the context of time. However, the logic of the approach takes on meaning when we realize that *earned value measures work performance*, and that when less work is performed than planned, schedule slippages ensue.

The viability of earned value in measuring schedule variance is seen clearly when earned value schedule variance is mapped to the Gantt chart. This is illustrated in Figures 11.3a, 11.3b, and 11.3c.

The Gantt chart in Figure 11.3a shows a two-task project that is experiencing schedule slippage. The first task (valued at $700) is complete, but the second task (valued at $300) is only half complete. Although the planned amount of effort to be accomplished is $1,000, earned value is only $850. Schedule slippage is thus $850 - $1,000 = -$150. In general, a negative schedule variance figure indicates schedule slippage and reflects a Gantt chart that shows such slippage, whether the Gantt chart has two tasks, twenty tasks, or two hundred tasks!

Figure 11.3b shows a project on which the planned work has been achieved. As of today, $1,000 in work was supposed to have been accomplished, and $1,000 in work has actually been finished. Schedule variance is $1,000 - $1,000 = 0. In general, a zero variance indicates that the planned effort has been accomplished.

Figure 11.3c shows a project on which work has been accelerated so that more work has been accomplished as of today than originally planned. The first task (valued at $700) is finished early, so work on the second task begins. This second task (valued at $300) is also finished early, so work on the third task (valued at $200) begins early. As of today, $1,000 of work was supposed to have been accomplished, whereas $1,200 has actually been achieved. Schedule

Figure 11.3. Earned Value: Examining Schedule Variance.

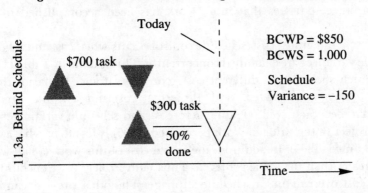

11.3a. Behind Schedule

Today

$700 task

$300 task

50% done

Time

BCWP = $850
BCWS = 1,000

Schedule
Variance = –150

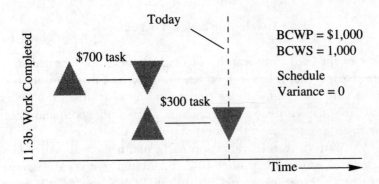

11.3b. Work Completed

Today

$700 task

$300 task

Time

BCWP = $1,000
BCWS = 1,000

Schedule
Variance = 0

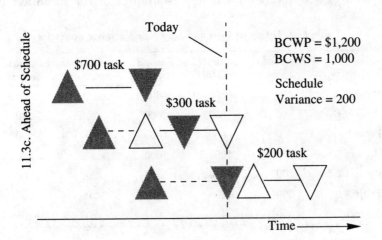

11.3c. Ahead of Schedule

Today

$700 task

$300 task

$200 task

Time

BCWP = $1,200
BCWS = 1,000

Schedule
Variance = 200

variance is $1,200 - $1,000 = $200. In general, a positive schedule variance indicates that more work has been accomplished than planned.

Integrated cost/schedule control occurs when cost and schedule variances are examined concurrently. This is done in Table 11.1, which shows seven different cost/schedule variance scenarios that might be encountered. With Project A, cost and schedule targets have been achieved, yielding zero cost and schedule variances. In Project B, the value of work performed ($600) is less than what was planned ($800). In addition, the actual cost of this work ($800) was greater than the value achieved. Thus with Project B we encounter a cost overrun and a schedule slippage. The other projects can be examined in like fashion.

Developing a New Vocabulary

One of the confusing features of the fully developed earned-value approach is that it has its own terminology, and this does not conform with the commonsense understanding of words. I find when teaching the earned-value approach that students spend more energy trying to master the vocabulary than the concepts.

With the earned-value approach, planned cost is called *budgeted cost of work scheduled* (BCWS). Actual cost is called *actual cost of work performed* (ACWP). Both BCWS and ACWP correspond exactly to traditional understandings of the meanings of

Table 11.1. Different Cost and Schedule Variance Scenarios.

	Planned cost	Actual costs	Earned value	Cost variance	Schedule variance
Project A	800	800	800	0	0
Project B	800	800	600	-200	-200
Project C	800	600	1000	200	200
Project D	800	1000	1000	0	200
Project E	800	600	800	200	0
Project F	800	1200	1000	-200	200
Project G	800	400	600	200	-200

planned and actual cost respectively. Earned value itself is called *budgeted cost of work performed* (BCWP).

With this new vocabulary, we define schedule variance as:

$$SV = BCWP - BCWS$$

We define cost variance as:

$$CV = BCWP - ACWP$$

The percent of a job achieved is computed as:

$$\% \text{ Complete} = 100 \times BCWP/BCWS$$

The "burn rate" at which we are spending money—it can also be interpreted as an efficiency rate—is called the *cost performance index* (CPI) and is computed as:

$$CPI = BCWP/ACWP$$

The estimate of final project cost is called *estimate at complete* (EAC) and is computed as:

$$EAC = BAC/CPI$$

where BAC stands for *budgeted at completion,* which is the total budgeted value of the project. EAC allows us to forecast final project costs on the basis of the efficiency with which work performance is achieved for each dollar actually spent. If a project is budgeted to cost $500,000 (that is, BAC = $500,000) and eighty cents of work is being generated for each dollar spent (that is, CPI = 0.8), the final estimated cost of the project will be $500,000/0.8 or $625,000 (that is, EAC = $625,000).

Case Study: The Bora Bora Officers Club

The power of the earned-value approach as an analytical tool is best seen through an example. The example employed here is a project to build the hypothetical Bora Bora Officers Club. Data on progress to date are provided in Table 11.2. The bottom line of this table shows that as of today, three phases of the construction project should have been completed, for a budgeted cost of $96,300 (BCWS). As of today, $87,100 has actually been spent (ACWP). The value of the work achieved is only $78,650 (BCWP). The data on schedule and cost variance tell us that this project is behind schedule and over cost. Schedule variance (BCWP - BCWS) is -$17,650 and cost variance (BCWP - ACWP) is -$8,450. The project has achieved 81.7 percent of the planned effort (78,650/96,300). The burn rate (cost performance index) for the expenditure of funds is .903 (78,650/ 87,100)—that is, for every dollar spent, the project is achieving ninety cents of value. Given this burn rate, the final project cost (that is, estimate at completion) of this $115,000 budgeted project could be $127,353 (115,000/0.903).

The analysis of the bottom line gives us a good sense of progress on this project. The verdict is that it is not doing very well. It has a substantial schedule variance, and its final cost will be greater than what has been budgeted.

A strength of the earned value approach is that we are not restricted to an aggregate overview of the project. Budget and schedule analysis can occur at any level of the work breakdown structure. To see this, consider the data on Phase I of the Bora Bora Officers' Club project. The schedule variances of zero for individual tasks shows that work on this phase is complete. At the end of the work, a small cost overrun of -$500 exists.

The Phase II data suggest some problems. Three tasks have negative schedule variances (finish roof, install plumbing, and attach siding), indicating that more work must be done before the phase is complete. The overall cost overrun for the phase is -$7,175. The lion's share of the cost overrun is tied to problems in framing the house (a -$6,000 overrun).

Phase III is in even greater trouble. Schedule variance data reveal that a whopping $16,075 of work remains undone. Although the cost variance appears small (-$775), the project is so far behind schedule that it is likely that it will incur substantial cost overruns before it is completed.

Table 11.2. Subcontractor Report on Progress-to-Date. Project: Bora Bora Officers Club.

	Planned costs	Actual costs	Estimated percent complete	BCWP	Schedule variance	Cost variance
PHASE I						
Clear 1/4th acre site	1,500	1,500	100	1,500	0	0
Excavate site	2,500	2,600	100	2,500	0	(100)
Pour concrete foundation	3,500	3,600	100	3,500	0	(100)
Emplace basic plumbing	1,000	1,200	100	1,000	0	(200)
Erect cinderblock foundation	2,500	2,500	100	2,500	0	0
Waterproof foundation	800	900	100	800	0	(100)
Total, Phase I	11,800	12,300		11,800	0	(500)
PHASE II						
Frame house	35,000	41,000	100	35,000	0	(6,000)
Finish roof	6,500	7,300	95	6,175	(325)	(1,125)
Insulate house	3,500	3,200	100	3,500	0	300
Install electrical wiring	3,000	3,000	100	3,000	0	0
Install plumbing	3,500	3,100	90	3,150	(350)	50
Attach siding	4,500	4,000	80	3,600	(900)	(400)
Total, Phase II	56,000	61,600		54,425	(1,575)	(7,175)
PHASE III						
Put up dry wall	12,000	6,000	50	6,000	(6,000)	0
Finish floor	6,000	5,200	80	4,800	(1,200)	(400)
Finish interior woodwork	6,500	2,000	25	1,625	(4,875)	(375)
Paint interior	3,00	0	0	0	(3,000)	0
Paint exterior	1,000	0	0	0	(1,000)	0
Total, Phase III	28,500	13,200		12,425	(16,075)	(775)
Total Project To Date	96,300	87,100		78,650	(17,650)	(8,450)
Total budget (BAC): $115,000.						

Note: All tasks listed were to have been completed by the time of this report.

Collecting Data

On very large, complex projects, data collection on work performed can become quite complicated. The way companies handle data collection is by assigning cost account managers (CAMs) the responsibility for gathering data. On large projects, an individual CAM may have responsibility for millions of dollars of effort.

The principal data CAMs focus on are figures that will enable them to estimate the amount of work performed (that is, earned value). They do this by walking around the organization asking task leaders how much of their work they have achieved. The CAMs know what the milestones are, so their inquiries focus largely on the achievement of planned milestones.

CAMs also have responsibility to take the raw data and fashion them into earned value reports. They are the first line of defense in identifying deficiencies in meeting the plan. Each month they highlight these deficiencies, alerting management to their existence.

On smaller projects, it is not cost effective to hire CAMs to track data. Work performance can be tracked a number of ways without incurring major administrative costs. By employing something like the fifty-fifty rule or the zero–one hundred rule, all that needs to be tracked is: Has a task begun? Has it ended? The clever use of milestones can also facilitate measurement of work performance (for example, "We have achieved twenty out of thirty milestones, where each milestone represents one hundred person-hours of work. Thus we have achieved two-thirds of our target"). As a last resort, work performance can be measured by guesswork (for example, "Experience tells me we have done about 85 percent of our planned effort").

Trend Analysis with the Earned-Value Approach

Earned-value analysis can be employed to determine general trends in work performance. This is illustrated in Figure 11.5, which shows trends in actual costs (ACWP), earned value (BCWP), and planned costs (BCWS). If everything is going exactly according to plan, the lines reflecting these three measures should be pictured as a single line. Deviations of the ACWP line from the earned value line indicate cost variance. Deviations of the BCWS line from the earned value line indicate schedule variance.

Figure 11.4 shows that in the early months of this project, there are abundant cost and schedule variances. Both ACWP and BCWS are substantially larger than BCWP, indicating negative variances. However, as time goes on, the size of these variances shrinks, and by Month 8 the variances have virtually disappeared, indicating that the project is under control.

Use of a chart such as this can offer managers a high-level view of project status at a glance. If the chart indicates that the project is generally faring well, there is no need to burden managers with detailed tables of numerical data. If the chart indicates problems, this might suggest a review of more detailed data.

Figure 11.4. Earned-Value Analysis over Time.

When Is the Earned-Value Approach Appropriate?

The earned-value approach was originally devised to provide government contractors and government program managers with guidance on how to track progress on large complex projects (see the historical note offered in the appendix to this chapter). Because the fully developed earned-value system is governed by detailed instructions that create a substantial administrative burden, the assumption has been that this approach is only appropriate on projects in the range of $100,000,000 or larger. Using it on smaller projects would be like trying to kill a mosquito with a shotgun.

The Bora Bora Officers Club case demonstrates that—stripped of unnecessary administrative requirements—the earned-value approach can give project managers valuable insights into project progress even on small projects. If a project has information on planned costs and if actual cost data are being reported accurately and promptly, the earned-value approach can be employed usefully. It offers a numerical substitute for the use of Gantt charts and cumulative cost curves. Although these graphic tools serve the purpose of communicating project progress visually, the earned-value approach is far more powerful analytically.

With well-maintained data, an earned-value system can measure precisely work performed, the proportion of our effort we have achieved, and the "burn rate" for the expenditures of project funds. It can even offer rough forecasting capabilities through the computation of the EAC. Note that these analyses can be carried out at any level of the WBS.

Use of the earned-value approach has two key limitations. One is the availability of accurate and timely cost data. Unfortunately, the majority of the organizations with which I work have not established systems to collect such data. I suspect that these organizations represent not the exception but the rule. It is difficult to fathom how an organization expects to manage its projects effectively without such data.

A second limitation is educational. For the earned value approach to work properly, everyone in the organization who touches the project management function should have an understanding of its mechanics. For example, they should be able to read and understand an earned value–based status report. "Everyone" includes upper management. If they do not study this approach and learn how it can yield improved insights into project performance, then much of its impact is lost.

A Historical Note

The earned-value approach was developed in the United States in the 1960s to help manage very large defense projects. Most of the effort in its development was driven by the U.S. Air Force. During the heyday of defense contracting in the 1950s and 1960s, it became apparent to the Defense Department that as projects get larger and more complex, it grows increasingly difficult to track what is happening on them. This problem is compounded by the fact that these large projects are being carried out in multiple contractor organizations, each of which employs its own peculiar planning and control system.

By the early 1960s, it was obvious that the Defense Department was no longer able to track adequately the efforts of its contractors. It decided that contractors on large, complex projects should be required to report their project efforts in a consistent fashion. It worked to develop rules for reporting project progress and in 1967 issued DODI, 7000.2, known also as the *Cost/Schedule Control System Criteria* (C/SCSC). In 1991, DODI 7000.2 was superseded by DODI 5000.2, which is virtually identical to DODI 7000.2. DODI 5000.2 tends to be a bit dry and abstract, so in order to put more meat on the bones, the Defense Department produced a document called the *Joint Implementation Guide,* which offers detailed and reasonably practical instructions on how to satisfy C/SCS requirements.

Today, DODI 5000.2 and the *Joint Implementation Guide* continue to offer the key guidance on how to report progress on large, complex projects. They focus on developing consistency and a tight management discipline in five areas:

- *Organization.* Instructions are provided on the development of work breakdown structures and organizational breakdown structures.

- *Planning.* Key planning requirements are highlighted—for example, the establishment of performance baselines.
- *Accounting.* Requirements are specified for the collection and maintenance of cost accounting data.
- *Analysis.* Guidance is offered on use of earned-value techniques for reporting budget variances, schedule variance, and EAC.
- *Reporting.* Instructions are given on reporting project status through cost performance reports (CPRs), which are required on very large projects, or cost/schedule status reports (C/SSRs), which are less burdensome to generate than CPRs and are required on smaller projects.

Because of the big-project focus of DODI 5000.2, coupled with its arcane nature, organizations outside of the defense community were unaware of its potential use to them on nondefense projects. This situation began to change in the late 1980s. As the Bora Bora Officer's Club example demonstrates, the earned-value approach can be used effectively on small projects when bureaucratic requirements—such as those found in DODI 5000.2—are stripped away. Non–U.S. project organizations have been studying DODI 5000.2 and the *Joint Implementation Guide* carefully in order to garner insights to help them manage their large, complex projects more effectively. One of the most savvy managers I know in the use of DODI 5000.2 is a Japanese fellow working on large construction projects in Japan.

Conclusions

There cannot be much accountability on projects if no one is sure how much work has been done. If project staff's rigor in reporting progress is restricted to "I think we're basically on target," they are not likely to know they are in trouble until it is too late.

This chapter argues that special effort must be made to measure work performance. Knowing how much work has been done is certainly one of the most important pieces of information a project manager can have. The good news is that well-tested methods exist for measuring work performed. These methods focus on what is called *integrated cost/schedule control.* They can entail something as simple as generating and comparing Gantt charts and cumulative cost curves. Or they may involve following the detailed instructions of Department of Defense Instruction (DODI) 5000.2 in order to track the world's largest, most complex projects. In any case, measuring work performed is vital if project staff desire to spot problems when they are little and can be fixed with few resources. The alternative is to be ignorant of problems until they are large and damaging.

Chapter Twelve

Evaluating Projects

to Maintain Goals,

Strengthen Accountability,

and Achieve Objectives

Good management requires accountability. Accountability means that people are answerable for their decisions and actions. To the extent that accountability is diffuse, we can expect to find things falling through the cracks, inadequate levels of follow-through, and finger-pointing when things go wrong.

The issue of accountability is particularly acute in project management for at least two reasons. First, projects are typically carried out with borrowed resources whose loyalties lie with their functional areas. Computer programmers are loyal to the data processing department, engineers to the engineering department, designers to the design shop, and so on. These resources drift in and out of projects on an as-needed basis. They do their jobs, then they are gone. Their functional bosses typically have little or no idea of what they do when they are farmed out to projects. Their project managers, who have little direct control over them, usually lack the technical knowledge to assess their efforts. In a sense, these borrowed resources are accountable to no one.

Second, as projects are carried out over their life cycles, the players continually change, and continuity in outlook is often lost. Requirements tend to drift according to the interpretation of the latest project players. Decisions are made whose rationale is almost immediately lost when a new set of players come on board. In the end, no one is quite sure who authorized or built what. No one is answerable for either good or bad decisions and actions.

This chapter explores one way to strengthen accountability in project organizations. Accountability can be bolstered by implementing fair, systematic, and rigorous evaluation procedures. With effective evaluation, people will find it difficult to sweep problems under the rug or to shrug off important decisions. They are answerable for their decisions and actions.

The value of evaluation extends beyond its contribution to accountability. Through evaluation, we are able to measure our progress according to some preestablished criteria. It should be recalled that evaluation is an integral part of management by objectives: first we establish objectives that we wish to achieve, then we periodically undertake evaluations to see whether they have been achieved in the prescribed fashion.

If evaluation is carried out regularly, we can identify problems when they are still small. We can act upon them immediately, before they become big problems. It is well known that it is much cheaper to fix a problem in the design phase than in the prototype phase, and that it is cheaper to fix it in the prototype phase than in the production phase. Evaluation provides us with a mechanism to fix problems relatively cheaply.

Unfortunately, a major constraint to effective evaluations is that they can be scary. They entail scrutiny of performance. Sometimes the scrutiny involves a detailed inspection of how things are going. Furthermore, a key goal of this scrutiny is to uncover problems. Even the friendliest evaluations can be painful when they unearth difficulties in planning, design, or execution. Nobody enjoys being inspected for flaws. Sadly, many evaluations are not friendly.

Early in my career, I spent six years as a professional evaluator. I became familiar with various methodologies, conducted numerous evaluations, read evaluation journals, wrote articles on

evaluation techniques, and attended symposia with other evaluators. Through this in-depth exposure to evaluation activities, I
became convinced that the key to success has little to do with the
specific techniques employed. Rather, successful evaluation hinges
on creating a nonthreatening environment so that people are willing—perhaps even eager—to share with others the details of some
of the problems they are encountering in their work. Consequently,
this chapter is more concerned with understanding the nature and
purposes of evaluation than with detailing evaluative techniques.

What Is Evaluation?

Evaluation involves periodic stock taking. With evaluation, we step
back and ask whether we are achieving a set of criteria we have
established. They may be schedule, budget, technical, or some other
kind of criteria. Evaluation is thus a mechanism to build follow-
through into project management. It is not enough simply to establish targets: staff must conduct tests to see whether the targets are
indeed being met.

Evaluations are ubiquitous. They are being carried out all
around us, although we may not recognize them to be evaluations
per se. To illustrate this point, I have had students in my management seminars list some of the activities they experience in their
organizations that could be construed to be evaluations. These lists
can grow to be quite long. Following is a scaled-down version that
highlights the most common kinds of evaluations my students have
experienced.

Bid/No-Bid Evaluation

For projects undertaken in a contractual environment, companies
cannot spend precious resources bidding on every contract opportunity they encounter. They must husband their resources and bid
only on those projects that are winnable and promise outstanding
rewards. Bid/no-bid decisions can be made after studying a number
of factors associated with a particular project. For example, if technical criteria are important, key questions to be addressed might be:

Will this project strengthen our technical capabilities? Will it enable us to use existing capabilities in the best way?

Business Case Evaluation

A significant portion of making bid/no-bid decisions may depend upon the business case that can be offered for pursuing a project. As the name suggests, a business case review focuses on the business implications of a project. A *competitive analysis* may be undertaken to identify strategies, goals, market presence, and capabilities of key competitors. Careful cost and revenue projections may be developed (these may be part of a *cost/pricing evaluation*). From these projections, insights into profitability can be inferred.

Feasibility Studies

The term *feasibility study* is used in many ways. Generally, it denotes undertaking a technical, economic, and commercial review of a project concept. In the international arena, it has a more focused meaning. It is associated with the financing of projects by public or private lenders. These lenders (for example, the World Bank, commercial banks, government development agencies) use the results of the feasibility study to determine whether they will support a project financially.

Technical Evaluation

Over the life of a project, the deliverable that is being developed and produced will undergo many technical reviews. In the development stage, for example, two critical technical reviews that are often undertaken are the *preliminary design review* (PDR) and *critical design review* (CDR).

The purpose of the PDR and CDR is to add an element of stability to the design process. In the earliest stages, the design will be very dynamic as project staff explore different design alternatives. At some point, however, the design team must settle on a particular design so that the project is not bogged down in an endless loop of design changes. With the PDR, a particular design choice is reviewed and approved. Since this is still early in the development process, this design will likely undergo substantial modification. Ultimately, to prevent endless modification the design is subject to a CDR. The result of the CDR is an approved design that will serve as the basis of building the physical deliverable.

Technical evaluation is closely associated with testing. For example, a piece of software may be tested to see whether it meets defined throughput standards, or an O-ring may be tested to see whether it performs effectively at low temperatures.

One clever technical evaluation approach that will be examined later in this chapter is the *structured walk-through*.

Proposal Evaluation

Companies that bid on large contracts often subject their proposals to evaluations to see whether or not they are credible. One way this is done is through the establishment of teams whose job is to tear the evolving proposal apart. In the early stages, a proposal may be put through a *pink team* review. This review is analogous to a PDR. Its purpose is to offer guidance on future directions the proposal should take before too much effort has gone into its development. Later, after the proposal is more fully developed, it may be put through a *red team* review. This review is analogous to a CDR. Its purpose is to make last minute adjustments to the proposal before it is submitted.

Acceptance Testing

Throughout its life, the project may be punctuated with acceptance test milestones. Generally, customers review the results of these tests to see whether the deliverable is making acceptable progress as it evolves. The most crucial of these tests is the final *customer acceptance test*. This last test will determine whether the customer is satisfied that the deliverable meets the specifications. This last test is often the basis of determining whether final payments should be made to the developer.

Root Cause Analysis

When projects get hopelessly bogged down, management may initiate a root cause analysis to identify the origins of the difficulties. If these can be perceived, then attention can focus on fixing the sources of the problems rather than the symptoms. The root cause analysis may show management that things are so bad that the best course of action might be to shut down the project.

Postmortems

After a project is ended, many companies undertake postmortems to see what went right and what went wrong. The postmortem can be a valuable exercise, particularly if the lessons learned are documented and incorporated into revisions of project methods and procedures. In this way, the organization can learn from its experiences and avoid making the same mistakes twice.

Unfortunately, the circumstances surrounding most projects often lead to ineffectual postmortems. For example, because of discontinuities typical of most projects, where new players continually replace old players, it may be difficult to reconstruct the project experience with any cogency. Who was working on the project during the design phase? Do they remember what went wrong and right? (Do they even care?) What were the specific circumstances under which the project was selected? Is any one around who remembers?

These problems are not insurmountable. However, to deal with them requires a major commitment by management and the project team to document decisions and actions throughout the project's life and to minimize staff turnover.

Performance Appraisals

All the evaluations mentioned up until this point focus on project performance. Performance appraisal focuses on the achievements of individual players. The chief problem with performance appraisal on projects is rooted in matrix management. Typically, project workers are borrowed resources who come from a functional area, do their job on the project, and then return to their functional homes.

The big question is: How do you evaluate their efforts? Their functional bosses are too far removed from the project to understand what they have done on it. Their project "bosses" usually do not contribute to their performance appraisal reviews, and even when they do, their contribution is questionable for a variety of reasons (for example, they are incapable of evaluating the technical contribution of the borrowed resource, or they do not understand the career development targets of the functional group).

The question of how to conduct performance appraisals of matrixed employees is one of the most significant questions facing project management today. Each of the three key players in the matrix has a great deal at stake in this matter. Project workers want to know how they will be evaluated. Their future in the organization depends on the outcome of their evaluations. They are nervous about being evaluated by functional managers who do not see them at work on projects. By the same token, they may be uneasy about being evaluated by project managers who are unaware of their career objectives and who lack the technical insights to assess their work.

Functional managers may be distressed that they are evaluating employees in a vacuum since they may not have firsthand exposure to the efforts of their workers. They also may be bothered by the fact that project managers are giving the functional workers guidance that runs contrary to accepted procedures within the functional department.

Because they typically have little or no role in the performance appraisal of project workers, project managers find themselves lacking the carrots and sticks needed to motivate their borrowed staff.

Unfortunately, there are no easy fixes on how to carry out performance appraisals in matrixed organizations.

Audits

A commonly encountered form of evaluation is the financial audit. This is carried out by outside auditors. Their job is to review project accounts to check their accuracy. Scheduled audits are not particularly frightening since they can be anticipated in advance. Surprise audits can be scary because they suggest a lack of trust in budget management procedures.

Quality Assurance

People may not realize it, but quality assurance is fundamentally an exercise in evaluation. Targets are set (for example, acceptable defect rates may be established), and then a process is periodically examined to see whether the targets are being achieved.

Evaluations and the Project Life Cycle

A review of the different kinds of evaluation commonly encountered on projects suggests a tie between the type of evaluation and the stage of the project life cycle. Evaluations that occur in the preproject phase are typically conducted to see whether the project is worth pursuing. Included here are approaches such as feasibility studies, bid/no-bid evaluations, and business case evaluations.

Evaluations that occur during the project phase are concerned with measuring performance. Is the project achieving its targets? Many of these evaluation efforts are technical and are associated with technical tests. If the project is in serious trouble, an evaluation may provide the rationale for making major course corrections or even for killing the project. Toward the end of the project phase, one evaluation stands out over all others: customer acceptance. Without customer acceptance, the project can lumber on endlessly.

Evaluations carried out in the postproject phase focus on lessons learned. Although they will not affect the outcome of the current project, if the lessons are captured and incorporated in project methods and procedures, they can affect how future projects are executed.

Problems with Evaluation

As I mentioned at the outset of this chapter, I spent six years early in my career developing evaluation systems for high-technology organizations. Through this experience, I gained firsthand insights into how evaluations are carried out in the real world. I was fortunate because the evaluation offices I worked with at places like the National Institutes of Health (NIH) and National Science Foundation (NSF) were staffed with professionals who were evaluation experts and were well acquainted with evaluation's pitfalls. Still, even when approached intelligently, evaluation had its share of pain.

Over the years I have reflected on why evaluations are so painful. Having been part of dozens of evaluation efforts and having witnessed scores more, I have perceived a number of common problems. Many of these are rooted in distortions of the purpose of evaluations. Others are tied to specific characteristics of evaluation, such as its disruptive nature and the threat inherent in it.

Distortions of Evaluation's Purposes

Few individuals in organizations understand what evaluation is about. Unfortunately, this is as true of upper level managers as of the rank and file.

One common misunderstanding is that evaluation is a tool to identify poor performers. By this reckoning, it is designed primarily to separate the wheat from the chaff. It is something to be feared. This perception arises from evaluation's focus on identifying problems when they are minor so that they do not grow into large problems. There is no question: with evaluation, we are looking for problems. However, this is not to say that we are looking for troublemakers.

Along these same lines, some managers see evaluation as a mechanism to keep their staff on their toes. They view it as something akin to a surprise audit. I once had a manager say to me: "I like to conduct surprise evaluations. This way I can see how my staff function at any given time, when they don't have the opportunity to prepare for an audit. I find it keeps them sharp since they never know when they will be scrutinized."

Actually, effective evaluation requires that surprises be kept to a minimum. Evaluation criteria should be clearly laid out. They should be reviewed according to a well-established schedule and clearly defined rules. In this way, project staff know what is expected of them. They can work to meet these expectations. This outlook on evaluation lies at the heart of management by objectives.

A third and highly destructive distortion is the use of evaluation to serve political ends. What happens here is that political players use it to support their political objectives. If it confirms their position, they employ it to strengthen themselves. If it contradicts their position, they ignore it. Evaluation in this case is simply an instrument of convenience. When used politically, its credibility as a management tool is destroyed. Project staff justifiably see it as a dangerous weapon.

Inherent Characteristics of Evaluation

Much of the pain of evaluation is tied to some of its inherent characteristics. The people being evaluated often do not see its value as a feedback mechanism designed to keep the project on track. At worst, they feel threatened by it; at best, they see it as a nuisance.

Perhaps the most negative feature of evaluation is its inherent threats. As mentioned earlier, evaluations look for problems. They are exercises in criticism. The people being evaluated are put into a defensive posture. Their natural tendency is to resist attacks on them. For evaluations to succeed, project staff must be made to realize that this criticism is not designed to hurt them. Management must convey a sense that it recognizes that problems occur naturally and that everyone faces them. The existence of problems should not be construed to indicate incompetence. If the need for evaluation is properly conveyed to staff and its level of threat is lowered, staff are more likely to participate fully and honestly in it.

Another problem with evaluation is that it is disruptive. Frequently, evaluations are carried out by teams of outsiders. The theory here is that we do not want conflicts of interest to arise—we do not want foxes guarding the chicken coop. Unfortunately, when outsiders come in to review project work, enormous amounts of time must often be dedicated to educating them about the project, its goals, its history, the composition of the team, and so forth. Project staff may find themselves pulled off project work in order to help in this effort. The act of evaluation may actually contribute to schedule and cost overruns.

A final problem with evaluation is that it can easily be carried out in an arbitrary and capricious fashion. Project staff are painfully aware that if the evaluation team arrives on a Monday rather than a Thursday, their conclusions might be different. They are also aware that evaluation Team A will likely come up with different conclusions than Teams B or C. What is present here is excessive subjectivity. What is lacking is consistency. If indeed the process is carried out in an arbitrary and capricious fashion, the results of the evaluation effort lack value. We might as well determine our conclusions by a throw of dice.

Incidentally, evaluations do not have to be highly subjective. Effective evaluation attempts to make the process as objective as possible. One way to do this is to specify the evaluation criteria long before the evaluation is carried out, so that the project team knows what is expected of it. Another way is to make the criteria objectively verifiable. For example, a criterion might read: "The team should finish all tasks associated with Phases A and B by March 15" (determining whether or not the tasks are complete should be relatively straightforward), or "Data entry errors should be no more than one error per five hundred key strokes."

Clearly, significant problems are often associated with the attempt to evaluate project work. To the extent that project staff perceive the evaluation to be dangerous to their future or a waste of time, they are unlikely to supply information needed to make it meaningful.

How to reduce the level of threat inherent in evaluation? How to eliminate the sense that it is carried out in an arbitrary and capricious fashion? There are various ways that evaluations can be conducted effectively. One example will be presented here. This approach, called the *structured walk-through*, has been employed heavily since the late 1960s. Those who have experienced it generally perceive it to be a useful exercise and do not see it as threatening. Consequently, they openly participate in the evaluation effort, greatly increasing the likelihood that it will result in meaningful conclusions.

The Structured Walk-Through

The structured walk-through technique was developed by IBM in the late 1960s as a relatively friendly approach to evaluating project efforts. It demonstrates that with a bit of creative thinking, management techniques can be developed to deal with seemingly intractable problems. In the case of evaluation, the intractable problem is that the negative aspects of evaluation discourage project staff from partaking forthrightly and readily in the evaluation process. The structured walk-through approach deals with this problem by giving the people who are being evaluated control over the evaluation process.

Following are the key rules for conducting a structured walk-through. These rules reflect the original rules created by IBM, as well as modifications to them that have evolved over the years. The following discussion also incorporates observations gleaned from interviews I conducted with project staff associated with some thirty structured walk-throughs.

Rule 1: The Group Being Evaluated Chooses Its Judge and Jury

This rule reduces the sense of threat felt by the people being evaluated. If they choose the evaluators, they cannot complain that the evaluation team was selected in an arbitrary fashion. They also can be assured that the team was not chosen in accordance with some hidden political agenda. Finally, they can select an evaluation team that is made up of people who are already educated as to how the organization functions and what is being developed. By doing so, they reduce the amount of time they must dedicate to bringing the evaluation team up to speed.

Obviously, there is a danger that the group being evaluated will rig the jury. That is, they can choose evaluation team members who are their close associates and who would be reluctant to criticize them too harshly. In practice, this potential abuse of privilege does not appear to be a serious problem. None of the people I interviewed suggested that they worked with a rigged jury. The structured walk-through approach creates a sense of trust, and the people being evaluated are reluctant to violate this trust. They recognize that it is a greater crime to distort the walk-through process than to experience difficulties on the project.

In addition, in many organizations, the team being evaluated is not given full latitude in choosing its evaluators. Rather, it is given the opportunity to select its evaluators from a list of candidates preapproved by the organization's evaluation office.

Rule 2: The Group Being Evaluated Determines the Rules of the Evaluation Effort

The people being evaluated continue to control the process by establishing the rules of the game. They identify the evaluation criteria. They send the evaluation packages with instructions to the evaluation team members. They set the agenda for the evaluation sessions.

As with Rule 1, there is the possibility that this rule can be abused. Specifically, the group being evaluated can create rules that steer the evaluation team away from problem areas. Once again, this does not appear to be a real problem in practice. They realize that by avoiding problems, they are defeating the whole rationale of the evaluation.

In addition, in many organizations, the rules the team can establish are governed by a set of guidelines established by the evaluation office.

Rule 3: The Group Being Evaluated Runs the Evaluation Meetings

The evaluation review occurs through one or more meetings. This constitutes the actual walk-through. The people being evaluated actually run the meetings. They determine who talks, when they talk, and how long they talk.

Interestingly, in my interviews, the greatest complaints about the structured walk-through focused on how the meetings were conducted. Typical complaints include:

- The people running the meetings are not experienced facilitators—they conduct the meetings in an amateurish fashion.
- The meetings do not stick to the agenda—for example, technical evaluators tend to go off on a technical tangent.
- Discussion is not effectively limited—some participants drone on endlessly.
- The evaluation meetings can provide a forum for different groups to grind their political axes—in selecting outside evaluators, it is important that people are chosen who get along with each other.

These complaints are not directed at the structured walk-through process itself. Rather, they are directed at the lack of skills many of us have in running a meeting.

Rule 4: No Upper-Level Managers Should Be Present at the Evaluation Sessions

The whole point of the structured walk-through process is to create an environment that engenders honesty. How honest will employees be if they are asked to discuss serious problems in their work in the presence of individuals who rate their performance? A substantial minority of the people I interviewed reported that higher-level managers occasionally would sit in on their structured walk-throughs. Most indicated that they were not pleased with this management presence and that they found it stifled the free flow of ideas.

Rule 5: Customers Should Not Be Present at the Evaluation Sessions

This fifth rule never appeared in the original IBM guidance on conducting a structured walk-through. Those who have experienced the presence of a customer during a walk-through session strongly recommend that customers be excluded. Their rationale is identical to the rationale underlying Rule 4. How honest will people be in uncovering problems when the customer is present? Furthermore, there is the danger that the customer may actively join in the criticism process and use the occasion to change project requirements.

This rule may sound as if it is anticustomer. It is not. Customer satisfaction remains a key objective of project management. However, there are many other avenues through which we can obtain customer inputs—for example, through customer walk-throughs.

In the nineties, we find one growing class of projects where we cannot exclude customers from the structured walk-throughs: those projects that involve intense partnering between customers and project staff. In these cases, the customer is already aware of the inevitable difficulties that arise on projects, so their presence during evaluation sessions will not be disruptive.

Rule 6: Maintain Good Documentation
Throughout the Whole Evaluation Process

Virtually everyone I interviewed believed strongly that the structured walk-through will not be effective unless the whole process is documented carefully. In particular, notes should be taken of comments and decisions made during the evaluation meetings, and action items should be created from these notes. These action items should detail what actions should be undertaken by what time. Follow-on reviews should be made to assure that the action items have been adequately addressed.

Organizations that employ the structured walk-through approach to evaluation are highly satisfied with the results they achieve. It is not a panacea and can be a bit painful to carry out. However, most employees are aware that the alternative is to bring in outsiders who they may not trust, and they much prefer the structured walk-through approach to this.

Conclusions

Projects are cybernetic systems. That is, feedback and control are essential to their proper execution. A major source of feedback information comes from evaluations. As we saw earlier in this chapter, these evaluations cover a broad range of topics—from performance appraisals to technical reviews to selection appraisals to postmortems. This reflects the fact that projects are driven by forces coming from a variety of sources, and feedback from each of these sources is needed to keep the project on track.

Without systematic evaluation procedures, the project will lose its way. It's like trying to drive a car in a severe rainstorm when the windshield wipers aren't functioning. The view of the road is so distorted by the raindrops that one cannot drive effectively. The driver can slow down to a crawling pace, but this may mean that he misses his appointments. He can continue driving at a speedy rate, but this makes it more likely that he will have an accident.

Evaluation systems must be developed with great care. Their purpose is to generate honest, timely, and accurate insights on project progress. If they are perceived to be threatening, the probability of obtaining honest information is diminished. If they are conducted in a disorganized, haphazard way, they certainly won't generate timely results. And if the instruments for measuring performance are no good—for example, if they depend on excessive use of subjective judgment—the conclusions will lack accuracy.

Evaluation serves an additional function, beyond providing feedback information to keep the project on track: it is an instrument to heighten accountability. Too many projects fail because accountability is diffuse. With properly conducted evaluations, people are answerable for their actions and decisions. They have no choice but to adopt a "buck stops here" outlook on their efforts.

Chapter Thirteen

Understanding and Using
Performance Metrics;

or,

Measuring the Right Stuff

Imagine driving an automobile with a nonfunctioning speedometer. You likely would feel very uncomfortable. As you passed posted speed limit signs, you would not know whether you were exceeding the limit, thus risking a speeding ticket. On the highway, you might decide to travel the same speed as the other cars on the road, but when you saw the police pulling over cars in your group, you might decide this was not a wise policy. Without the speedometer, you would have high levels of uncertainty about your driving performance.

Our lives are filled with measurement. Upon awakening in the morning, we check our weight by standing on a scale. We then go into the kitchen where we measure out two scoops of ground coffee, which we put into our coffee brewer. We set the brewer for "extra-strong" coffee. The newspaper delivery boy drops by, and we pay him for two months of newspaper deliveries. We look at our watch and realize with horror that we have only fifteen minutes left before we should leave for the office. The office is located ten miles away. Given an average commuting speed of thirty miles per hour, we estimate that it should take us twenty minutes to reach the office.

Clearly, using measures is an important part of our daily lives. Lord Kelvin emphasized this importance in a famous statement when he said that if something in science cannot be measured, it has little value. Kelvin was a renowned scientist. The role of measurement in science and engineering is obvious. Less obvious is the role of measurement in management.

Measurement is highly important for effective management. Imagine a for-profit company trying to manage its affairs without cost and income data. Or imagine it trying to plan its affairs without any knowledge of the time it takes to carry out its activities. Despite their obvious importance, many organizations appear to be content to fly blind without the measures they need to track their efforts and to make reasonable decisions.

Occasionally, one encounters stiff resistance to attempts to measure work effort. The grounds for this resistance are frequently stated as: "There are some things that are just not amenable to measurement!" I suspect that this resistance to measurement is largely rooted in what John Allen Paulos calls the "innumeracy" of management and the work force. In his insightful and entertaining book *Innumeracy* (1988), Paulos convincingly demonstrates that Americans often lack the most basic grasp of what measurement is about. They simply do not understand numbers and what they can do. Consequently, they have little appreciation of the power of measurement to help them function more effectively—or they accept numerical results too readily because they lack the competency to assess the genuine pitfalls of measurement.

Some of the key topics discussed in this book—estimation, risk management, evaluation, integrated cost/schedule control, accountability—have a strong measurement component to them. If one is to get a firm grasp of estimating time and cost performance, evaluating work performance, or determining the range of risk associated with a decision, one must have some sense of how measurement plays a role in each of these areas. What makes for a good measure as opposed to a bad one? How are measurement data collected? What measures can we employ when "hard" measures are lacking? What are the pitfalls of measurement?

This chapter should be viewed as a primer on measurement in project management. The reader who has taken a doctoral-level research methodology course will be comfortable with the topics covered here since they are standard fare in such courses. The approach I employ is commonsensical rather than formal and rigorous. The objective of this exercise is to heighten the awareness of project managers and staff of the role that measurement does and should play on their projects.

The Role of Measurement in Managing Projects

Measures serve a variety of functions in project management. Their uses range from the establishment of unambiguous targets to the tracking of accomplishments to modeling project processes. The common thread running through these different uses is *accountability*. When something is measured, its fundamental features are laid bare. Measurement implies clarity, replicability and verifiability. With proper measurement, vagueness and obfuscation are no longer viable recourses for the inept manager. Accountability reigns!

Some of the key uses of measurement in projects are the following.

Establishing Clear Targets

An important feature of management by objectives is the creation of unambiguous goals. A goal is ambiguous when five people reviewing it come up with multiple interpretations of its meaning. When a goal is clear, the five people hold a single view of its meaning.

A good way to establish an unambiguous goal is to build verifiable measures into it. The goal "to arrive at grandma's house as fast as possible" is considerably strengthened when phrased, "to arrive at grandma's house within half an hour." Similarly, the goal "to carry a lot of grocery bags into the house from the car" is less ambiguous when stated, "to carry into the house a minimum of four grocery bags taken from the car."

By establishing measurable goals, we create more clearly defined targets toward which we can direct our efforts. With clear targets, there is less chance of misinterpreting what should be done.

Tracking Performance

Without clearly defined targets and well-defined performance measures, it is impossible to track performance effectively. How does one determine whether the vague goal "to do the job as quickly as possible" is actually being achieved?

By allowing people to track performance effectively, measures provide feedback about the achievement of specified goals. This feedback gives people a sense of what they have accomplished and what it will take to complete the job. To see this, consider the following simple example.

George is told that he has two weeks to write Chapter Three of a user's manual for a software system his organization is developing. The specified length of the chapter is thirty pages, including eight drawings. By the end of Week 1, he finds that he has written only ten pages of manuscript and has completed two drawings. When the project manager contacts him to determine what progress he is making, how should he report his progress?

He could say, "I'm slipping a bit, but with a little more effort I might be able to meet the deadline." The problem with this answer is that it provides little insight into the actual status of George's effort. Furthermore, it offers no real insight into what will be needed to complete the job on time.

By phrasing his response in terms of work measurement, George can provide the project manager with a better sense of the project's status. For example, he may estimate that for this chapter, it is taking him one person-week of effort to produce ten manuscript pages and two or three drawings. If he continues to work alone at this rate, he calculates that he will slip his deadline date by one week since the job entails producing thirty pages of text and eight drawings in two weeks and he will actually have completed only twenty pages and five or six drawings in this time. His computation of his actual work performance rate suggests how he can achieve the two-week deadline: if an additional person can be assigned to the effort, the job can be finished by the deadline date.

George's analysis can be extended to compute the cost implications of his schedule slippage—for example, he can compare the additional costs of adding a new person to the project and contrast that to the costs associated with extending the project one week. The point is that by examining the quantitative implications of George's work performance, the project manager now has key data to allow for rational decisions.

Rewarding/Punishing Behavior

The achievement or nonachievement of defined measurable goals often serves as the basis of individual performance appraisals. For this approach to be viable, those being appraised should play a role in defining the measurable goals. If they do not play such a role, they may feel they are being held accountable to an unrealistic yardstick. They are not likely to feel a personal commitment to achieving the goals. They may even distort their reporting of data because they do not want to be punished for failing to achieve unrealistic goals. The dictum that workers be part of the goal-setting process is a fundamental precept of MBO.

With individual performance appraisal, qualitative factors clearly play an important role. That is, such hard-to-measure things as attitude, energy, and team orientation of employees are important evaluation criteria. However, these subjective judgments should be reinforced with objective measures. A subjectively determined criterion such as energy level (or a good attitude) is not by itself useful if the evaluated worker is consistently deficient in meeting his or her defined goals. Without the use of measurable performance indicators, we run the risk of rewarding substandard behavior on the basis of "feel good" sentiments or punishing basically good behavior because of "bad" feelings.

There is nothing new in the use of measurable performance indicators to reward good behavior. The best known example of this is the commission paid to sales personnel. The more sales made, the greater the commission. To encourage superperformance, commission rates may be accelerated for a sales volume above a threshold.

Modeling and Predicting Project Performance

With the creation and employment of performance measurements, it becomes possible to develop quantitative models of project activities. The advantage of modeling the project process is that it allows project staff to generate "what if?" scenarios associated with different situations. Through modeling, a change of the value of such things as the number of human resources available or the estimated duration of a task can provide staff with important information about the cost, schedule, or quality implications of specific changes.

The models created need not be elaborate. A simple budget maintained on an electronic spreadsheet is an example of a rudimentary but useful computerized model. By changing wage rates on the spreadsheet, the analyst has instant data on what project costs will be with the new rates.

A commonly employed modeling tool in project management is the PERT/CPM network. These networks can be built using a wide variety of PERT/CPM software packages. Today's packages integrate budget, schedule, and human resource data, thus creating a truly robust overview of project performance. Some of these packages are easy to learn, requiring only a morning of instructional effort. Of course, the more sophisticated packages require more time to master.

Of recent interest to project managers are analytical approaches that allow them to model risk. A variety of software packages have emerged in recent years that permit even mathematically naive managers to estimate the range of possible budget, schedule, and human resource outcomes facing them under conditions of uncertainty. This topic is discussed in more detail in Chapter Four.

The Nature of Measurement

Not all measures are good. If the instrument that records data is defective, this will lead to the generation of bad measures. For example, a miscalibrated thermometer will consistently yield incorrect temperature readings. If a measure is used inappropriately, it will also provide bad results. For example, using blood pressure measures as an indicator of anxiety will yield poor results since high blood pressure has other causes beyond intense anxiety.

In order to use measures effectively, we should have some appreciation of their fundamental nature. In this section we explore some basic features of measures, an understanding of which can allow us to use them more effectively.

"Strength" of Measurement

Numerical data that serve as the basis of measurement can be viewed as possessing varying degrees of "strength." The "softest" data are *nominal scale* data. These are nothing more than labels. The numbers on the shirts of athletes are nominal data. Basically, nominal data are useful in categorizing phenomena. Counts of boys versus girls in a room, counts of Catholics versus Protestants, and counts of blue dresses versus green and yellow dresses all exemplify the use of nominal data.

Ordinal scale data are more powerful than nominal data. They allow us to rank things in some order. When we say that ice is colder than tap water, we are making an ordinal comparison. Similarly, when we say that Jackie ranks first in her class, whereas Myron ranks second and Marsha ranks third, we are engaging in ordinal measurement. These measures are commonly employed in performance appraisal and often take the form of "Greatly exceeds standards," "Exceeds standards," "Meets standards," and "Falls short of standards." They are also frequently encountered on evaluation questionnaires when we are asked to rank something on a scale of one to seven, where one represents the worst case and seven the best case.

One thing to keep in mind when dealing with ordinal data is that they are not additive or subject to the full range of arithmetic manipulation. You cannot add first place to fourth place to tally to fifth place. Neither does it make sense to subtract, multiply, or divide ordinal measures.

Interval scale data are numbers that can be employed fully in arithmetic manipulations. The price of a piece of pie, the temperature on a winter day, and the number of days it takes to carry out a task are examples of interval scale data. These data can be added and subtracted together meaningfully ($2.00 + $3.00 + $4.00 = $9.00; $5.00 - $2.00 = $3.00), multiplied and divided (2 × $5.00 = $10.00; $10.00/2 = $5.00), and manipulated in every conceivable way. Because of this versatility in their employment, they are considered to be the most powerful of the three scales of data discussed here.

Most attempts at gathering work performance measures on projects focus on collecting interval scale data. Task durations, budget expenditures, number of resources available, fraction of effort achieved, efficiency measures, technical performance data, and so on are common measures employed on projects, and they all employ interval scale data.

When such measures are not readily available, project staff often shrug their shoulders and give up trying to collect data, arguing that what they are looking at is fundamentally nonmeasurble. Before they give up, they should attempt to see whether the thing they are trying to assay can be measured ordinally. I may not be able to say that customer satisfaction with Feature A of my software system is twice as high as with Feature B, but I can make the ordinal statement, "Satisfaction with Feature A far exceeds satisfaction with Feature B." Not a precise insight, but at least it gives us a sense of what is happening.

If something appears to be difficult to measure ordinally, an attempt to measure it nominally might be undertaken. The mere classification of something is a form of measurement and can provide project staff with valuable insights. For example, categorizing activities by risk factor is a form of nominal measurement that is valuable on projects.

Subjective Versus Objective Measures

A great drive to quantify human behavior arose in the 1960s. At that time, the social sciences were titillated by the possibility that social science could be carried out with the same degree of precision as the physical sciences. The prevailing view was that the chief difference between human behavior and physical action is one of degree rather than kind. That is, human behavior is sloppier than physical behavior because it is more complex, made up of a myriad of variables that affect outcomes. Although in the physical sciences we actually encounter parsimonious relationships such as $E = MC^2$, the complexity of human activity makes such relationships unlikely in the social sciences. However, the advent of the computer made the handling of complex relationships easier. From the computer's perspective, manipulating fifty variables is only marginally more burdensome than manipulating three. The power of the computer to harness massive quantities of data that allow for social engineering was captured in the pop culture of the time in Michael Crichton's science fiction thriller *The Andromeda Strain* (1969), which portrayed computers as capable of measuring all aspects of human activity.

In their attempts to quantify human behavior, social scientists focused on developing measures that were as objective as possible. Objectivity was seen to be "scientific" because of its association with replicability. It also implied the absence of human judgment in making the measure; this detachment in arriving at judgments was also seen to be "scientific."

The following simple example illustrates the objective versus subjective dichotomy: determining temperature by employing a well-calibrated thermometer is viewed to be objective, whereas asking someone to describe it based on their personal sensations is considered subjective. Objective measures tend to give consistent results, whereas subjective ones do not.

In management, the drive toward objectivity reached an extreme form in the Delphi process that emerged in the 1960s. Delphi is a forecasting tool that attempts to convert subjective judgments into objective data. To see how the Delphi process works, consider the problem of estimating how long it will take before the United States has operational factories in space. Let us suppose that a panel of fifteen experts on the economics and technology of space commercialization and manufacturing is identified. With Delphi, the views of each panelist are collected independently, typically by means of a questionnaire. That is, the panelists are not permitted to interact with each other directly. Their views are statistically analyzed and summarized. The statistical summary is then returned to the panelists, who are instructed to study the results. In view of the summary—which, in effect, reflects the collective judgment of all the panelists—the individual panelists are asked to reconsider their original estimates and adjust them accordingly. The panelists' revised views are then analyzed and summarized, and the latest results are sent back out to them. This procedure continues in this iterative fashion until some preestablished degree of convergence of views is achieved.

The striking feature of the Delphi approach is that in the interest of maintaining objectivity, direct interaction of the panelists with each other is proscribed. The rationale for such a "sanitary" procedure is to avoid "contamination" of judgments that might arise if the panelists were permitted to interact directly and thereby be influenced by personality factors.

The obsession with objectivity characteristic of the 1960s appears a bit quaint from today's perspective. For one thing, viewing human judgment and interaction as a contaminant seems rather short-sighted. Today, we tend to feel strongly that through human interaction, new insights are achieved. Ideas are less likely to grow stale because they are continually challenged. Interestingly, one of the most popular contemporary tools for converting subjective judgments into objective data is the analytical hierarchy process (AHP), a fairly sophisticated mathematical approach that requires the heavy interaction of people in a face-to-face forum.

For another thing, the whole concept of what is objective and what is not has turned out to be harder to define than people thought back in the 1960s. Even the most seemingly objective judgment is ultimately based on premises that are rooted in human biases. This is seen clearly in the public debates on standardized examinations of human capabilities, such as IQ tests and the SATs. Several decades ago, the objectivity of such exams was widely accepted. Today, however, these and other similar examinations are under severe attack for being culturally biased. It has reached the point where the Educational Testing Service (the developer of the SAT) has agreed to include a subjective essay component in future editions of the examination in order to make the examinations less biased. In this case, subjectivity is seen to be more scientifically valid than objectivity.

Reliability

The measurement of anything but the most trivial objects often results in some measurement error. If I ask five people to count the number of bricks visible on the front elevation of a brick house, I will be likely to get five separate numbers. Some of the variance might be attributable to definitional problems. For example, what constitutes a "brick" for counting purposes? At the corners of the house or along window frames many bricks are cut in half in order to allow them to fit properly into the structure. Should these be counted as whole bricks or half bricks? Some of the variance is simply a result of counting error. A number of bricks might be double counted, and others might be skipped entirely.

The big issue here is not whether everyone comes up with the same count. Chances are, they won't. The issue really is, How much variance is there in their counts? If one individual reports that the house has 3,500 bricks, another 6,200 bricks, and still another 8,200 bricks, there is a large variance in the counts. In this case, we say the measures have low reliability. On the other hand, if the reported number of bricks coming from three estimates are 6,150, 6,200, and 6,225, there is a high degree of consistency in the counts, and we say the measures are highly reliable.

A measure is reliable, then, if after repeated samplings, the results we achieve are close to each other. If a measure has low reliability, then it is not much use to us. Wild "guesstimates," common on projects, typically have low reliability. They often exemplify the old data processing adage "garbage in, garbage out."

Reliability can be enhanced by developing careful methods and procedures for collecting data. Substantial attention should focus on defining carefully what should be counted. In the example given above, data collection procedures might specify that bricks that have been split in half should be counted as half bricks. If data gatherers are allowed to make up their own rules as they do their jobs, then there will be inconsistency in the measures.

Validity

Validity addresses the question, Are we really measuring what we think we are measuring? For example, temperature is not a valid measure of humidity (although it may be correlated with humidity). It *is* a valid measure of the hotness or coldness of a body or environment. GNP is not a valid measure of national economic well-being because a country can have a high GNP, but national wealth may be concentrated in the hands of an elite, leaving the majority of the population in desperate poverty. GNP *is* a valid measure of the market value of goods and services produced in a country.

The issue of validity is particularly relevant in our attempts to develop measures for performance appraisal. Is absenteeism a valid measure of a worker's commitment to doing a good job? Is the worker's consistent achievement of objectives a measure of effectiveness? Is the frequency of complaints directed at a worker a valid measure of his or her concern for customer satisfaction?

The validity of a measure must be determined in the context in which it is used. Consider the three measures mentioned in the paragraph immediately above. In general, absenteeism reasonably reflects worker commitment to doing a good job. Clearly, the hotel clerk who constantly calls in sick in order to create time to visit the beach is not heavily committed to doing a good job. However, during flu season, absenteeism may reflect nothing more than the fact that some workers had the misfortune to be exposed to the flu virus. In this case, its validity is suspect.

The consistent achievement of objectives *can* accurately reflect an employee's effectiveness, particularly if he or she played a role in defining them. On the other hand, if unrealistic objectives are imposed upon the employee, failure to achieve them may be more strongly rooted in the fact that they are poorly specified than in the employee's lack of effectiveness.

Frequent complaints directed at an employee *might* indicate that he or she lacks a commitment to customer satisfaction. They might also indicate that the organization in which the employee works is not adequately supporting its workers to do a good job. For example, if only one employee is assigned to deal with a multitude of complaints and this results in slow response to individual complaints, it is likely that customers will focus their anger on that employee.

One way to test for the validity of a measure is to see whether it correlates positively with other closely related measures. For example, if we find that measures of absenteeism do not correspond at all to other measures of employee commitment (for example, hours of unpaid overtime worked or employee attitude), then they probably are not valid measures of commitment.

Another way to deal with the matter of validity is to constantly scrutinize the measures we employ and ask: Are they really measuring what we say they are measuring? This scrutiny should be carried out by a wide array of people, including different members of the management team, the individuals being evaluated, and "disinterested" outsiders.

Generating Measures

Most organizations are sitting on a gold mine of useful measures, but they do not realize it. Quite frequently, when I ask a project manager, "How long does it take you to test the XYZ component on your products?" I get the answer, "I'm not sure. We don't have that data." I know for a fact that in this organization, a dozen projects have been carried out that have tested the XYZ component, yet basic data on its duration, resource requirements, and costs are not handy. In actuality, the organization *does* have the basic data, but they are buried in a morass of other facts and figures. The problem is that no one has taken the effort to retrieve the data and put them into a useful form.

When I suggest to people that they begin collecting data that can serve them well on their projects, they often look at me in wonder.

"We've never done that," they say.

"Why not begin now?" I respond.

The greatest obstacle to the effective generation of measures is ignorance. The vast majority of people I encounter do not have a clue as to how they should begin the data generation process. They see it as a highly complex undertaking requiring specialized skills that they simply lack. They are overwhelmed by the effort involved, so they deal with it in the most convenient way possible: they avoid it.

In this section, I examine a number of ways that people can generate useful measures on their projects. The key point is that there is nothing magical about developing good measures. They lie all around us. Our job is first to identify them and then to put them into a usable form. In developing good measures, we should take some guidance from the great French cubist painter, Georges Braque. When asked how he came up with his vision for his pictures, he responded, "It's easy. With my paint brush, I brush away the white surface of the canvas, and the painting emerges from beneath the surface."

We here examine two broad approaches to generating measures: one is to make use of existing data, and the other is to create new data.

Generating Measures from Existing Data

The file cabinets and mass storage media of most organizations are filled with data that can lead to improved project management if employed productively. It is merely a question of identifying which data can be used effectively and then massaging them to make them useful. Following is a list of untapped data sources that can be found in most project organizations.

Time Sheets. Well-constructed time sheets provide valuable information on how project staff allocate their time. They show the variations in the usage of different categories of personnel. Technical support personnel (such as testers, maintenance personnel, statisticians, and editors) will be allocated across several projects. Core personnel (such as designers and developers) will commit their time to fewer projects. Drawing on past patterns of personnel usage that emerge from a review of time sheets, project planners can predict future allocations of people to tasks.

Other valuable information can be extracted from time sheets. For example, they might indicate which workers and categories of work have high levels of administrative overhead associated with them. By examining overtime allocations, they can provide information on how realistic the organization has been in estimating work requirements for tasks. They also show work cycles, alerting management that there are predictable times when staff might be underemployed or overemployed. All this information can be used to help project organizations make better resource allocation decisions.

The key problem with time sheets is one of reliability. In many organizations, the rules on how to fill out a time sheet are very loose. For example, if administrative time is not carefully defined by the organization, one employee may count a half-hour conversation with the accounting department as administrative time while another may deem it a legitimate charge against a project. For time sheets to be a valuable source of project data, organizations must carefully define how they should be used and should apply the rules consistently across all employees and projects.

Budgets. Like time sheets, budgets have locked in them valuable information nuggets that can help us manage our projects more effectively. For example, a careful review of past project budgets may allow cost estimators to establish cost standards for carrying out various tasks, such as report production, testing, and data analysis. These standards permit more consistent cost estimating in the future. Instead of creating brand new estimates of how much it should cost for data entry tasks each time a new project is conceived, estimators can review standards generated from past experience and adjust them according to the specific characteristics of the new project in question. Incidentally, these new standards should not be cast in concrete. They should be updated constantly to reflect more recent project experiences.

In collecting data from budget forms, analysts should pay special attention to what it actually cost to do work and contrast that with what was initially budgeted. The actual expenses will play an important role in formulating our cost standards. They also provide us with insights into the adequacy of previous estimates. If we find that in our budget projections we consistently understate project costs by 15 percent, we should take this information into account in future projections.

Previous Schedules. Most organizations have voluminous project reports stashed away in their file cabinets, and a good number of these contain schedules for previous projects. With the advent of microcomputer-based scheduling software, we increasingly find that historical data on schedules are archived electronically. These old schedules contain valuable information that can be employed on future projects. At a minimum, they list activities and milestones that arise on the organization's projects. These activities and milestones can be scanned across a broad range of previous projects and used to create punch lists of "things to consider" in scheduling future projects.

The old schedules may also contain estimates of the duration of tasks. These estimates can be checked against actual performance (gleaned from old status reports) and can lead to the development of estimating baselines.

Organizations interested in employing good project metrics should certainly establish consistent procedures for reporting schedules so that scheduling data can be readily fed into a historical data base for projects.

Status Reports. Status reports come in a variety of shapes and sizes. A well-configured status report clearly establishes actual performance against planned performance. If this information is readily accessible in the status report, it becomes a treasure trove of valuable project measures. For example, planned versus actual cost and schedule data can be derived from twelve months of status reports and plotted graphically. The plots show visually the extent to which previous plans were met. If we find that previous plans consistently understated costs by 20 percent, this information should be reviewed and future plans might be adjusted accordingly. Furthermore, the "actuals" data can be collected task by task and can serve as the basis of creating cost and scheduling standards against which future performance can be assessed.

Postmortems. Postmortems are conducted after projects have concluded and serve a lessons learned function. Well-executed postmortems often contain thoughtful insights as to what worked well and what did not work on projects. In addition, the insights typically are backed up with tabular and graphical data. Postmortem reports should be scanned to determine whether they contain useful measures.

Generating New Measures

Project staff should not feel constrained to work only with existing measures garnered from time sheets, schedules, status reports, and the like. In certain situations, they may find it useful to generate wholly new measures. In this section, we review two approaches to generating such measures.

Questionnaires and Interviews. A common way to collect data about human activity is through questionnaires and interviews. These are ubiquitous in modern societies. At home, pollsters phone at inconvenient hours—usually at dinner time—to determine the opinions of home owners regarding a new tax initiative. In the supermarket, customers are queried in the aisles about their buying preferences. In the mail, people receive all manner of questionnaires soliciting their views on everything from their satisfaction with the service they received at the auto repair shop to their opinions on alternative candidates for the presidency.

Questionnaires and interviews also have their place on projects. One obvious way to determine how project staff spend their time is to ask them directly: How long does it typically take you to review client needs? How much time do you spend filling out forms? How many hours a week do you spend on project work? (this can be a check on data gathered through time sheets). Questionnaires and interviews can also be used to assess the risk of a set of activities, to identify when a set of resources will be freed up, to determine satisfaction with project management procedures, and so on.

Questionnaires and interviews generally fall into one of two categories. Some are open-ended and are designed to generate information in an unstructured fashion. Examples of questions associated with this approach are: What do you think are the three most significant quality problems the design department faces? How can response time to customer queries be shortened? Who are the individuals in your department who have the greatest impact on generating effective project procedures?

A second set of questionnaires and interviews are structured and are geared toward generating information that can be analyzed objectively. Examples of questions associated with this approach are: On a scale of one to five (where one represents "poor" and five represents "excellent"), how would you rank the probability of technical success for this project? Given the following five options, which most accurately describes the factors that result in better formulated documentation? How many years have you been a project manager?

With structured data, it becomes possible to conduct sophisticated inquiries into important issues. Results can be reported as percentages ("Seventy-two percent of the respondents stated that work conditions have not improved in the department"), reported as cross-tabs ("Of the 72 percent who stated that work conditions have not improved in the department, three-quarters had been with the company less than two years"), or analyzed according to any of a large number of sophisticated statistical methodologies (analysis of variance, regression analysis, factor analysis, discriminant analysis).

Individuals employing questionnaires and interviews should be aware of a number of potential pitfalls. Some of these are based on the mechanics of questionnaire design. Are the questions unambiguous? Are they biased? Do they really measure what they set out to measure? On a structured questionnaire, are the structured responses clearly written? Do they reflect the broad universe of potential responses? Is the questionnaire or interview too long? If so, respondents may be reluctant to cooperate with the query. Is it too superficial?

Other pitfalls stem from the environment in which the query is carried out. Are people willing to "speak for the record"? Will confidentiality be maintained? Has an attempt been made to query a random sample of respondents, or is the sample biased?

Direct Measures. Modern management owes a large debt to the scientific management principles of Frederick Taylor. Taylor was obsessed with measuring work performance. He invented the concept of time and motion studies, where trained observers systematically scrutinize the work efforts of workers. The tools of the trade were the clipboard, a pad of paper, a pencil, and a stopwatch. Work would be broken down into its most elemental parts and then measured.

Direct measures of work effort are often appropriate on projects. Consider the situation facing the designer of a new information system. One important design consideration is the usability of the new system. To test for usability, a number of experiments might be set up. One experiment might test to see which of several data entry forms best facilitates data entry. The performance of data entry clerks on the different forms might be measured on a number of criteria: Which form has the least number of data entry errors associated with it? How quickly can a standard set of data be entered into each of the forms? Which forms allow for the speediest correction of errors?

Project staff should be trained to see how they can generate direct measures when appropriate. This training need not be elaborate. It can include simple exercises in measurement. For example, staff might be required to track in a diary how they use their time over a week. Or they might count the pieces of mail they receive, sorting letters into appropriate categories (for example, project related, department related, demands response, junk mail). Or they can tabulate the durations of everyday tasks (How long does it take to brush my teeth? To prepare breakfast? To travel between three stations on the subway? On the average, how long is the queue at the sandwich stand in the cafeteria at 12:15 P.M.? On the average, how long does it take before the fourth person in the queue is fully served?).

The Shadow Side of Measures

Numbers seldom speak for themselves. In an amusing book titled *How to Lie with Statistics* (1954), Darrell Huff shows how a given set of numbers can be employed in countless self-serving ways. When manipulated skillfully, statistics can be used to make practically any desired argument. When used carelessly, well-intentioned analyses can produce erroneous results that lead to disaster. Clearly, metrics have their shadow side. In this section, we look at some common problems.

Measurable Performance Targets: Unintended Consequences

Earlier in this chapter, it was stated that an important use of metrics in projects is to establish performance targets. A pharmaceutical company may set a target to enroll forty new patients a month in its clinical trials. A telecommunications company may set a target to spend no more than two days per site to install its low-end telephone switches. Sales staff are given quarterly sales targets to achieve. When used effectively, these targets greatly strengthen the project management process. However, experience shows that great care must be taken in establishing them, since poorly formulated targets can lead to unintended consequences. This point is illustrated in the following examples.

Case 1: Sorry . . . Wrong Number. In keeping with the new focus on customer satisfaction, ABC Electronics Co. established a telephone hot line to field customer complaints and queries. Some concern was expressed that operators might linger in their chats with customers, so the number of calls handled was computed, and rewards were offered to those operators who handled the most calls. In order to give visibility to the superlative performers, an Operator of the Quarter was identified quarterly. Ms. Smith won the first Operator of the Quarter award. Everyone was amazed at her performance: she handled 25 percent more calls in the quarter than the runner-up. Ms. Smith also won the second Operator of the Quarter Award. This time she topped the runner-up by 30 percent.

Management became suspicious of Ms. Smith's performance. In a horse race, horses typically win by a nose or a horse length. Ms. Smith was consistently winning by the equivalent of ten horse lengths, an incredible performance. They did some investigating and determined how their star operator achieved her prize-winning performance. They determined that each time Ms. Smith received a phone call from a caller with a foreign accent, she would hang up on him or her. She reasoned correctly that talking to someone who was struggling with English would be time consuming and would reduce her calls-per-quarter performance. In her drive to satisfy the metrics, she unwittingly was defeating the whole purpose of the telephone hot line, which was to increase customer satisfaction.

Case 2: Killing the Messenger. Otto Stuttgart was a District Manager at a Fortune 50 company. He was a firm believer in the efficacy of management training. He was generous in offering his employees training opportunities, and he took advantage of such opportunities himself. Early in his career, he made a rule that whenever he attended a training session, he would return to work with at least one lesson that he would apply. In this way, he assured himself that he got something useful out of the training effort.

In the early 1990s, Otto attended a one-week course on total quality management (TQM). He enjoyed the course enormously. He was particularly impressed with the instructor's discussion of zero defects programs. Otto's understanding of this concept was that organizations should constantly strive to reduce defects, no matter how low the defect level is. The ultimate goal is to have no defects.

Otto resolved to apply the zero defects concept to his district. The only problem was that zero defects programs were implemented in manufacturing environments, where defects in products are obvious, whereas he worked in services. Suddenly it hit him what he could do: he would implement a zero complaints program. He could hardly wait to return to the office to launch this initiative.

The day he returned to the office, Otto announced to his staff that they would undertake a zero complaints program. That is, all staff members would work consciously to reduce customer complaints to zero. In order to give the program some teeth, individual performance evaluations would be tied in part to complaint levels.

The program was seemingly an astounding success. Within a month, complaints dropped to near zero levels. Otto was very pleased with the initiative. His faith in the conscious application of management training was reaffirmed.

Of course, complaints did not magically disappear. Otto's employees were not about to report complaints if in doing so they would jeopardize their careers. Otto had resurrected the ancient practice of killing the messenger who conveyed bad news. (One can surmise that in ancient times only extremely stupid messengers actually wound up dead. The survivors would lie through their teeth.)

What his staff did was to creatively redefine the concept of "complaint." Were they being dishonest? In a sense, yes. They were misrepresenting data. However, this dishonesty was forced on them when Otto tied complaints to their performance appraisals. While Otto returned to his office with the concept of zero defects, he neglected to bring home another key lesson in quality management: recognition that 85 percent of quality problems lie out of the control of workers. They are systemic. Only upper management has the power to correct them. If this is true, then 85 percent of the complaints arising in Otto's district were associated with problems out of the control of his employees. By themselves, they could not correct most of these problems. Realizing this, they refused to play Otto's game in the way he intended. Otto's scheme might have worked had he established a process for distinguishing system-induced complaints from those tied directly to employee actions.

Garbage in, Garbage out

Clearly, the effective use of measures in project management requires good data. If the data are not good, the analysis of the measures will yield erroneous conclusions. We have already explored earlier in this chapter two criteria of goodness of data. One is that the data should be reliable. That is, repeated measures of some phenomenon should give consistent results. Another is that the data should be valid. That is, it should be demonstrated that the measures do indeed reflect what they purport to measure. In particular, we should guard against biased measures that tilt our conclusions in a particular direction.

Every attempt should be made to collect reliable and valid data. This requires the establishment of clear data collection methods and procedures. It also requires constant quality checks on the data to make sure they are good.

Problems of Misspecified Models

Even when we have good measures, we may derive false conclusions from them if they are employed in models that poorly reflect reality. In statistics, this difficulty is called the *specification problem*. One common source of the specification problem is the assumption that we can predict future events by extrapolating from the past with a straight line. The technical name for this is the *assumption of linearity*. Forecasters and statisticians have traditionally assumed that the variables they deal with are linearly related because it has been convenient to do so. It has been much easier to deal with a linear relationship such as $y = mx + b$ than with relationships filled with square roots, trigonometric functions, power functions, and the like. Today, much of the problem of nonlinearity has disappeared since modern computer algorithms make it as simple to work with nonlinear relationships as linear ones.

Another variant of the specification problem is employment of the wrong variables in the model. Key variables may be left out. Irrelevant variables may be included. In both cases, the model will provide a poor reflection of reality.

Conclusions

Innumerate managers are at a disadvantage. Because they do not understand the nature of measurement, they do not know how to use measures to help them function more effectively. They also do not know how to assess whether the numbers being presented to them by others are meaningful. A common strategy they employ to deal with their innumeracy is to deny the value of measures for management. "We are dealing with people," they say, "and people are unpredictable and defy attempts to tag them with numbers." The implication is that they are humanists struggling against the exertions of technocrats to digitize humans.

The real issue is not one of humanism versus technocracy. The discussion offered in this chapter is not designed to deny people their humanity. The real issue is: Do we have effective information upon which we can make informed judgments? By effective, we mean: Is it objective? Is it replicable? Does it allow us to determine whether we are doing our jobs properly? Can it clarify accountability on the project?

As we have seen, projects contain plenty of information that meet the criteria of effectiveness. Much of this information is in the form of measures. The challenge is to collect data and present it in a usable manner. The innumerate manager can do neither.

Chapter Fourteen

Carpe Diem:

Seize the Day!

In *The Dead Poets' Society,* a fine motion picture released in 1989, a teacher in a private boy's school admonishes his students to follow the Latin dictum *carpe diem*: "seize the day." His point is that they should avoid being overly restricted by the old rules. Those who travel down a familiar path may have a comfortable, safe journey, but they miss seizing the astonishing opportunities that exist off the beaten path.

People working in project management today are positioned to "seize the day," to take advantage of the central role project management has taken in the management of organizations. A review of some of our most perceptive management thinkers—Charles Handy, Peter Drucker, Tom Peters, Peter Vaill, Robert Reich— shows that the capabilities they have identified as necessary to survive and thrive in today's chaotic world are the very competencies that have long been associated with effective project managers. For decades, these men and women have had to function in environments where chains of command are fragmented or nonexistent, where they have had large amounts of responsibility without commensurate authority, and where flexibility is a requirement for effective action. The project manager's world has long been governed by Murphy's Law.

The central position of project management today is largely a consequence of historical accident. So long as the world of commerce was governed by regularity and standardization, project management's position was on the periphery. This was the state of affairs from the beginnings of the industrial revolution in the early nineteenth century. But with the explosive intrusions of global competition that occurred in the 1980s, regularity and standardization became artifacts of a bygone age. *Customization* and *chaos* are the new watchwords.

So today's project professionals are in a position to seize the day. However, they won't be able to do this unless they redefine their roles. If they see themselves in the traditional way, as mere implementers of other people's initiatives, then nothing will change. They must see themselves with new eyes. They must recognize that their skills and insights have great value in today's chaotic business climate.

They must be eager to play the role of initiator rather than reactor. For example, if their customers expect the project team to help them develop business solutions, they must be prepared to fill this new role. Certainly, when challenged to help the customer, they should not respond, "Our job is to provide technical solutions, not business solutions."

A central theme of this book has been that for project professionals to function effectively in their new roles, they must develop new skills. Traditionally, the key skills they were expected to possess lay in the areas of scheduling, budgeting, and allocating human and material resources. Basically, if they knew how to create Gantt charts, PERT/CPM networks, cumulative cost curves, and responsibility matrices, they were judged to possess the core skills needed to fulfill their role as mere implementers.

The new project management has far more challenging skills requirements. Necessary scheduling and budgeting proficiency now extends to integrated cost/schedule control. More than ever, project professionals need to develop people skills to deal effectively with their customers, their staff, and their managers. Similarly, the new project managers should develop capabilities in the areas of risk analysis, decision making, basic financial analysis, and requirements analysis.

If today's project professionals invest in learning and mastering the new skills, they will find that their efforts pay off handsomely. However, as this book has suggested, project success depends upon more than simple mastery of tools. One attitudinal holdover from traditional project management that they should keep is a can-do attitude. The traditional project management obsession with getting the job done must persist in this new era. The marriage of the results-oriented, can-do attitude and the new skills set make for a valuable project professional.

What does the future hold? Is project management simply a passing fad? Will project professionals gain recognition in their organizations for their special capabilities?

Project management assuredly is not a passing fad. As I stated at the outset of this book, humans have been carrying out sophisticated projects for millenia. There is no sign that projects will fade away. If anything, we are seeing a growth in the number of projects being undertaken. As we move away from standardization to customization, the volume of projects organizations try to manage will continue to grow explosively. Consequently, the need for men and women possessing the skills to handle projects effectively will also increase.

As project management becomes more important to organizations, we are witnessing pressures to professionalize it. Much of this pressure comes from major organizations desperately attempting to develop cadres of effective project professionals. Companies like AT&T, NCR, IBM, Computer Science Corporation, Fannie Mae, Hughes Aircraft, and Hewlett-Packard now put employees through both internal and external project management certification programs. It was in response to this pressure that the Project Management Institute initiated a project management certification examination in 1984. It started slowly, but by 1990 the number of people sitting for the exam began to grow exponentially. Today, thousands of people have become certified Project Management Professionals. Interest in certification continues to grow dramatically.

A predictable side effect has accompanied the growing demand for the most capable project professionals: their salaries are climbing. At the time of the publication of this book, I find people asking me if I can recommend experienced project managers to them in such varied industries as software development, telecommunications, electronics, finance, and pharmaceuticals. When I ask, "What salary are you offering?" I'm occasionally stunned by the answers. One organization in the Far East was willing to offer $130,000 for a senior project manager experienced with systems development.

What are these highly paid project managers doing to justify their generous incomes? Interestingly, many of them are operating like independent businesspeople running their own businesses. Many have profit and loss responsibilities. All are charged to work closely with their customers. Most are given impossible deadlines to achieve—and somehow they achieve them. All are practitioners of the new project management. They certainly do not see themselves as mere implementers of other people's initiatives. They have defined their roles broadly in order to serve their organizations and customers well.

The future looks bright for project management and project professionals. The individuals who will fare best in these exciting, chaotic times will be those who follow the old Latin dictum: *carpe diem*. So, seize the day.

Appendix

An Annotated Reading List
for the New
Project Management

There are currently many books available about project management. A data base search I recently carried out at George Washington University provided a list of hundreds of titles. For the most part, the books tend to focus on the standard project management topics of budgeting, scheduling, resource allocation, and managing with borrowed resources (matrix management).

In compiling a bibliography for *The New Project Management*, I consciously resisted the temptation to generate a data dump from computerized bibliographic sources. While an impressively long listing of project management works would emerge from such a step, readers would not have any idea of which books have value and which do not. Furthermore, in the era of the new project management, some of the most helpful books lie outside the domain of traditional project management. I refer here to books that focus on the new chaotic business environment, as well as works on such topics as risk management, management metrics, and human relations management.

I have put together a highly personal bibliography. The books listed here are ones that I have found to be valuable in my own thinking about project management. The reader does not have to worry about which books are worth reading and which are not, because *all* the books in this bibliography are worthwhile. Has this bibliography excluded other books that can provide project professionals with good insights into today's project management? Absolutely. There's a lot of good material out there. However, most readers have neither the time nor the inclination to pore over massive volumes of instructive and inspiring literature. This bibliography is founded on Italian economist Wilfredo Pareto's 80-20 rule, which holds that a small number of items cover most of the information needed to understand a broad range of phenomena.

I have organized the bibliography according to key themes developed in the text of The New Project Management. The themes roughly correspond to the chapters contained in this book.

Understanding the New Business Environment

Some of our most influential business thinkers have written perceptively about the revolutionary changes that are occurring in today's business environment. These changes include downsizing, flattening, reliance on outsourcing, and empowerment of employees. The general environment is characterized by chaos and complexity.

The following books provide good insights into the nature of the new management climate and offer constructive guidance on how to deal with it:

Cohen, A. R., and Bradford, D. L. *Influence Without Authority.* New York: Wiley, 1990.

Cohen and Bradford recognize that one of the frustrations facing today's managers is that they have high levels of responsibility without commensurate levels of authority. This, of course, is the situation project managers have been facing for decades. The authors offer pointers on how to build influence in an environment where managers have little authority.

Drucker, P. *Managing in Turbulent Times.* New York: HarperCollins, 1980.

As usual, Drucker recognized the new forces at work long before others. This prescient book, written at the outset of the truly turbulent 1980s, calls for managers to recognize that business-as-usual outlooks no longer work.

Hammer, M., and Champy, J. *Reengineering the Corporation.* New York: Harper Business, 1993.

Hammer and Champy offer specific guidance on how organizations can perform radical surgery on their efforts, enabling them to experience dramatic improvements in their operations. They argue forcefully that traditional reorganization leads only to small improvements. Their focus is on redefining and improving the processes carried out by the organization.

Handy, C. *The Age of Unreason.* Boston: Harvard Business School Press, 1989.

Handy points out that the old management paradigms are obsolete. In particular, the changing nature of work coupled with the evolution of more dynamic organizational structures have altered the workplace dramatically. At the heart of the new enterprise are knowledge workers. A major challenge they face is to motivate and lead other workers whose loyalties to the organization have grown tenuous in these turbulent times. To survive and thrive in this environment, managers must be capable of engaging in "upside-down thinking."

Peters, T. J. *Thriving on Chaos.* New York: Knopf, 1987.
Peters, T. J. *Liberation Management.* New York: Knopf, 1992.

Peters is best known for his book, *In Search of Excellence.* While *In Search of Excellence* focused on the traits of the "best" firms, these two books recognize that in a chaotic world, "best" is a highly dynamic concept. As its title indicates, *Thriving on Chaos* offers advice on how to make the most of the revolutionary changes facing organizations today. *Liberation Management* basically says that there are no rules anymore. It sees project management approaches as a key to managing chaos.

Reich, R. B. *The Work of Nations.* New York: Knopf, 1991.
Reich wrote this book before becoming secretary of labor in the Clinton administration. Like Handy, he considers the key players in today's successful organizations to be knowledge workers, whom he calls "symbolic analysts." Also like Handy, he sees the effective employment of other workers (such as in-service providers and repetitive process workers) to be a major challenge in the new environment.

Vaill, P. B. *Managing as a Performing Art: New Ideas for a World of Chaotic Change.* San Francisco: Jossey-Bass, 1989.
Vaill is well-known for his work on high-performing systems. This book is a compilation of essays on managing in the new organizational environment. Of particular interest to project professionals is his metaphor of management as "permanent white water rafting."

Understanding Chaos and Complexity

Until recent times, the view of Western thinkers was that the world is fundamentally an orderly place. Consequently, a major objective of reflective men and women should be to determine the rules that lead to order. Recently, scholars in the scientific, policy, and management disciplines have come to view the world as fundamentally disordered, with chaotic processes disrupting the best-laid plans. At the root of much of this chaos is complexity. In the 1990s, it is generally acknowledged that effective management requires an understanding of chaos and complexity. Some worthwhile books dealing with these subjects include the following:

Gleick, J. *Chaos.* New York: Viking, 1987.
Although this book is basically a scientific work, it became a best-seller. It describes in lay terms the scientific roots of

chaos and indeterminacy. Its implications for management in chaotic times are very clear.

Petroski, H. *To Engineer Is Human: The Role of Failure in Successful Design.* New York: St. Martin's Press, 1985.
Petroski describes how engineers have managed to build ever more complex systems over the past several millennia. Their secret: to learn from their failures. The engineering approach to managing complexity has been to design more complex systems, experience failure, and document new procedures to bypass failure in the future. Petroski explains how this process works, with examples ranging from the collapse of bridges to the disaster of the space shuttle Challenger.

Senge, P. *The Fifth Discipline.* New York: Doubleday, 1990.
Senge suggests that the principal way to deal with today's complexity is by employing a systems perspective. He uses various examples to illustrate how commonsense, non-systems approaches to problem solving can lead to erroneous conclusions. He shows how employment of such systems tools as influence diagrams enables managers to deal with the dynamic aspects of complexity.

Sinha, D. K. *Catastrophe Theory and Applications.* New York: Wiley, 1981.
Traditional approaches to modeling nature and human behavior have focused on continuity. Rene Thom, the principal driving force behind catastrophe theory, points out that many phenomena are, in fact, governed by discontinuities. Examples include the points at which a glass rod snaps, stock markets collapse, and dogs bite the hands that feed them. Sinha's book describes catastrophe theory, an approach to modeling systems that looks for discontinuities.

Managing Change, Risk, and the Future

To my way of thinking, the concepts of change, risk, and the future are closely interrelated. If people knew the future with high levels

of certainty, risk would be reduced. Furthermore, they could anticipate change and prepare to deal with it in advance. Each of these
concepts is given a separate chapter in this book (see Chapter Three,
on managing change, Chapter Four, on managing risk, and Chapter Nine, on estimation). Some worthwhile books dealing with these
topics include the following:

Buckley, F. J. *Configuration Management: Hardware, Software,
and Firmware*. New York: Institute of Electrical and Electronic Engineers, 1993.
An up-to-date overview of a highly disciplined approach to
managing change. While configuration management has
been employed in the defense community for nearly four
decades, it has only recently become a hot growth area in the
management of commercial projects.

Casti, J. L. *Searching for Certainty*. New York: Morrow, 1990.
Casti presents a highly readable work on the limits to predicting the future based on findings in the areas of science,
mathematics, and statistics. Some phenomena are highly predictable, such as the amount of time it takes for a ball to drop
from a height of ten feet. As German physicist Werner Karl
Heisenberg demonstrated, the prediction of other phenomena may be very chancy. Casti does not restrict his discussion
to purely scientific topics, but addresses prediction in business areas as well.

Kanter, R. M. *The Change Masters*. New York: Touchstone, 1983.
Kanter examines companies that leverage change rather than
resist it. She shows that effective adaptation to change lies at
the root of innovation and offers strategies for dealing with
change in a chaotic world.

Stacey, R. D. *Managing the Unknowable: Strategic Boundaries Be-
tween Order and Chaos in Organizations*. San Francisco:
Jossey-Bass, 1992.
Stacey employs some of the findings emerging from chaos

theory to the matter of strategic management. He offers guidance on how to plan in an environment of uncertainty.

Samaras, T. T., and Czerwinski, F. L. *Fundamentals of Configuration Management*. New York: Wiley-Interscience, 1970.
Although this book is a quarter of a century old, it was written at a time when configuration management was relatively new, so it carries with it a sense of urgency for getting a handle on managing change in highly complex projects. The lessons explicated in the book are as pertinent today as they were when the book was originally published.

Wideman, R. M. *Project Risk Management*. Drexel Hill, Pa.: Project Management Institute, 1992.
In this relatively short work, Wideman lays out the basic principles of risk management as applied to the management of projects. Readers should be alerted to the fact that risk management comes in many guises. Particular perspectives on risk management have emerged in widely diverse fields, ranging from finance to pharmaceuticals to nuclear power. Wideman's book focuses specifically on project risks.

Dealing with Customers

One of the chief areas where the new project management differs from traditional project management is in its view of the role of customers. The new perspective holds that customers stand at the center of project processes and that customer satisfaction should be the primary objective of project management. Lack of a customer focus may well lead to the production of deliverables that are not used, or are underused, or are employed incorrectly.

Many books have been written about the development of good customer relations. Most of these books are geared toward sales personnel. They often offer valuable guidance on what it takes to keep customers happy. Readers who feel that they lack a general understanding of customer relations should certainly feel free to read this literature.

My suggested readings list is quite short. It looks at works that have a direct bearing on situations facing project professionals.

Frame, J. D. *Managing Projects in Organizations: How to Make the Best Use of Time, Techniques, and People.* San Francisco: Jossey-Bass, 1987.

At the risk of appearing self-serving, I have included one of my own books in this bibliography. One of my obsessions in project management is to understand customer needs, wants, and requirements. *Managing Projects in Organizations* focuses heavily on developing skills in the areas of needs and requirements analysis.

Hanan, M. *Consultative Selling.* (4th ed.) New York: American Management Association, 1990.

This is one of the truly prescient management books of all time. When the first edition was published in 1970, it offered two important insights that anticipated outlooks that would become dominant two decades later. One was that the most effective hardware vendors recognized that they were really in the business of selling solutions, not physical products. (IBM did not learn this lesson until the late 1980s, much to its detriment!) The second was that account teams must view their customers as partners, not as opponents. Taken together, these two insights suggest that to be effective, project staff must develop general business skills. The solutions that customers are looking for are those that improve their profitability, so project staff must know the basic rudiments of financial thinking.

Juran, J. M. *Juran on Planning for Quality.* New York: Free Press, 1988.

Juran is one of the giants of the quality movement (the others are Demming, Crosby, Feigenbaum, and Ishigara). At the heart of Juran's definition of quality is customer satisfaction. Juran recognizes that the concept of *the* customer is a fiction. For any product or service, there are in fact multiple customers. In this book, he offers a methodology for improving quality by systematically addressing the needs of multiple customers.

Project Metrics, Control, and Evaluation

Control and evaluation cannot be undertaken effectively if organizations lack basic data. An important goal of modern project organizations should be the collection and analysis of data pertinent to project operations. Included here are data on costs, schedules, and resource utilization. Today's project professionals must develop an appreciation for the collection and interpretation of numerical data. The following books will help them develop better capabilities in dealing with project metrics:

Huff, D. *How to Lie with Statistics.* New York: Norton, 1954.
> Four decades ago, Huff produced this book of enduring value. He demonstrated that the idea that "the numbers will speak for themselves" is nonsense. A given set of data can be interpreted in multiple ways, depending upon how the analyst chooses to manipulate the numbers. This work should alert managers to their need to develop capabilities for understanding what data actually mean. On a personal note, I can illustrate the value of this book by pointing out that at George Washington University it is nearly impossible to access the book at the library since it is constantly checked out by students. Clearly, when it comes to lying with statistics, there is no generation gap between eighteen-year-olds in the mid 1990s and those in the mid 1950s.

Kerlinger, F.N. *Foundations of Behavioral Research.* (3rd ed.) New York: Holt, Rinehart & Winston, 1986.
> Kerlinger's book is a standard work used in graduate-level courses that focus on research methodology. He discusses issues of measurement in a highly readable and rigorous way. Included in his discussion are descriptions of how data can be collected through a broad range of mechanisms, from interviews to questionnaires to unobtrusive indicators.

Paulos, J. A. *Innumeracy: Mathematical Illiteracy and Its Consequences.* New York: Hill and Wang, 1988.
This book is a must-read for any managers who purport to
be interested in using data to help them better understand
what is happening in their organizations. In a humorous and
informative fashion, it shows that common sense approaches
to interpreting data often lead to incorrect conclusions.

Managing People on Projects

Clearly, people lie at the heart of project management. Projects
seldom fail because a PERT system crashes. Almost inevitably, success and failure are determined by the actions of people. Hundreds
of books exist on people management. The selection of books listed
here is obviously highly restricted. I have focused on a handful of
works that I have personally found useful in enabling project professionals to deal explicitly with managing people in a project
environment.

Block, R. *The Politics of Projects.* New York: Yourdon Press, 1983.
Block recognizes that a key problem facing project professionals is that they have high levels of responsibility without
corresponding levels of authority. To get the job done, they
must develop good influence skills. Block reminds us that
politics is the art of influence. His book provides readers with
a useful methodology for improving influence/political
skills.

Brooks, F. P. *The Mythical Man-Month.* New York: Addison-
Wesley, 1975.
Frederick Brooks is renowned for his work developing the
operating system of the IBM 360 mainframe computer system. In their effort, Brooks and his team at IBM virtually
invented modern software project management. In this book,
Brooks offers a personal view of what it takes to manage
complex projects.

House, R. S. *The Human Side of Project Management.* New York: Addison-Wesley, 1988.

This work is an innovative, case-focused approach to dealing with people in projects, including bosses, peers, staff, and customers.

Keirsey, D., and Bates, M. *Please Understand Me.* Del Mar, Calif.: Prometheus Nemesis Books, 1978.

Keirsey and Bates present a readable account of Myers-Briggs psychological typing, which is based on the work of Carl Jung. Knowledge of psychological types enables project professionals to understand the roots of so much of the conflict they encounter in their work. It also offers them insights into steps they can take to motivate project staff. *Please Understand Me* contains a self-scoring version of the Myers-Briggs test, so that readers can determine their own psychological types.

Nadler, D. A., Gerstein, M. S., Shaw, R. B., and Associates. *Organizational Architecture: Designs for Changing Organizations.* San Francisco: Jossey-Bass, 1992.

Nadler and his associates show how organizational structure has inevitable consequences. In structuring teams, project professionals should be sensitive to the organizational consequences of the structure.

Thomsett, R. *People and Project Management.* New York: Yourdon Press, 1980.

Thomsett addresses the issue of the roles of people on projects. He discusses many common problems project managers face in motivating their team members. He provides a number of team-building exercises that can be employed on projects.

Weinberg, G. M. *The Psychology of Computer Programming.* New York: Van Nostrand Reinhold, 1971.

This classic work is based on the premise that project success and failure are tied to human factors, so that the understanding of human psychology becomes vital to ensuring project success. Weinberg provides many real examples of how human factors affect project outcomes.

Techniques

University and public libraries contain hundreds of books that describe various management and decision-making techniques that can be employed effectively by project professionals. A good source for achieving a quick grasp of the rudiments of key techniques is a college textbook. A nice feature of textbooks is that they are a compendium of a broad range of possibly useful topics.

- Managers who want to become familiar with current decision-making techniques need merely acquire a copy of a competent managerial decision-making text (try Rowe, A. J., and Bougarides, J. D. *Managerial Decision Making: A Guide to Successful Business Decisions.* New York: Macmillan, 1992).
- A more technical overview of decision making can be gained from operations research textbooks (such as Hillier, F. S., and Liebermann, G. J. *Introduction to Operations Research.* [5th ed.] New York: McGraw Hill, 1990).
- If you want to gain an appreciation of customer relations, purchase an introductory marketing text (for instance, Armstrong, G. *Principles of Marketing.* [4th ed.] Englewood Cliffs, N.J.: Prentice Hall, 1989).
- If you want to learn about basic business finance, get your hands on an introductory finance text (try Seitz, N. *Finance for Nonfinancial Managers.* Reston, Va.: Reston Publishing Co., 1983).
- A good suggestion for gaining basic knowledge on contracting concepts is to acquire Ralph C. Nash and Steven L. Schooner's *The Government Contracts Reference Book: A Comprehensive Guide to the Language of Procurement* (Washington, D.C.: The George Washington University's Government Contracts Program, 1992). Although this work focuses on government contracting, the principles covered pertain to contracting in all realms, private and public.

I suggest that readers examine a number of texts in an area of interest to them and then choose the one with the simplest, most readable explanations. With text in hand, you can selectively get up to speed on such topics as linear programming, Monte Carlo simulations, the analytical hierarchy process, capital budgeting, principles of market research, contracting basics, and so on. The idea is not to become a noted scholar who is an expert in some arcane area; rather, it is to acquire a quick understanding of methods that can lead to better decision making.

References

Abernathy, W. J., Clark, K. B., and Kantrow, A. M. *Industrial Renaissance*. New York: Basic Books, 1983.

American Heritage Dictionary of the English Language. Boston: Houghton Mifflin, 1978.

Block, R. *The Politics of Projects*. New York: Yourdon Press, 1983.

Boehm, B. "Industrial Software Metrics Top Ten List," *IEEE Software*, Sept. 1987, pp. 264–271.

Bolles, R. N. *What Color Is Your Parachute? 1993: A Practical Manual for Job Hunters and Career Changers*. Berkeley, Calif.: Ten Speed Press, 1992.

Buss, M.D.J. "How to Rank Computer Projects." *Harvard Business Review*, 1983, *61*, pp. 118–125.

Cohen, A. R., and Bradford, D. L. *Influence Without Authority*. New York: Wiley, 1990.

Crichton, M. *The Andromeda Strain*. New York: Knopf, 1969.

Drucker, P. F. *Managing in Turbulent Times*. New York: Harper-Collins, 1980.

Duncan, W. R., and Nevison, J. M., *The Project Manager's Toolkit*, Spring 1994, *1*(2), 3.

Frame, J. D. *Managing Projects in Organizations: How to Make the Best Use of Time, Techniques, and People.* San Francisco: Jossey-Bass, 1987.

Gleick, J. *Chaos.* New York: Viking Penguin, 1987.

Hammer, M., and Champy, J. *Reengineering the Corporation.* New York: Harper Business, 1993.

Handy, C. B. *The Age of Unreason.* Boston: Harvard Business School Press, 1989.

Hanon, M., Cribbin, J. J., and Heiser, H. C. *Consultative Selling.* New York: American Management Association, 1970.

Hersberg, F., Mauser, B., and Snyderman, B. *The Motivation to Work,* 2nd ed. New York: Wiley, 1959.

Huff, D. *How to Lie with Statistics.* New York: W. W. Norton, 1954.

Jewkes, J., Sawers, D., and Stillerman, R. *The Sources of Invention.* (2nd ed.) New York: W. W. Norton, 1969.

Kanter, R. M. *Change Masters: Innovation for Productivity in the American Corporation.* New York: Simon & Schuster, 1983.

Keirsey, D., and Bates, M. *Please Understand Me: Character and Temperament Types.* Del Mar, Calif.: Prometheus Nemesis Books, 1978.

Maslow, A. H. *Motivation and Personality.* New York: Harper & Row, 1954.

Nadler, D. A., Gerstein, M. S., Shaw, R. B., and Associates. *Organizational Architecture: Designs for Changing Organizations.* San Francisco: Jossey-Bass, 1992.

O'Connell, P. M. An Analysis of DoD Requirement Handling Procedures and Major Program Overruns. Unpublished doctoral dissertation, George Washington University, 1990.

Paulos, J. A. *Innumeracy.* New York: Hill & Wang, 1988.

Peters, T. J. *Liberation Management: Necessary Disorganization for the Nanosecond Nineties.* New York: Knopf, 1992.

Peters, T. J. *Thriving on Chaos.* New York: Knopf, 1987.

Petroski, H. *To Engineer Is Human: The Role of Failure in Successful Design.* New York: St. Martin's Press, 1985.

Price, D. D. *Little Science, Big Science.* New York: Columbia University Press, 1963.

Reich, R. B. *The Work of Nations: Preparing Ourselves for 21st Century Capitalism.* New York: Knopf, 1991.

Saaty, T. L. *Decision Making for Leaders: The Analytical Hierarchy Process for Decisions in a Complex World.* Belmont, Calif.: Lifetime Learning Publications, 1982.

Senge, P. *The Fifth Discipline.* New York: Doubleday, 1990.

Solomon, J. *The Signs of Our Time.* Los Angeles: Tarcher, 1988.

Tyler, P. *Running Critical: The Silent War, Rickover, and General Dynamics.* New York: HarperCollins, 1986.

U.S. General Accounting Office. *Automated Information Systems: Schedule Delays and Cost Overruns Plague DOD Systems.* Report to the Chairman, Legislation and National Security Subcommittee, Committee on Government Operations, House of Representatives. May 1989 (GAO/IMTEC-89-36).

Vaill, P. B. *Managing as a Performing Art: New Ideas for a World of Chaotic Change.* San Francisco: Jossey-Bass, 1989.

von Clausewitz, K. *On War.* New York: Marboro Books, 1992. (Originally published in 1833.)

Webster's New World Dictionary of the American Language. Cleveland: World, 1964.

Weber, M. *The Theory of Social and Economic Organization.* New York: Free Press, 1964.

Weinberg, G. M. *The Psychology of Computer Programming.* New York: Van Nostrand Reinhold, 1971.

Wideman, R. M. *Project Risk Management.* Drexel Hill, Pa.: Project Management Institute, 1992.

Index